MAN,

SPORT and EXISTENCE:

A Critical Analysis

Health Education,
Physical Education, and
Recreation Series

RUTH ABERNATHY, Ph.D., EDITORIAL ADVISER
Chairman, Department for Women, School of Physical and Health Education, University of Washington, Seattle, Washington, 98105.

MAN,

SPORT and EXISTENCE:

A Critical Analysis

HOWARD S. SLUSHER

Foreword by Edgar Z. Friedenberg
Introduction by Eleanor Metheny

LEA & FEBIGER

PHILADELPHIA, 1967

Library of Congress Catalog Card Number 67:25095
Printed in the United States of America

To my wife, Nancy

Who lives as she is . . .

One cannot treat either an individual or a social organism as a means to an end absolutely, without robbing it of its life substance. . . . One cannot in the nature of things expect a little tree that has been turned into a club to put forth leaves.

Martin Buber

FOREWORD

Man, *Sport and Existence* is a unique work. So far as I know, it is the only book yet written that raises and explores serious philosophical questions about the role of conventional, organized sport in the individual life experience of contemporary American participants, from surfers to football players. Countless authors have dealt with the social psychology of sport; and some, like Reuel Denney, have written perceptively about the involvement of spectators in terms that are philosophical as well as sociological. But only Professor Slusher has explored the state of being of the athlete in the course of his participation in American sport today, attending, with faint irony, to the continuous contrast between the sense of authenticity that athletic competence affords and the sense of instrumentality—of using oneself or being used as a thing—imposed on the player by the way sport is institutionalized in America and even by the rules and purpose of the game itself.

Philosophically, Slusher represents a pure existential position; he is nowhere concerned with establishing that athletics have a pragmatic function for the athlete, though he is, of course, interested in their value to the athlete as a form of self-realization. Nor is he interested in the social or psychological functions of athletics except insofar as these affect the athlete's sense of self. In fact, he does rather less with this aspect of the matter than might have been useful. So much of what a player experiences depends precisely on the way society uses sport and on the way players use it to establish or alter their position in society that even a strictly existential critique of sport requires a more concrete description of the athlete's life than Slusher gives. The book would be enriched by the kind of anecdotal detail found in such a work as George Plimpton's *The Paper Lion*, for example, which, at one level, depicts what it *is to be* a professional football player.

But experience of sporting life at the level described by Plimpton has been fully and vividly discussed by many other authors, while Slusher is the first to extend to the world of sport the kinds of questions about being and relationship that Buber, Heidegger, Kierkegaard and Sartre—to name only the most familiar of Slusher's rather technical array of sources—have raised. He extends these questions without being either pompous or patronizing about sport; he does not exaggerate the role of sport in the life of man in order to justify taking sport seriously; he does not deride sport in order to establish his philosophical gravity. He never sentimentalizes sport either through nostalgia for the lost Hellenic ideal of youthful physical perfection or, as has been more common since Victorian times, by attributing to it unusual power to build character or even sportsmanship. Sportsmanship is, no doubt, properly so called; but most sportsmen, as Slusher notes, play to win.

Since Slusher assumes, I think correctly, that existential philosophy deals with the key issues that affect central aspects of the athlete's experience, he has no occasion to be pretentious. The most important of these issues is *authenticity*. The terms, and even the idea, have become cliché, but few modern writers who have dealt with sport have considered how one's sense of one's own body contributes to one's sense of self, except in social-psychological terms, *e.g.*, whether one feels inadequate, or inferior, and compensates by pseudomasculine aggression, or whether athletes who are admired for their prowess tend to become alienated from their bodies and regard them as equipment that they own, polish, and display. Both these processes are common enough and, sometimes, important, but Slusher is more interested in how the athlete's sense of the peculiar grace that he brings to his life-space becomes a part of his consciousness and identity. In George Herbert Mead's terms, this book is almost totally concerned with how being an athlete affects the "I" rather than the "me."

Sport is a kind of applied art. Aesthetically, it resembles ballet in that the human body is the medium, but the limitations that the athlete must accept are more like those that are binding the sculptor whose work is to become part of a public building of traditional design. The expressive function of the athlete is subordinate to spectacle and profitability, while his performance must fit completely within a framework of rigid convention if it is to have any meaning at all. If the athlete insists on presenting a virtuoso performance without regard for its place in the total structure, he mars the whole work. Athletics, therefore, is among the most formal of the arts; and team-sports are more convention-bound than are athletic activities such as track-and-field or surfing in which the rules that govern what may be done, like those that govern classical ballet, grow out of the function of the human body in relation to the task rather than out of the need to create and regulate a contest. In German, track-meets are termed *Leichtathletik*, in the sense in which Mozart's music is light and easy.

Formality, however, does not make sport inexpressive; by limiting and channeling expression into previously established modes it makes expression more forceful. "Art is not a plaything, but a necessity," Rebecca West observed in *Black Lamb and Gray Falcon*, "and its essence, form, is not a decorative adjustment but a cup into which life can be poured, and lifted to the lips, and be tasted." Sport provides a rather shallow cup, but one which nevertheless tells us a great deal about the people who designed it and choose to drink from it. Societies reveal much of themselves, and of their differences from other societies, in their preferences among sports. Basketball, for example, seems to me to provide an abstract parody of American middle-class life. I have written elsewhere about what I think it reveals concerning the quality of adolescence itself, through its tempo and vividness; but it also mirrors the society we live in. How else could one dramatize so effectively our legalism and the intricate web of regulations among which we live and on which we climb? Who but contemporary Americans could have designed a sport in which status changes so swiftly that no lead can be considered commanding until the last few seconds of play, and in which the officials run back and forth like agitated ferrets looking for breaches of regulations? Basketball rules in fact affect the game quite differently from the way in which the rules of most other sports do. In football, for example, the actions defined as illegal, such as being offside or holding, generally either disrupt the game or are dangerous to the players, such as clipping or unnecessary roughness, and the penalities assessed are genuinely intended to discourage illegal play. But the basketball player—or, certainly, the coach—must respond to the rules of his game as a business executive does to the Internal Revenue and Fair Labor Practices codes. He wins, not by obeying them, but by cannily balancing the penalties risked by each violation against the strategic advantage that might be gained by, say, a back-court foul committed so as to interrupt a probable scoring drive by the team in possession, thus giving his opponents a chance to win one point instead of two, and gaining possession of the ball afterward on more favorable terms. Slusher quotes one of the early pioneers of basketball as having been dismayed that the present-day sport should have become the kind of game it has, with The Man blowing the whistle at every turn and the play so harrassed by interruption that it becomes all tactics and no strategy, as has become our life. A more leisurely sport would make us envious of the players and get on our nerves.

Perhaps the most peculiar thing about basketball is the way it reflects the anxiety about homosexuality that pervades our society. Is there any other sport in which bodily contact between opposing players is *itself* an offense? Certain kinds of body contact, which might be dangerous or which impede play, are forbidden in all sports in which such contact might occur. But to design a game in such a way that it provides its "thinclads" with continuous occasion for physical encounter, but must be stopped the instant an encounter occurs, so that the boy judged more aggressive may be punished surely is a dramatic acting-out of a widespread anxiety in our society which could never, I think, accept high school or college wrestling as a genuinely popular sport. Among Americans, wrestlers must be ugly clowns who seek no real victory and yield no real submission.

Man, Sport and Existence has in it many valid and original observations about the silences—true moments of truth—in sports, and their relation to the players' occasional ecstasy. But it touches only by implication, and then gingerly, on the erotic function of athletics, which seems to me a regrettable omission from a book that includes a brilliant chapter on the related question of "Sport and the Religious." Athletic events occur, and always have occurred, in an atmosphere of erotic tension and excitement that enriches their contribution either to sacred or secular occasions. Our conception of physical beauty is still primarily that of the athlete, while the epithet "jock" applied to a young man expresses as much envy as scorn even now, in a bureaucratic, technically developed, utilitarian society in which physical prowess has little practical utility. Our religious tradition puts the athlete down; a beautiful body is regarded as either sinful in itself or a temptation to sin in others—to be valued only as evidence of physical fitness. Still, there it is; the pupils dilate, along with certain of the smaller blood vessels, and the heart sings on beholding it—but not so loudly as it once did, for many young people have become aware that the heart of the athlete is less likely to sing back than is that of a wilder, hippier creature, who is less comely but more comforting, if you want somebody to love. So, the concept of beauty is changing its emphasis and becoming more various; Allen Ginsberg, people say, is a beautiful man—and it is true.

But the athlete is losing his status and part of his charisma in the course of the same reappraisal; much of this loss is attributable to the way sports have become institutionalized in this country. By experiencing himself as an athlete, a young man learns what it can mean to live fully in his body joyfully and exuberantly, though under self-imposed discipline. I cannot myself express how this feels nearly as well as a fifteen-year-old high-school athlete whom I interviewed a few years ago in the course of a research study:

> Well, I think there's no feeling quite like running down the track or something and winning. Or going out on the football field and suddenly deciding you liked this, and you do it and you feel kinda crazy. Like I was in a fall game last year that we lost by a very bad score but in the midst of it I was, seemed to be, having a fairly good day. And I just felt light-headed, and I just didn't play—I played for the heck of it, for the fun of it, because I just wanted to. And I was very, I mean, I'd be schmeared a couple of times—I'd get up and laugh my head off and I wouldn't know why I was laughing, and I certainly shouldn't have been laughing because I really got schmeared. And I'd go back to the huddle and I'd be dying laughing, and they'd think I was crazy, but I enjoyed it. And it was just, I couldn't stop it and I, I mean, after the game was over I felt terrible because we lost so bad. But during the game it was just this feeling

> of exuberance; I was having fun and nothing much could do anything about it, you know? And I was having fun because I was just—I was able to have fun; I was doing something that, at the time, I was doing reasonably well. And I just enjoyed it. During that game I was happy. But after the game I was not so happy, because we lost so badly. And that's the thing, I think that it's a temporary thing, when you're not realizing it, you're not really trying to think about it; you just know that you're enjoying what you're doing right now. . . . I just enjoyed it. And I don't see how, I mean we were getting schmeared all over the field. I was going out there; I was doing a fairly good job. It seems the fellow in front of me that was supposed to be first string wasn't doing so good; so I played. And I did a pretty good job; but I just enjoyed it, and I couldn't help it, and I'd get hit and bounced all over the ground and I'd get up laughing and the guys would think I was crazy . . . but I enjoyed it; it's a release. And you feel as if you don't have to worry about anything, it's too—I don't know, it's just exuberance. As if there's something that really can touch you. And you're running toward this . . . you're doing it because right then and there you're enjoying it. . . . You're not getting rid of anything, it's just *now*, and you're hoping that two seconds from now will be just like that. And that's the thing.

The inner glow from this experience is an important part of erotic attractiveness but to say this is to say little more than that being a good athlete contributes to animal, and therefore human, vitality. It is precisely this vitality, however, which the institutions that socialize youth are designed to stifle. Where, as in America, exuberant youth are regarded as a threat to good order and good adjustment, athletic activity will be channeled into organized sport; and organized sport will be dominated by authorities—usually school authorities—who will administer it in such a way as to deprive their students of the sense of themselves as beautifully coordinated aggressive young animals—the sense that they might otherwise have gained from participation.

The same thing happens outside of school also. In our society, it occurs wherever athletics are controlled by business-like—not necessarily puritanical—adults. Some of Slusher's most penetrating comments pertain to Little League sports, which he sees as frequently alienating the children who take part in them from any sporting sense they might develop: the children do not feel that they are doing their own *thing* and either go about the game as if driven or develop a slick professional approach inappropriate to their age and actual level of competence. Compared to the influence of the schools, however, Little League is peanuts.

Judging from the behavior of many high-school athletic coaches, and even the way the plant is designed, the characteristic attitude of physical education instruction toward the body, and the joy it may yield, is not merely repressive—it is truly counterphobic. It is the "phys ed" men, typically, who are the school disciplinarians—who snarl at "wise guys" and put down "troublemakers." It is they among teachers who show the most hostility to boys with long hair or odd, mod dress, and who encourage the members of their teams to harass these youths; if the "gung-ho" young athletes are provoked into assaulting the "long-hairs" verbally or physically, school authorities then use the incident as a pretext for forbidding long hair or mod clothes on the basis that they are conducive to violence. School authorities, moreover, are increasingly recruited from former "phys ed" personnel; a large proportion of vice-principals and principals formerly were coaches. These men bring to school administration the spirit of the informal martinet, superficially jolly but intolerant of spirit in young people and of poetry in anything—especially in athletics itself. Generally speaking, sport as a social institution is hostile to precisely the existential values that Professor Slusher stresses in this book and that provide the occasion for writing it.

This is a paradox, for the athlete and the flower-children ought to be allies. It is only possible to be a first-rate athlete if you can allow yourself to feel sport in your blood and open up to what it means. As Slusher makes clear, you have to "dig" the experience. The best athletes, in short, are "hippy" about sport; they hang loose but tough—relax and let it "turn them on." This implies, perhaps, that athletics is to the world of organized sport what creative scholarship is to the university. Great universities need real scholars, and great teams need real athletes, but the universities' deans and coaches will never admit without regret that this is so; they will continue to try to use substitutes instead, thus permitting excellence to be more widely shared, and widely feared.

Edgar Z. Friedenberg

Davis, California

PREFACE

Man, Sport and Existence was conceived out of my desire to pursue a theoretical analysis of the modern world of sport. This work is directly concerned with the total *concept and spirit* of sport in its present form. The critical development of this book is an outcome of subjecting sport to existential positions; however, in no way should this work be considered an "existentialistic interpretation" of sport since I refused to limit myself to one area of philosophic inquiry. The projected direction was not simply to investigate specific sports or, for that matter, a philosophic position. Although it is hoped that salient features of both will be clarified as the analysis proceeds, the primary hope is for the reader to perceive the depth of sport in a new dimension—one in which man learns of the potential of sport in the development of a meaningful humanity.

In a way, this effort is representative of a "Model-T" of things to come. To expect this work to be a definitive analysis of sport is to forget the present stage of relative infancy in the conceptual literature germane to this area. I feel certain the next decade will see greater development and increased sophistication in this most intriguing element of our culture.

The design of this book forms but one model in the continuum of this developmental process. The problems herein presented and their implications could lead into a lifetime of study and speculations. I have limited my discussion to what I presently consider relevant and personally stimulating, while at the same time satisfying accepted scholarly criteria.

There is no doubt in my mind that this is a very "tight" book of disturbing brevity and oversimplification. I attempted to study selected concepts of sport and, through a process of philosophic deduction and induction, arrive at some tenable positions. This process was completed without strict adherence to definitions of terms or even justification of preliminary assumptions. I am certain this will disturb and perhaps anger the more traditional in the reading audience. This form of development presents problems of clarity and structure. But my purpose was not merely to *define* (if introductory material is desired the reader is directed to the many outstanding sources listed in the bibliography). It was hoped the reader would *totally* appropriate the self, beyond cognition, and sense a meaningful involvement. Sport cannot be simply *known*, it must be experienced in a *felt* way. To say it incorporates forms of mysticism is perhaps most explanatory of my present thoughts.

In keeping with the theme stressing the *personal* quality of sport, I have often written in the first person singular. This was not due to my unawareness of traditional usage of collective and impersonal forms, but rather to my strong desire to communicate with the immediate and very personal dimension of man—about an immediate and very personal subject called sport. Likewise, discussion frequently proceeds in highly theoretical areas without the benefit of specific examples and references within the world of sport. It is hoped this will afford the reader some freedom to bring to the presented concepts experiences that are both personal and creative. In this way, true meaning may well be established. What follows is but one man's interpretation of sport.

Those individuals who come to this source looking for a technical "cook book" approach to sport and/or philosophy might well close the covers now! My concern is with *man;* and no recipe, incorporating all his ingredients, is offered. Nor am I interested in technique or mechanization. About this I make no apologies. For it is my belief that technique and mechanization *follow* understanding. This work deals with ideas, hopefully not too abstract, about man and his encounter within the realms of sport. Certainly, there is no attempt to relate to specific events or programs. In the development of this book man is viewed as a *participant*. The relationships of other roles are only mentioned as a tangential association to man—as a being within a movement experience. Furthermore, while the subtle and at times overt differences between play and other associated forms of movement are more than hinted at, this work is directly related to the meaningful and *commonly* accepted activities we call sport.

PREFACE

Since one of the basic concerns of this book is the relative *meaning* of sport in man's existence all forms of categorical absolutes are dismissed as non-real—for meaning can come from any modality. Sport is herein seen as a function of the individual's *derived* meaning; therefore, by definition, it is a subjective experience that is not completely admissible to objective inquiry. Sport is a product of man. He develops it. He modifies it. And he participates in it. The task is to uncover experiences that are personal and therein a *lived* state. To be certain, science has a high priority in the solution of man's problems, but my projected task is to discover the possibility of what is *beyond* the objective world. My concerns immediately focus on *being-in-itself*. However, meaning is not limited to being, it extends to all aspects of man's freedom. Therefore, my presented thesis is one of the unification of *Man, Sport and Existence*.

Howard S. Slusher

Los Angeles, California

ACKNOWLEDGMENTS

I wish to acknowledge, with extreme gratitude, the help of my colleague and consulting editor, Professor Ruth Abernathy, who demonstrated trust in my ability and allowed me the necessary freedom to pursue my desired aims. And I am grateful to John F. Spahr, of Lea & Febiger, for his patience and encouragement in the completion of this manuscript.

A special note of appreciation must be extended to Professor Eleanor Metheny who has been more than generous with her personal and professional support. This book *truly* could not have been written without her encouragement, insights and assistance. Her ideas have stimulated much that is within this work. And to Edgar Z. Friedenberg for sharing with me his sensitive understanding of man and society. He *is*, in his life and thoughts, a man of authenticity.

I am grateful to my teachers, ND, CH, JM, MM and DO, who in their own but different ways contributed so much more than they could ever know to my total development. I am also indebted to Professors Erich Fromm and the late Paul Tillich for giving me scholarly guidance and personal encouragement at a critical moment in my writing concerning the worthwhileness of continuing my study in the conceptualization of sport. I have also gleaned much from my discussions with my colleagues and especially the graduate students at the University of Southern California. Their fruitful ideas and willingness to participate in lively and long discussions, often into the late of night (without a "break"), have greatly assisted my efforts.

I would like to thank the Department of Philosophy at the University of Southern California for making office space and services available to me. For their criticism and kindly professional services I am especially appreciative to Wallace Nethery, Librarian of the Hoose Library of Philosophy, his assistant, Clayton Kradjian, and Professor Craig Walton who know and feel more about sport than they would care to admit. It is a pleasure to thank Ahmed Essa and Mrs. Misao Okino for their editorial and technical assistance in the preparation of the manuscript.

To more than any other person, I am most grateful to my wife, Nancy. Not only do I appreciate her reading and criticizing the manuscript and her inestimable assistance in scrupulously checking references, but also for her unselfish attitude in delaying her own work and denying herself certain pleasures of life until this work reached its completion.

For permission to quote copyrighted books and periodicals, I am indebted to:

New Directions Publishing Corporation for reprinting
"To Nike" from Rainer Maria Rilke, *Selected Works, II;* translated by J. B. Leishman. © The Hogarth Press Ltd, 1960. All rights reserved.

Philosophy Today. Messenger Press for quotations from
Lavelle, L.: Introduction to Ontology, *9*, 182–189, 1965.

Journal of Philosophy and Phenomenological Research. State University of New York at Buffalo for quotations from
Van Den Berg, J. H.: The Human Body and the Significance of Human Movement, *13*, 159–183, 1952.

E. P. Dutton & Company, Inc. for quotations from
Harrer, H.: *The White Spider*, 1960.

Wayne State University Press for quotation from
Salvan, J.: *To Be and Not To Be*, p. 66, 1962.

Philosophical Library for quotations from
Sartre, J.: *Being and Nothingness: An Essay on Phenomenological Ontology*, translated by H. E. Barnes, 1956.

Basic Books, Inc. for quotations from
Fingarette, H.: *The Self in Transformation: Psychoanalysis, Philosophy, and the Life of the Spirit*, 1963.

Houghton Mifflin Company for quotations from
Wilson, C.: *Stature of Man*, 1959.

Dover Publications, Inc. for quotation from
Olson, Robert G.: *An Introduction to Existentialism*, 1962.

Los Angeles Times for quotation from
Murray, Jim, Fleck's Infamy, June 17, 1966.

McIntosh and Otis, Inc. for quotations from
Then My Arm Glassed Up, by John Steinbeck. © 1965 by John Steinbeck. Appeared originally in *Sports Illustrated.*

Sports Illustrated for quotations from
Rogin, G.: An Odd Sport . . . and an Unusual Champion, October 18, 1965.

The New American Library for quotations from
Langer, S.: *Philosophy in A New Key*, 1948.

Librairie P. Tequi for quotation from
Maritain, J.: *Neuf Lecons sur les Notions Premieres de la Philosophie Morale*, 1949.

H.S.S.

CONTENTS

INTRODUCTION

PLATO knew himself as an athlete long before he recognized himself as a philosopher. As a young man in the palestra, he wrestled with all the powers of his body as vigorously as later, in the academy, he used the powers of his mind to wrestle with the questions of its existence. The author of *Man, Sport and Existence* was also an athlete before he became a philosopher, but he does not make Plato's distinction between the wrestling body and the wrestling mind. For him, the concerns of sport and the concerns of philosophy are not only inseparable, they are one and the same within the athlete's concern for defining the terms of his own human existence.

As an athlete, Dr. Slusher has long wrestled with the questions of philosophy in bodily form within the sports arena. Now, as a philosopher, he is wrestling with the problem of trying to describe the meanings he has found in these sport experiences. This is a brave attempt, courageously pursued in certainty of ultimate defeat. Dr. Slusher knows at the outset that meanings cannot be reduced to words. But the meanings he has experienced within his own being-in-sport are so compelling that he must try to express them as best he can.

In his struggle with words, Dr. Slusher spares neither himself nor the reader. His descriptions of the intimate dynamics of meaning in sport are often as involved and tortuous as the meanings he seeks to expose. They do not make easy reading, but they serve the reader's purpose by forcing him to examine the terms of his own existence, not only in sport but in his own being-in-the-world.

In his acknowledgments, Dr. Slusher has been generous in crediting me with facilitating the writing of this book. If our association has served that purpose, then I am doubly grateful for it. But I know that Dr. Slusher would have written this book sooner or later in any event, because it was the book he had to write. How else could be bring his vital involvement in sport and his equally vital involvement in philosophy together within the meaningful frame of his own being? In writing this book, I believe that he has made a substantial contribution to the literature of both fields of endeavour. I hope that many people, both in and out of sport, will find it as meaningful as I do.

Eleanor Metheny

Los Angeles, California

SPORT AND BEING

SPORT, for many individuals, is a cult. It fulfills generalized and specific need gratifications. However, this is not to imply that man necessarily participates in sport *because* of these ends. This is to assume motivation as a prior encounter to matter, an assumption one might have difficulty in logically supporting.

Sport, itself, represents a specific and externalized value system. It inculcates its own form of good and evil, rewards and punishments, as well as a complete matrix of individualized normative outcomes. In a way it can be said that sport determines its own situation in the context of culture. Frequently generalizations are made to "life" but the result is a specific and removed aspect of human involvement. I like to think of the sportsman as one who maintains the absorbing values of the culture within his organism and emerges with a totality of being that both reflects and reveals life.

The practical participation in sport is one of *doing*. Man simply bowls by knocking down pins. He plays golf by hitting the ball into the hole. He skates by maintaining his balance. And he plays tennis by a series of strokes. For the most part it is not *essential* activity. He does not earn his bread in this manner. He is not aware of spiritual concerns. Nor does he usually participate with the vigor that assists his health to any significant degree. They are simply activities of *interest*. Yet for man to attain being he must go beyond interest. His involvement must be marked by deep *concern*. He needs to sense the totality of the cosmos in order to initiate the bonds of relationship, the relationship between himself and the world. Of course it is not assumed that he is always aware of all, or should be. But to attain *being* he must encompass sport as inherent to his totality.

The history of sport evolves out of a mass of influences—war, survival, relaxation, recreation, etc. Today, through increased leisure time, if not free time, sport makes conspicuous and varied appearances within the culture. As a universal phenomenon, the intensity of concern with the sport experience is within the experience of each man. Thus, the totality of personal existence is available to one who exerts effort toward this end.

Although an act of sporting participation can be planned or spontaneous, it generally requires time, effort and expense of energy. To a degree it expresses individuality, no matter what form is attained. In a manner of speaking we actually live ourselves *into* the act of sport. We approach the act internally but we are immensely *social* in our endeavors, especially at the start of our "play" experiences. However, whatever its characteristics, *sport possesses a meaning of its own* (Fink, 1960, p. 101).

Sport frees man, not *from* other activities (*i.e.*, work) but *by* it. Each encounter provides a reason for being; but more than justification of existence sport provides its own rationale. Sport is more than simply what one does in his leisure; it is more than an escape from everyday life; and certainly it is more than a mere socially desirable avenue for release of one's aggressions. The *understanding of being* is clarified by sport. It affords man direction in his attainment of being. The man of sport soon learns that fundamental concepts of modern life do not necessarily bring about authentic conceptualizations of being. Concomitantly, however, he learns these elements are not made possible by the normal methods of *becoming*. Thus, normally when one reaches "defeat" and realizes it is real, he attains a maturity that can be explained only as "awareness of the truth." It is at this point that one experiences the relief of carrying the burden of hope. Despair might well set in; however, it is recognized as the end of futile dreams. In a cathartic way man is *happy;* he no longer needs to carry the burden of foolish and unrealistic hopes. Thus, the paradoxical expression of joy and despair are both present. This point is well expressed by Miss Becky Parks, an Olympic hopeful, as she tells about her intensive involvement in skiing, coupled with the realization of the truth of becoming.

> Glancing quickly at the steel-blue sky overhead, I decided that the snow which had been forecast wouldn't ruin the ski race after all. The almost-nonexistent breeze barely moved the pines lining the race course below me.
>
> My interest in my surroundings gradually changed to a feeling of excited anticipation as I awaited the starting signal. The explosion from the starter startled me momentarily as I pushed myself forward onto the course with my poles. With these first movements downward came an icy sting of air blowing against my face and a sensation of unrestricted speed. My eyes tried to focus on the first gate which was fast approaching to my left. I forced myself to concentrate on my form and timing as I entered the gate; "Plant pole, shift weight, edge downhill ski, lean into hill," I repeated to myself as I coordinated my movements with my thoughts. Coming out of the gate, I gathered speed again and set my skis for the next gate. It came up faster than I had expected, and I lost control for a moment sensing the total helplessness of falling. Luckily I caught myself and regained my proper position of the moment before.
>
> Gate after gate I mentally repeated my instructions as I coordinated movement with words, "Plant pole, shift weight, edge downhill ski, not so much into the hill, *faster*." On I went: first to the right, then to the left. I was oblivious to my surroundings and intent only upon a world of whiteness intermittently dotted with bamboo poles. Judges and spectators flashed by me in splashes of kaleidoscopic color. Ice-crusted pines were mere blurs of green as I shot through gate after gate.
>
> Suddenly I saw the final gate and the finish line beyond. Momentary relief spread through me as I realized the race was almost over. Quickly, *through* I forced the pleasant thoughts from my mind as I dutifully repeated my silent instructions and fought to gain speed. Three more gates behind me, and I was nearly upon the poles which marked the final gate. Now, fighting madly for extra speed, I thrust my poles into the snow and shoved myself forward. As I pulled my poles back to my sides, I realized that the push had been a bit overdone and had cost me my balance. My next sensation was a horribly delightful feeling of tumbling over and over as I rolled down the hill. Mixed with my joy at such complete freedom of movement was the sickening realization that this fall had cost me the most important race of my life: the Winter Olympics. (Parks, 1966)

At a time when one might think all is lost, this young athlete feels "momentary relief," "horribly delightful," "joy at such complete freedom of movement," and "sickening realization." Yes, the world of sport is often goal oriented. A world that says sacrifice, work, suffer, it will all be worth it. Yet, when it is over, and defeat is brought to consciousness, man often experiences the feeling of despair, a feeling that is not all negative in that it symbolizes the "end," which is almost what Western man is always seeking.

Sport is *not* a supplement to life but rather an essential concomitant to that that we attribute to existence. Yet it is not as much essential to life as life is essential to sport.

Play is the "raw material" for sport. But sport is more than play. It includes devotion, care, respect, concern and responsiveness toward the desired outcomes. It is serious. Sport is woven into man's existence and like most phases of life it has evolved into a "task" of the living. Therefore, the concept of sport as recreation is no more than artificially assigning function to existence, when indeed such function is not innate. This type of dualistic argument is a further admission of the division of logical discourse. Man lives in one world. There might be many facets of the one world, but they all contribute to the totality. It is as if to say, man first works and *then* he plays. No! Man is his being! All his spheres have meaning in their own domain, but all are also integrally connected in something we call life. This concept of being-in-the-world composes man's very existence. It is foolish to think the tennis player knows how to perform prior to knowing both his racket, the ball and his self. All the variables are a total composite of the existing world.

Man in his search for meaning of existence may indeed need others. This concept of being-with-others is not always a social situation for man. Indeed the feeling of loneliness might often be highlighted when man encounters the sport situation. Man rarely finds himself as alone as when he represents the crucial "out." Few men have felt the magnitude of loneliness that is an everyday occurrence for the football player who needs to "cooperate," yet is almost fully the one responsible for *his* own actions. The wrestler becomes immediately aware of his body as he grapples with his opponent: tension, stress, interpersonal reflection, closeness of another, yet really very much alone. Thus, being *through* the body is not inferred, as some would lead us to believe, but is a quality of *immediacy*. Man is his body and by knowing it directly and immediately he comes to realization of being.

This awareness of being can be intentional or not, but the immediate experience of sport, centered around the physical body, is developed by the "other" until the present world has structure and meaning. Now we see the relationship between the subject and the object. The man of sport, by definition of the activity, must relate to the object. Now he attempts to reconcile his position, as subject, with the objects, namely, the implements of the sport. Simply, he must determine which is *really* the tool!

The answer for most men of the Western world is to relate to an "end"; to someway or somehow say I am aware of *becoming* and cannot simply think of myself as *only* here. So it is in sport. All is relative to the self. All depends upon the supposition that awareness of being is purely a relation of personal identity. The result is what each man *thinks* and acts it to be.

This is not to indicate that sport serves as a *means*. For it does not; if one commits himself to the concept that the appearance of any phenomenon, as distinct for what it *is*, is really a separate entity, than he feels being. It must be the sport itself and not its instrumental attempt, that makes it worthy of human involvement. In its own mode sport provides man with an *arena* for *living* (not the transfer of lessons learned on the field to problems of "life")—yielding its own ends for its own sake. Values, attitudes and structures for living derived from sport *cannot* be applied to other avenues of existence without the risk of losing "philosophic specificity." If sport is of value, and it is to me, it is so because of sport and not because of what it may teach me in life! The idea that sport teaches one to "get up off the ground of life" is a fallacy of man's desire to idealize his existence. Reading Frank Merriwell as a child, man almost comes to believe in bedtime fairy tales. Sport must be conceived in its own context, without a superimposed value structure. In this way, *sport* has meaning for each person who engages in the specified activity. It is not what it appears to be, but it is sport itself. I, as an individual, might wish it to appear in a specific manner, but in so doing I deceive not only the object but the subject as well.

In a way, sport *is* different from all that composes life. It is dynamic without fear of shame. It is aggressive without psychologic disdain. It is emotional without self-consciousness. And its means have a high degree of relationship with its end.

For many of us, sport has traditionally provided us with the present situation. Its future stops at the end of the period or the sound of the gun. Thus, we tend to look at sport with something less than *real* seriousness. To be sure, sport provides us with a potential form for meaning, authenticity, and reality—all leading to being-in-the-self. Thus, sport as more than a link with life, is a vital aspect of existence, one which opens the self to the mystery of being. One cannot expect a logical and rational deduction from sport Happenings are simply what they are.

To hypothesize that all is true from sport is to talk nonsense. Analysts of sport must turn their attention to the data of sport—or the phenomena. "What is given us to start with is a sort of unnamed and unnameable confusion where abstractions not yet elaborated are like so many little unseparated clots of matter" (Marcel, 1952a, p. 119). While it is true that most immediate experiences may indeed be vague, it would be a mistake to assume that being in sport is either all things to all men or, conversely, nothing.

Sport is not necessarily, as some have inferred, a courtyard for happiness. In reality sport, as life, is a place for happiness as well as grief. Through activity man builds anxieties, suffers pain, engages the tensions of life, and frequently challenges actual death. The emotions of fear, joy, terror, exhilaration are nothing but what is involved in life. Sport, at times, is a mixture of comedy and tragedy. It includes the pleasures of success and the afflictions of defeat. Sport is complete with the emotions of life. One day one loses what he has *worked* a lifetime to achieve. Emotions are so strong that they are expressed in tears of happiness upon selections of honor. Sport does provide real pain. For some it is play, but sport is never *just* play. The design forces man to make inferential decisions upon what is known and at the same time demand mystical allegiance to the obscure.

"There is no way to explain that baseball is not a sport or a game or a contest. It is a state of mind, and you can't learn it" (Steinbeck, 1965, p. 100).

It all has to do with the *one* world, expression of the real world. Each dimension places personal existence forward, not passively but with full involvement, so that we are shaped by the experience. We fill our lives with experiences of pleasure *in* sport but also a feeling of ecstasy *about* sport.

Each encounter with sport provides a specific meaning. Running, jumping, hitting, being hit, throwing, etc., are all "spokes" of the wheel of sport. They are significant to the degree they develop meaning in the individual. Of course, meanings can be instrinsic and thereby refer to those significant interpretations of persons, objects and relationships that exist within the individual; or meanings can be extrinsic and refer to outwardly manifested interests of the participant and spectator.

It has been more than hinted at that sport is essentially an activity engaged in with others. The stress of communal ends will be dealt with in some detail in a later section; however, it should be indicated that sport deeply recognizes man's profound relationships with others. Of course, critics of this point of view will be quick to counter with the so-called "individual sports," not to mention the many activities that are essentially solitary. The very meaning of sport negates this thesis and encourages "the other." "The solitary player is often playing with imaginary partners" (Fink, 1960, p. 102). Man needs a *real* game but not the presence of real people, either participating or "spectating."

Realms of Being

It is necessary, at this point, to face the idea of *existence* with a statement of *being*.

> Being could be defined as the source of all possible modes of participation, existence as the act of participation to being with a finite being capable of saying "I and Me" and reality also as being completely present to the I or to the me, yet surpassing them and becoming for them a being which is given. (Lavelle, 1965, p. 182)

Again, it is good to recall the sense of urgency and necessity inherently connotated by the word "being." In consideration of a sport situation, being encompasses *all* felt experiences, both empirical and mystical. Man is excluded from nothing within the potential of his own awareness as it *fits* the sport situation. There is present in the sport experience a physical involvement that simultaneously is more than physical. The body makes us present in the environment in a special way, but somehow there is something that is beyond the body. The situation, potentially, tells man to unite with himself. Frequently, the feeling is one of frustration. It is as if my body understands what I am attempting to achieve but it *really* does not understand me. I might add, parenthetically, that it is this sensation that differentiates to me, a nonenlightened but highly interested spectator of the dance, the performance that *is*, from the one that just *is not*! On the other hand, when the performance is "right," it is frequently because I *know*, really know, that the dancer has revitalized my life. She has created, not repeated! Something is apparent to me that says I am more of my self because of this experience. In a real sense, "Being is, non-being is not" (Lavelle, 1965, p. 183).

In some ways, sport appears to be an answer to the discontentment that man feels. Life is not all it should be. There is a great void that the daily activities of life simply do not fill. Some turn to religion to take care of this need. Others just work harder at their daily tasks, thinking they can avoid the "pain" of life by doing just a little more. Still others turn to sport to provide that something extra in life.

> It is a wild illusion to believe that life on this earth continues to become better and better in some way when we refuse to it all the continuation beyond the grave. Man and life, indeed, far from finding, according to this view, any expansion, become miserably restricted. (Parain-Vail, 1960, p. 637)

An objective factor that is both potent and realistic is needed to clearly direct man's rising disappointment into a phase of life wherein he may achieve "victory."

The sport phenomena can be visualized as basic to a philosophy of *being*. As man participates within the limits of force, space and time, it makes him aware of the limitations of life. All that is *now* is soon in the past. To be *in* the *instant* is the process of sport. To recognize the opportunity, to move *now*, to "swing" precisely—in a word, to recognize the *instant* and point to the frustration of not dealing with the composite of life. Sport illustrates that man is just a small part of the totality. We do not nor will we ever reach the point of importance; we are just one on a team. Thus, the limitations of man are so judged because of the stress on the partial and not complete. In seeking the "perfect game" man is asking for eternity, something that he knows no one will ever attain. But this is *never* achieved; for the performance of man can never really be perfect. Even if it does not allow a man to reach "base," his perfection is limited. It is limited to the quality of another and the conditions of the attainable life. In this way sport is little but a promisory note; a promise of the *eventual*.

The question of *being* and existence must now be asked. What is being? What is the relationship between being and existence? How do both realms relate to sport?

First, we can understand that the "happenings" of sport make up the being of the participant. When the individual attempts to attain being through the *act*, we recognize the difficulty of separating the act from the totality of *action:* together they comprise an identifiable reality. "Man is not an object, a determined sum of qualities, his being is intermingled with his activity of participation; it is his own manner of laying himself open to being" (Parain-Vail, 1960, p. 638). The man of sport takes part in the activity. His being is determined by his quality of *authentic involvement* in the sport. Therefore, being is relative. Thus, the differentiation between being and existence. Existence is an absolute essential—in potential. It is specific, exact, definitive and finite. Existence is descriptive of "having." Being is a formulation of process.

Man's existence, by definition, is specific in sport. He is made available to move toward being. To open oneself up, and, in the process, transcend the self is one potential contribution of sport. Rusty Miller, a champion surfer, explains this tenet.

> You're in a contest against yourself. . . . It's you and the sea, and the sea is eternal. You're alone for a little while in a crowded world, out under a big sky with the wind blowing on you. It's . . . learning to depend solely upon yourself, of trusting your muscles and endurance and nerve. . . . It's a way of reminding yourself that life is, or can be, basically simple. (Mitchell, 1964, p. 123)

Sport provides the challenge of existence, the situation for attainment of high level being. It lets you know how good you *really* are. Man learns to determine his existence—to find what he has!

It may be self-evident; however, it must be seen that sport facilitates identification of each participant's existence. It allows man to identify his potential within the elements. If we do not participate in sport or have minimal involvement, the world of sport is perceived as little but object and subject. It takes an involvement, and a certain degree of skill, to be capable of attaining being.

In many ways, American sport with its emphasis on records, commercialization, college "scholarships," fame, and size of the catch has prostituted the very existence of sport. Instead of seeing man, at the center of concern, his external concomitants are placed in the limelight. Man becomes an object of his object! Man becomes a pawn in the world of athletics and sport. He is reduced to a *thing* that performs a function. He loses his role as a subject and in so doing dismisses his potential for being. Existence loses its priority to essence as man loses his being in a frantic effort to *become*! Man, as an object, engulfs his possessor and leaves little doubt that he is anything more than the ensemble of his act. Yet, he knows "the object is always evil; only the subject can be good" (Berdiaev, 1944, p. 26).

When participation in sport is authentic, when it is rid of superficiality and selfish desires, man attains being. Available to being, the performer is *given* a rebirth of existence. Being is fulfilled and quickly transcends *the* situation, leaving man with anything but discontent. To know one as a wrestler *and* as a man and to have *really* pinned the shoulders of another to the mat is to sense fulfillment and actualization, of not only the self, but of all of another. It is to experience *his* being as yours.

This cannot be achieved if the action is detached from the person, when man centers his thoughts on the object. One might still win the bout, but he loses the "war." The experience of wrestling with man's being is more than is human. Anything becomes possible as *the one* reaches for the other. This becomes the challenge of sport. It is the challenge of existence. To understand that bodily conflict is but convenience and the real match is the determination and control of the other's being is to approach the deep penetration of sport as a synthesis of life.

Being, as a goal, might not be absolute but it is complete. It is the perfect explanation of man's involvement in sport. It is a *total* expression of the *wholeness* of man. Any argument relative to dualistic concerns of mind-body and reason-emotion is simply not valid to the intelligent critic of sport. Man cannot *fully* engage in sport activities by engagement of polarities of action. But if man, in sport, is complete, it is paradoxically true that nothing can be added. The question then becomes one of perpetuation. Thus, the next logical question must be asked. Does man, or indeed will man, participate in sport in order to *maintain* what he is? Upon self examination we discover the being of each *one* is specific to his own concreteness. The being of the participant lies in the milieu of relationships which unify things to and for man. Listen to the words of a body-surfer. A person keenly aware of the completeness *and* availability of being.

> In his struggle *to be*, man finds that sport is available to him when *he* is accessible to sport. He will find authenticity and transcendence through sport . . . he challenges the waves with his naked body; there is no intermediary. The body may lie inert and passive in the water, flirting a bit with the *safe* ones; or he can commit himself to the *big* ones by actively swimming out to confront the wave, choosing consciously to match his skill with Nature who is often unpredictable and relentlessly cruel.
>
> The surfer places his sensitive fingers on the pulse of the ocean, and from its surge becomes *aware* of its physical being. . . . he commits himself to the wave; he involves himself with it. He has allowed himself to become accessible to the being of the wave. Man exists . . . the wave exists . . . both meet in a confrontation. The wave causes subjective impressions within the mind of the surfer; the

> synthesis of these impressions allows the wave to be revealed as object . . . thus each surfer projects upon the wave different impressions. As he rides the wave, he is aware of a sense of freedom which comes from mastery over one's body. He reigns subject over the wave . . . he grasps the being of the wave . . . he and the wave become an autonomous unity. (Tyner, 1966)

Certainly the experience of this individual is not to infer that *being* is the goal of sport nor even the object of sport. Being is both subject and object. It *is* wholeness. It is that to be actualized and also that which affords realization.

The awesome primacy of sport rests in the premise that man is really removed from himself and at the same time made more of what he is to be. The self is present and it is the responsibility of man to reflect upon sport as an immediate situation in his *life*—in all its fullness.

Being-Within-Sport

To "capture" being, the sports performer needs to retain a unification or a feeling of *oneness* of personal being and the *be-ing* qualities of the sport. It is this sensation that tells man that "today is my day." The touch is right; everything seems to fit; and there exists a degree of *appropriateness.*

In order to reach this level of *oneness* man's self needs to be complete. Each *one* is an entity of reality. While he is *in* the game situation, man *presents* himself as complex organism. His "presence" is not, in itself, the identity of the person. It appears that not only can you not tell a player without a scorecard, you might not be able to *really* tell him with one! In other words, an appreciation of *the* individual's place within the immediate context of sport is quite distinct from *one's* place. Existence is not handed to man as if it were distinct from totality. Man, as a priority, exists. Awareness of self affords the potential for being. Throughout the world of sport, *the* man is surrounded by dynamic concerns, concerns that challenge man to realize his potential. Existence is before him. To the degree that he is available to the world will, in part, determine the *quality* of being-within-the-world attained in the sport situation. His *true* nature within the world is a necessary prerequisite to comprehension of self in the sport.[7]

> One sticks one's finger into the soil to tell by the smell in what land one is: I stick my finger into existence—it smells of nothing. Where am I? Who am I? How come I am here? What is this thing called the world? What does the world mean? (Kierkegaard, 1941, p. 141)

For the man attempting to analyze sport as a phenomenon these are questions of urgent necessity.

Man's natural presence within sport must be so conceived that sensitivity to awareness will accrue. The *being* of the athlete pertains to the relatively limited structure of the game, with all its regulations and traditions. Each time the ball is hit, the puck is shot, each specific event brings with it a partially hidden reality. Each event is truly a phenomenon and as such is *less than* the totality. Being is achieved through widest horizons of experience. Being is conscious involvement and commitment to the activity in a "purposeful" (intentional) manner. The man of sport is not simply in space and propelled by force but simultaneously aware and concerned with time. Together with goal orientation, he uses the matrix of time, force and space to *order* his world. Thus, in subject-object language, man is both mover and moved in sport.

From the prior discussion the reader might have been led erroneously to believe there is *nothing*, in the actual performance of sport, that lends itself to learning. One could argue if truth is intuitive and being is personal then the act is *all* the individual decides it to be. Nothing could be more incorrect.

All "knowledges" are within the modalities of being. In other words, the fact that there is something "to learn" about hitting a baseball, catching a fish, stroking a tennis ball, riding a horse, etc., is indicative that these are the "things" that demonstrate that there is *being*. It is *what* is to be known that brings on being and concomitantly what is learned as true is so because of the human (*being*) element.

The performer does not change that *which is* (knowledge); all he can do is relate to what is known by choosing and acting. The multitude of choice that is afforded to man, as he encounters the sport phenomenon, is quickly transferred to man as he now is, in totality. This is expressed well by Roger Bannister, the man who with use of systematically applied knowledge broke one of the greatest barriers in sport, the four minute mile. "I sometimes think that running has given me a glimpse of the greatest freedom a man can ever know, because it results in the simultaneous liberation of both body and mind. . . . Running is creative. The runner does not know how or why he runs. He only knows that he must run, and in so doing he expresses himself as he can in no other way" (Bannister, 1955, p. 265). He is his freedom. He might not be capable of explaining but he knows the act requires *all* of him. The "more" within his imagination, the more he is—and this is a dimension of knowledge, a foundation and necessity for truth.

The participant must focus his main attention on the activity. The "things" that occur in the specific sport situation are not calculable or even objective. They are objects of *intentional* existence. In a pedestrian way, it could be said they were meant or designed to happen by *man*. Thus, through actualization of purpose, reality is apparent and being is attained.

For some this is not sufficient reason. They want to know *why being* is attained in sport. It is not that the potential is doubted as much as the inquiry aims at more depth for human envolvement. One could give all sorts of verbal answers. To be glib, one might claim that freedom of sport sets man apart from nature and thus open to subjective necessity. But even the most superficial analysis would demonstrate that this skirts the problem of existence.

Simply, they are as is! Being is without reason, without cause, and without necessity (Sartre, 1956a, p. 619). "We run, not because we think it is doing us good, but because . . . we cannot help ourselves" (Bannister, 1955, p. 265). On the surface sport appears to reject ontological truth. The sport situation calls for man to be constantly evaluated, judged and measured. At times the world of sport appears to rest on a "second hand" and tape measure. Man's dive is worth 8.5 (note it is not 8.0 but 8.5) which of course is multiplied by the degree of difficulty of 2.6. Others bowl "perfect" games. That is they knock down all the pins with minimal opportunities. Others run 3:54.2 seconds for the mile. It would appear that we objectify the sublime! Within broad limits we ignore conditions of playing surfaces, ignore weather factors, and competitive factors. We objectively measure that which is subjectively determinable. But, in reality, these acts are after the fact. Being is judged as a prior commitment and as such is divorced from results. This does not deny causation as much as it attempts to emphasize the truth of an action for what it *is*. What the athlete *is* and what he intuitively feels while performing is the *summum bonum* of sport. Precedence is placed on being and not on results. To *sum ergo cogito*—"I am therefore, I think" (Sartre, 1956a, p. passim)—one might add, "Therefore, I *do*!"

Man's world, although filled with "doing," is often a bit less than he would wish it to be. Sport affords man the opportunity to go beyond the everyday. In any sport event, there is always the *real* chance to become. In a way, *life* is restored to man. The individual *is* important and even error brings its reward. Simply, man is important.

As sport is pursued, it is finally not what man believes he is as much as what indeed he really is. Thus, sport provides a dimension of being. Through participation in sport-like activities man searches for a dimension of his existence. Man needs to find out what he is. Man asks what does it mean to be.

The deep concern indicated by this imperative question is often hidden in the competitive nature of the activity. In the process of the contest it is easy for man not to be. He simply assumes the superficial elements of the mode of his selected activity and avoids the questions of seriousness. Yet, when one is involved in sport one faces a critical reflection of life. Within the drama of the activity all of existence is revealed—joy and sorrow, excitement and boredom, hope and despair, victory and defeat, and ultimately life and death. When man is faced with situations of this magnitude, the question of being is fundamental. It is a question of truth of self and authenticity of purpose. However, unless man is ultimately naive and avoids the actual, it is obvious that modern man suffers greatly over the anxiety of being which results in a sense of meaninglessness and absurdity of action.

In sport man searches, or may search, for being. Man exists and concomitantly sport exists. Both are results of human perception. Altered observations, of either, bring about changed results. "The real world and human experience are . . . correlatives" (Van Peurson, 1959, p. 39). This volume pertains to the phenomena of sport *itself;* and the meaning sport makes available to man. By definitino, this development is *personal.* It is a perception of what sport is. The concern, for the most part, is not the *potential* of sport or what one *wishes* it to be. It is what *is.*

There is no attempt to arrive at the validity of being through naturalistic or idealistic systems. In the sport situation man is presence unto himself *and* is the object of things. Both must be considered. "That (which) I achieve within my own body by recognizing myself, spreads out into a relationship with things about me, so that they manifest *their* meaning" (De Waelhens, 1959, p. 59). Analysis of being, as presented in sport, needs to go beyond fancy verbalization. Reality is the basis of being. Therefore, it becomes necessary to draw upon the real experiences of sport, those that *do* happen, if man is authentically to locate his *real* being.

The discussion presented here postulates that sport is a function of personal meaning. Therefore, the meaning of sport is *relative* to the individual; however, this form of subjectivity is not to be incorrectly identified as the antithesis of objectivity. It is simply a matter of a *personal*, and not scientific, relationships. All forms of categorical absolutes are dismissed as *non-real*, "Being is, non-being is not" (Brenton, 1961, pp. 65–66).

While it is true that sport *itself* does not possess a being divorced from man, it has an *essence* that affords a potential for meaning. Thus, sport is not only *what-it-is* but possesses a *being-of-itself* and a *being-for-itself.* The participator and the sport are cognates. This quality of *of-itself* and *for-itself* accounts for some of the special kinds of experiences in which the performer projects himself in the activity. Man says I partake in the experience with my skills and my will. This constitutes the *being-of-self* of sport; yet, because of the involvement between man and nature, sport might yield a world calling for man to bow to the sport. The gymnastic attempt at the "perfect" crucifix might well be a *being-for-itself* quality of sport. Either or both qualities might yield a reply to the question, "Who is man?"

This is not to indicate that sport elicits a meaning to man that is, in some way, unique or novel. For this might or might not be true. To the man of sport, there is not just the question of *specific* meaning but of *man* as the being who performs an operation in *and* of itself. To be sure, certain elements of sport can be scientifically objectified. But as long as the internal experiences of the performer are personal, we must settle for answers of truth as opposed to reason. Assuming the existence of objectivity, *meaning* becomes a dimension of subjective necessity. Real worth, in participation, comes from voluntary release of meaning, a propulsion from the "inner self."

To discuss the being of sport presupposes the assumption of the being of man, for there could be no sport without the presence of man. To assume the presence of man in "sport-like" activities is not to assume the being of sport. Being, as a word, indicates necessity. In consideration of a "being of sport" all is available to man within the context of the essence. Being is complete. It says what is *real*. And what is real is necessary, for if it is not real there is *nothing*. It is the explanation *and* the goal of man's involvement in sport. Simply defined, being is the basic source of all potential modalities of participation within the sport situation. Consequently, sport necessarily exists; that is to say, if man exists. Since we start the argument with the assumption that man exists, it logically follows that sport has an ontological facet.

The actual verb *to be* presents a most striking dilemma. I could use the verb in a limiting manner (*i.e.*, there exist two balls on the field) or in a universal form (*i.e.*, there are many balls in the world). The difference is striking! When I say *it exists*, I assert an absolute attribute of specific dimension. The implication is one of confinement (two balls on the table)—an extension of the theoretical absolute of sport. However, when I say *there is*, I indicate a being of sport. I assert the presence of essence and commit myself to realization of being. I admit to the availability, relativity and openness of being. Sport makes being *available* to man. He is open. He is accessible. He is ready. *There is* being in sport. Sport does not *give* being. If man is available and open, he *may* attain the being available in sport.

The water skier, at the end of a towline, might be *skiing* or he might simply be riding. In the *sport* of water skiing *there is* an authentic involvement, a concern which makes *being* available to man. On the other hand, man can merely "ride" on water skis. Being is not an assigned value. Thus, man *is given* that which there is. Existence is accidental to essence. Because of the lack of commitment to the form or activity and the delimited choice, a state of non-being is present. There is nothing! Why? In a word, there is no *life*.

In sport *all* is potentially *available* to man. This assumes a concern with what is, in reality, and not what could be, potentially or ideally. To be committed to sport, the skier must spiritually transcend the *actual* experience. It is more than mere thinking. In fact, it is more than mere action. There must be a sense of the forces of nature upon man; he must have passion for the brutality of the waves; he needs to sense the magnificence of the tension of the line; and he must encompass the ecstasy and beauty of *that* which the experience is symbolic of. Skiing becomes a question of *can* one exist and the *quality* of the existence. The choice of taking part in sport or taking a mere ride is the choice of being and non-being. Thus, *to be* a man of sport is to actualize that which *there is* in sport.

The *mere existence* quality of being is a limiting factor of sport. In denying relativity, it asserts negation of individual meaning. It says, take sport as it *is given*. Specifically, it assumes the way it appears to *one* is the way it is to *all*. To argue what is recognized is what is universal is to admit the "oneness" of essences. John Steinbeck's words are a reminder of this fallacy.

> My feeling about hunting has made me pretty unpopular. I have nothing against the killing of animals if there is any need . . . But the killing of large animals just to prove we can does not indicate to me that we are superior to animals but a kind of keep-down feeling that we are not. A room full of stuffed and glass eyed heads always gives me a feeling of sadness for the man so unsure of himself that he has constantly to prove himself and to keep the evidence for others to see. (Steinbeck, 1965, p. 99)

Indeed, the meaning of sport is personal. Sport is an integral part of humanity. But what is, perhaps, more important is that man, as a human, is an indivisible part of sport.

In sport man quickly becomes aware of his existence. He stands out, both literally and figuratively. "Man, at the same time he *is* presence unto himself, *is* object of things" (De Waelhens, 1958, p. 57). The man of sport, although engaging in a multitude of social encounters achieves meaning and yields same, maintains one of the last frontiers of the "rugged man." Here he is, not what he *says* he is, nor what he *hopes* he is, but what he reveals himself *to be*—in action!

Furthermore, when the being of sport is conceived as *there is*, man is challenged to transcend the situation and locate *all* that is personally meaningful. "I sought God and found him easily there in the waves and people of surfing" (Quinn, 1965, p. 82). The athlete is aware both of self and nature as existing objects. This, in itself, provides a resource of meaning for the perceptive and committed individual. It is the *doing* of sport that develops the mecca for *knowledge* of man, but it is the critical awareness of the act that brings about *meaning*. "This inscription, this self-realization that I achieve within my own body by recognizing myself, spreads out into a relationship with the things about me, so that they manifest *their* meaning" (De Waelhens, 1959, p. 59). The man of sport is provided with instant feedback of the immediate experience (not often available in other forms of life) of affirming the self. He extends meaning to the lives of others as well as his own. His existence has reality, truth and, most important, it provides extensive immediate potential for meaning.

The quality of being of sport can now be viewed relative to the essences of sport, which concomitantly relate the *specific* phenomena to the *totality*. Dualistic concerns normally associated with sport such as existence-essence, objectivity-subjectivity, spirit-matter, freedom-dictate, and mind-body are not as much a duality of *sport* as much as a residue of the duality of the *being* of sport. Meaning *is* to be derived from the essences of sport.

It should be remembered that *being* applies to all things, individuals and activities. No matter how abstract or concrete is the mode, being is potentially applicable. All sports and the implements are capable of being; however, it is the relationship of man to the "it" that determines the quality of the being.

Only *nothingness* lies beyond being. For man in sport to *not* locate what *is* in sport is to participate in a state of nothing.

Meaning is excluded and man flounders *through* life, never stopping to appreciate, to be aware, and be sensitive to the importance of existence. Therefore, in all acts, excepting nothingness, there is a potential for that which is beyond cognition. If movement is to be meaningful, man must endeavor to search and derive meaning from the specific situation.

A word of caution must follow. Much like Estragon and Vladimir the "recipient" individual spends much time in *Waiting for Godot.* To accept sport fully and *only* as a "vehicle" is sad because of the inherent suggestion that man can do nothing to alter fate. Sport, as is, makes man act. To attain *nothingness* is "safer" than to die; but it is also not to live.

True, the movement of sport must be considered as a quality of being that is as is. To really attain the wholeness of act and action man needs to commit himself to the activity. To ski is to attempt the symbolic appropriation of a snowfield, to project ascendancy over the *in-itself* in the guise of sport (O'Neill, 1958, p. 69). But being also encompasses an element of possession. The skier learns to move so that he will be more of what he is. Similarly, the movement *itself* can be *more* of a movement if man is committed to it. Two objectified movements could be quite dissimilar in *reality.* Through encompassing part of the environs, man truly is more of what he is. Just to *do* the movement or *have* the movement as part of you is not enough. Both are reducible to the quality of *being.* Man participates in sport *for-itself.* Certainly the skier is not skiing *because of* the desire to become physically fit. He might in skiing become so, but this could not be his rational desire for the commitment to skiing. If "fitness" was his end, he could find a more direct method to approach this goal. Nor does one ski to make social contacts or to strengthen one's moral fiber. One skis! He performs because he *is* and the movement *is.* Thus, he is more (O'Neill, 1958, p. 69)!

To be in sport is more than the abstraction of self-fulfillment. In a sense it is release from all earthly holds. It is the exhilarating feeling of knowing that the experience is holistic. It is more than physical. It is more than conscious. It is the complete act. It is the quality that both sees being as a necessity through perceptual affirmation, and at the same time recognizes the existence of voluntary reality. Thus, the question of the interior and exterior man, a question which belongs to both the man of metaphysics and the man of sport.

Obviously, our interests and endless dedication to sport cannot be glibly passed over through stimulus-response explanations. Behavioral theories, stressing source and/or origin, have enjoyed too long a reign. We have been brought up steeped in scientific methodology with its subtle, and at times not too subtle, insistence on *causation*. Man is not a conscience that can be restricted and broken down into elements. In sport man is present to the world as a total being. If he is bound to his past or to any other structure that divides him for the supposed purpose of reducing ambiguity, he is no longer the man of freedom who is within his potential integration. We must consider man as he is, a human being-in-the-world.

> Every desire if presented as an irreducible is an absurd contingency and involves in absurdity human reality taken as a whole. For example, if I declare of one of my friends that he "likes to go rowing," I deliberately intend to stop my investigation there. . . . I can not in fact consider this fondness for rowing as the fundamental project of Pierre; it contains something secondary and derived. Those who portray a character in this way by successive strokes come close to holding that each of these strokes—each one of the desires confronted—is bound to the others by connections which are purely contingent and simply external. . . . Someone will say, for example, that the subject considered is a sportsman who likes violent exercise and is in addition a man of the outdoors who especially likes open air sports. . . . To explain Pierre's fondness for rowing is to make it a member of the family of fondness for open air sports and to attach this family to that of fondness for sport in general. Moreover we will be able to find still more general and barren rubrics if we classify the taste for sports as one aspect of the love of chance, which will itself be given as a specific instance of the fundamental fondness for play. It is obvious that this so-called explanatory classification has no more value or interest than the classifications in ancient botany; like the latter it amounts to assuming the priority of the abstract over the concrete, as if the fondness for play existed first in general to be subsequently made specific by the action of these circumstances in the lover of sport, the latter in the fondness for rowing, and finally

> the rowing in the desire to row on a particular stream, under certain circumstances in a particular season—and like the ancient classifications it fails to explain the concrete enrichment which at each stage is undergone by the abstract inclination considered.
>
> Furthermore how are we to believe that a desire to row is only a desire to row? Can we truthfully admit that it can be reduced so simply to what it is? The most discerning ethicists have shown how a desire reaches beyond itself. (Sartre, 1956a, pp. 561–62)

I must concur with Sartre. Reduction of an activity is indeed not proper. Man is a totality, although he might show varied "faces of Eve" at any given time. To assume causation is to admit a priorness to man and therefore an expression of less than unity.

> Thus if I am rowing on the river, I am nothing—either here or in any other world—save this concrete project of rowing. But this project itself inasmuch as it is the totality of my being, expresses my original choice in particular circumstances; it is nothing other than the choice of myself as a totality in these circumstances. That is why a special method must aim at detaching the fundamental meaning which the project admits and which can be only the individual secret of the subject's being-in-the-world. (Sartre, 1956a, p. 564)

Perhaps the solution is so simple that man has need "to muddy the waters." Simply, sport like any other act of volition is a matter of choice. To categorize by causation is to admit to the unauthenticity of the evolvement. We find our meaning in varied forms but we do not necessarily select these forms because of our intended desires. To assume this much rational thought, from the irrational men of our world, is to exceed even the dominance of history! Man is in sport because he is and sport is in man because of its presence. In revealing himself to sport he admits his situation as human. He is nothing more and nothing less.

In this approach we can view the distinction between existence and essence as applicable to the athlete. The quality of *performance* is now perceived as more than just achievement of skill development but is a dimension of the *truth of being*. The development of a performer, in keeping with broad parameters of maturation, is a dilemma of eventualizing essence. It is that certain "something" that is to be reached or realized. The existence of the performer is localized in the *search.* The participant's existence is a product of the constant "looking out" (and being open to) for self-actualization. Essence for the individual is indigenous to that quality of existence which possesses its own being to be; also it has it as its own (Heidegger, 1962, pp. 32–33). Man faces sport with a potential for a degree of actualization. Being thus becomes a portion of that which is fulfilled in his world. In a way, he searches for his own development toward maximized internal existence. Man's *being* comes to sport prior to him, for existence has a prior presence to essence! The problem is one of great difficulty but is relatively simple to state. How does the participant find *truth,* in sport; that is, how does man locate the truth of his *own* being?

Truth of Being

In common usage one often refers to the *truth* of *something* as a concomitant of knowledge. For example, the *truth* of shooting an arrow is somewhat related to one's knowledge of factors inherent in the act. One has to know about the true conditions of wind variance, poundage, and other variables. It is obvious, however, that knowledge is not *all* there is to the attainment of truth. The "end" of truth is not attained within the object itself as a climax or fulfillment of knowledge. It is found in the *something* that enjoys a mixture of objective validity and personal *feel,* a *something* that goes beyond all scientific knowledge. One could say it is, to a degree, a symbol that makes *being* a reality.

To be knowledgeable in sport man, by design, needs an object. To locate truth within the media he needs to attain valid perceptions of the object. However, the truth of being does not happen because the participant is *there* perceiving the object. In fact, it is the opposite. The being of man as necessary, develops out of the subjective necessity of the object. Awareness of being of truth in sport arrives when man grasps the object.

If an *idea* is judged true, it must be representative of its object. If a form is true, it represents its essence. If a hypothesis is considered true, it must agree with observed and tested data. If a statement is true, it must concur with the statement of the case (Hofstadter, 1965, p. 167). In sport truth encompasses all the dimensions of ideas, essences and data as well as uniting the symbolic to the literal. The truth of a dive might very well extend outside the realm of what is *known*. Truth is more than mere attempts at attainment of reality or predetermined accepted patterns. In reality all that is empirically observable and all that is scientifically sensitized is included within the truth of sport movements. In this way sport resembles a two-sided coin. On one side, it bows to the world of science, a world that pays homage to sport as an observed and empirical reality. Thus, objectivity provides a picture of the support of being. However, there is the other side of the coin. The "flip-side" recognizes the value of experience as a personal encounter. Being is a personal matter. It is not enough for baseball to be considered the "All-American Game." It must be so considered by me. Like a coin there is no *real* duality between subjectivity and objectivity. It must be realized that one side may be viewed alone; however, the coin *itself* possesses two sides which in essence "back-up" on each other.

In a superficial way sport may be viewed as intimately involved with attaining truth. Games, movements, strategy are all related to regulations, established patterns and standards for action. Man is told to "adjust" to the system. In reality the system is frequently adjusted to man. For example, the "spit-ball" has been illegal for many years in professional baseball; however, there are few pitching staffs without at least one man who throws the "wet one." Umpires, managers, players all know the *truth of the matter* but they look the other way. The system conforms to the reality of the situation. Example after example could be given: excessive body contact in basketball, holding in football, the "near touch" of second base on a double-play in baseball, and the "save" in diving. But let us not belabor the point. Suffice to say that trueness in sport is frequently what *is* and what *is* is so because of its conformity to the precedent of existence. Thus, true movements are not only *genuine* but also *proper*. In a word, they fit.

From the previous discussion it follows that the participant's awareness of being is both a subjective and objective development. Therefore, ultimate truth of form, or dimensions of movement in sport, is as much a factor of the personal as the empirical. In fact, when one faces the situation of sport, it becomes obvious that the object has, within its potential, the opportunity to achieve *absolute* being; however, the individual, founded on the subjective, never attains the absolute.

Now for the obvious. Truth, as applicable to sport, has a special connotation or, if you please, meaning. In most forms of life, what man *thinks* actually is reality. But not so in sport. In many ways it can be said that sport is concerned with a *practical* truth. Generally, the interest is in *things* attaining *rightness* rather than *authenticity*. Rightness implies a direct path with a minimum of deviation from the expected. A "righted" arrow (not necessarily a *true* one) goes straight for its goal, thereby conforming to the reality. To shoot the *righted* arrow is to do more than participate in thought. One has to *act* in order that the thought of preparation become actualized.

Individuals involved in sporting activities have been traditionally concerned with *practical* truth, perhaps to the point of neglecting the *theoretical* truth. That is to say, a concern with the *rightness* which is directly attached to the practice of *thought*. In sport we give little but naive credence to the truth of a movement, be it a dive, the flight of the arrow, or the smash of a fullback into the line, *perceived to and by the intellect*. This is quite different from our usual emphasis upon the perception of the senses. When man *knows* his movement is right he, himself, desires existence. He craves to be. He wants to remain as is. Perhaps this is most dramatically demonstrated when the performer "holds" his follow-through after actual release of the performance, whether it be the golfer, discus thrower, or baseball pitcher. He desires himself, as a being, to *feel* himself and to kinesthetically as well as totally continue in the present form of existence. It is almost as if he were afraid to move for fear of losing the self he now so much enjoys. All of man is now *right*. He now knows what being *really* is.

It is my contention that truth in sport needs to be visualized as one of being. Being-in-object and being-in-man are both imperative. The performer, to attain all within the potential of the sport, must be vitally concerned with truth as inclusive of the real and the authentic. Ontology is broad in its concept of truth and, as such, a most suitable frame for sport. It is applicable to practice as well as to thought. Man seeks satisfaction in knowing the basics of any activity. Through the natural and immediate feedback of the sport situation, man comes to learn what being is.

To say one is a *real* skier is little more than to assert he *is*, to be sure, a skier. But this is not always valid. A *real* skier implies *trueness* and thereby connotes quality. In using the adjective *real* I am also demonstrating cognizance of the *existence* of the individual as opposed to simply recognition of my concept of his *essence*. In other words, I am not saying the individual *appears* to be a skier but in fact he *is* a skier. The reader will realize this viewpoint is quite different from traditional philosophic positions. The present analysis stresses being-in-itself, where most formulations stress the essence of being.

In further development of this thesis, I might desire to refer to the individual as a *genuine* skier. Now I give depth to the concept of existence. No longer am I referring to *just* a skier or even *merely* a real skier. Now I am inferring something that *is* what it seems *to be*. The genuine skier is not a deceiver or a cheat. He is, in a sense, representative of the *original* or perfect (in an ideal sense, much like a genuine diamond) skier. He now can be said to possess the quality of *being-in-itself*. Now being is tenaciously retained *within* the skier as an *original* quality.

Furthermore, to state one is an *authentic* skier is to indicate awareness of the original quality of skiing *itself*. "The thing's meaning agrees with its reality, and its reality conforms to its meaning" (Hofstadter, 1965, p. 170). The movements of the performer now are actualized through the operation. Being is now "full" and can be both recognized and communicated through *thought* of the sender and the receiver. Simply, the action is *so* identifiable that *thinking* is now a prevalent ingredient for being-in-itself. Being is easily grasped in this dimension since the symbol is easily recognizable as that which is.

The *true* skier is no longer such because of qualities that are attributed to the *external* self. Trueness is now accorded to he who has internalized truth. The skier is true not because what *appears* to be but what is in "theory of reality." The fact his edging is perfect, he skis lightly, his reactions are rhythmical and quick, he is a "stylist" and his movements are precise, is in itself not indicative of a true skier. Both theoretical and practical means must be applied before one analyzes the truth of a movement. It is necessary for the skier to *purport* that which he is. Of course this is a far cry from "appearing" to be. The skier must be *indicative* of the representation (theoretically) as well as *conform* to what is purported (practically). The skier might well transcend the actual experience, but he must remain in contact with the snow in order to bring about this mystical quality. Thus, the performer quickly tends to remain *in* the world but with a greater awareness of self, object and the world. He is not only available to being but becomes saturated with being.

It must be stressed that the *truth* of a skier is *not* a simple and ideal version that is externalized. It is the skier's own *meaning* for that which is *purported* to be. In the words of the experimentalist, the skier is *valid*. Thus truth of being in sport has been attained. The performer is still what he is. He maintains his essence—tissue and bones. However, this new dimension *extends* the skier from something of *matter* which is to a complete being with personification of *meaning*. The skier is now not only human but he is *humane*.

When the skier is accorded truth of being, his being is *possessive* of truth and not the *object* of truth. It is not truth *about* being (the truth of representation of an object) but that which comprises elements to genuineness and authenticity (Hofstadter, 1965, p. 173). Not only is he *aware* of his situation, but he remains ready to assume the responsibility of his choice. Skiing is a *placement* of being and no matter how *perfect* his choice he recognizes the limitations of the real world that *might* in the "long-run" (pun intended) bring tragedy to his existence. The skier who internally attains elements of ontological truth *really is*—a skier.

Ontological Truth: Foundation of Form

Sport provides the performer with a composite of relatives and absolutes. Truth can be attained *in* the specific movement, *in* the specific contest, *in* any and/or all encounters; however, the process of validity is not one of scientific process. Again, empiricism is a function of the observed-known rather than repetition.

A performer, desiring the *truth in form*, must, to a relative degree, be concerned with *simulation* of action. A diver considering the *essential* (without which none would be recognizable) form of the world of objects must certainly commence his creation from the senses, most frequently the visual. However, he needs to go further in order to accomplish inner achievement through the creation of form. Perhaps it is sufficient to say that there are aspects of the "objective" which are not available to perception, but might well be accessible to a different type of *apperception*. Perhaps this is akin to Husserl's development of "essences." Although the desired dive is beyond perception, there is no *mystical* element suggested here. What will determine the "degree" of the dive, beyond expected physical difficulty, is the individual's ability to *build* on the *idealized* form a new dimension of truth to the dive. To one and to all the "true" dive is recognized for its validity. The diver perceives the real object, the dive. It has essence and form. The diver incorporates into the self all the integral segments of the immediate environment. The spectators are perceived as a mass of colors, shapes, fusions, and emotions. The trickled water, beneath the board, fades in and out of consciousness. The towels on the deck, the feel of an occasional draft of air, the unique appearance of ceiling and the mass of fellow performers, all integrate the "whole" for the performer. Now the movement is more than even complete consciousness. Awareness is present.

There are those who contend that the athlete, for purposes of maximum performance, should free self from the environment: rid oneself of all that immediately exists and leave remaining the *contents* of the perceived dive. Thus, all connected experiences are expelled. Nothing remains except one's memory of the dive, removed from the specific setting of performance. Thus, the performance is left with an identification of characteristics of the desired movements. Admitting that I know little of the "strategy" employed in high level diving competition, I must admit my great concern with the segmentation of man from his total environment. No athletic cause could be so important. Certainly man needs to *transcend the everyday*.

Recognition of Truth in Sport

To determine the *absolute truth* of a movement one must eliminate the concept of the *absolute*. If this sounds like double-talk, it is not. Simply, the absolute truth is *beyond* the idealized absolute which is representative of mechanical and technical perfection. The abolution of the absolute is necessitated due to the recognition of no *finite* extensions of man's mind. Every judgment is arbitrary. Any attempt at objective evaluation of truth (certainly including the "verdict of the scoreboard") is impossible. This is not to say that the idealized does not *exist* as much as it is an indication of the *end* being beyond the sensation and knowledge of man.

Judgments are not all rational. Like the *actual* the *evaluation* includes the totality of the environment. Thus, the truth of a dive is to be judged from part substance and part intuition. It appears, in this regard, that intuition, perhaps, is more vital than logic based on established regulations.

What does it mean when the individual performer can say, because of inner communication developed *in* the dive, "I am"? Is it similar to the assertion that "the pool is"? Can one mean the same thing when he says: "the water is"; "the deck is"; and "the board is"? I think not. While it is granted that "non-beings" exist, they have no way of communicating their meaning of existence. The diver, in the dive and via the dive, has a means of expression. In a sense, being is the *composite* of the dive and diver. Again, we see the unification or wholeness of sport. Man cannot be considered as entity divorced from his action. He is the composite.

Within the action of the task, being is realized through the infinite choices available to the diver. The diver can demonstrate the *true* dive by uniting and organizing *all* the necessary elements into perceivable forms. If this is not accomplished, he tears into the very heart of existence through segmentation of that which is true. Of course, passing mention needs be directed to the skill of the performer. If one is just not capable of performing the dive, obviously the "perceivable form" will be anything but complete. The greater degree of sophistication of skill, the greater the opportunity to attain being. However, the mere mystery of skill certainly does not guarantee being. The diver must demonstrate awareness of the depths the dive may achieve. He needs to communicate with authenticity. His involvement needs to be genuine if the dive is to be really *true*.

> In the intellectual knowledge of being intellect recognizes that all that is, is something, a quiddity that exists. This aspect of existence cannot express quidditatively though it tends to so express it. . . . "to be" is expressed as an intelligibility in the judgment. Both the quidditative aspect and the existential aspect of being are understood by intellect as act. "To be" is recognized as the act of all acts even of forms. It is the act of essence which is seen like a formal perfection yet different. (Maritain, 1949, p. 20)

Truth is not *in* the action as much as it is revealed in and by the performer. This is not to deny relevance toward outcomes, for without the *object* there are no "relatives" and thus no truths. To think of a dive within the frame of universal and idealistic realities is to subordinate man. It is *in* man and *between* men that the truth of the dive, or any other sport movement, comes *to be*. There are no absolute truths in sport but only "concrete truth, willed, created, maintained, and conquered through social struggle" (Sartre, 1955, p. 238). The truth of being is a matter of choice. It is a matter of authentic choice. Finally, one could well agree with Heidegger's concept of "being there." The act, in this case the dive, does not stand *in* and alone by itself. It "stands out," thereby receiving and giving meaning to the individual and the immediate environment. Thus, man differs from other "existents"; in the dive, he gains knowledge into existence and thereby comes to terms with eventual realized being.

It becomes obvious that the sport participant cannot isolate himself from his fellow man, not if he is to discover being. Looking from the outside, in a form of detachment, will no doubt lead to a lack of meaning—a deficiency our world can ill afford. It is communicated only too frequently in many dives, as in other forms of sport action, that something less than *truth* is demonstrated. The diver, in this instance, might well operate his totality of performance *within* "space" and not from within the "self."

In a way, it is this aspect of *withinness* that speaks to the totality of the dive. It, partially, explains the difference between the *everyday* dive and the *real* dive. When the performer practices, day-in-day-out, the dive might develop toward perfection but it lacks that "certain something" that often comes in moments of competition. It is almost as if the practice dives were "fake" and the performance during the meet were "real." During practice the dives are completed in earnest; however, a type of "absence" or non-personalized identification with the act somehow always appears to be present. The dives are performed as "one does," expressing a level of "like so many others" that have been repeated and repeated and repeated. To be sure, there are certain rare performers who, in practice sessions, do not divorce themselves from achieving the range of human potentiality, but they are rare indeed (it is interesting to note that many coaches warn their athletes "not to leave their game on the practice field"). It appears that existence achieved through the "trueness" of the dive affords the performer an opportunity to see himself in a totally new perspective. When the diver "stands there" and "stands here," he is, by implication, totally *concerned* with the infiniteness of human possibilities.

We can see that, through the use of intellect, the act of sport affords being in its own right. Similarly, in the process of existence, all man's acts are realized not only on the cognitive level but in *actuality*. The dive shows to man *an* expression of his being. Certainly, "to know" is to encounter the importance of being. But the existence of man exists *prior* to the dive; therefore, the dive is there. One could really not expect anything else. Since there is nothing beyond existence, only the being of the totality, man and the dive, can satisfy. In truth, man must *apprehend* the being of the composite. He must locate its significance and admit this to the self. The end is a richer more noble life for man. Being is all there is—it is life.

The Body as an Entity

To discuss the body as an entity is to admit its existence. The temptation of dualistic analysis is there, but it is still imperative that the human body be viewed whenever man studies sport.

This separation does not presuppose segmentation of mind and body as much as it facilitates the view of the whole.

There can be little doubt that, in sport, the body is brought into conscious awareness. Through a sport activity, such as long jumping, man locates his body as *belonging* to him. As the jumper sprints down the runway of an approach that is seemingly endless, the body is "self-experienced." The body is all that *does* exist. It really *is*. In its concreteness, the jumper knows *it* must be propelled with maximum efficiency.

"Can I get the trajectory? Can I get that initial kick that will send me soaring?" The body, at this point, is certainly not separated from the mind; theoretically, both elements are *incorporated*. The performer's concern is apparently on the pit ("How far will I leap?"), but not really. The *intended* is nothing more than a target. If the mark were not there, the action might well be *absurd*. But the presence of the goal does not restrict man's action as much as it provides for a controlling of energies. Upon close inspection one could well see that the focus *is* on the *body*. "I experience my body first as a complex of life-movements which are indistinguishable from any experience of selfness" (Schrag, 1962, p. 204). *Man* makes the association of body to jump. But that is what it is, an association. The *imperativeness* of the *complete* act is localized in the body. The body is the *shell* for all that is real; it is not the *object*. That is to say, it is not that which is to be propelled into space. It is important to stress this point. *This is my body*. It might resemble others. It might appear to be some other form. But in the concrete, in its existence, it is the location for all that occurs to me. As an object it might well appear weak and prone to injury but as an *entity* it is most durable. In this way we can see the body belongs to me. *Others* might well experience *my* body but it is my body.

Frequently the athlete does not perceive his body as do others. Due to modern technology he might watch himself perform on film or even "instant replay," but in truth he is now *outside* of his body looking in. The body is either an entity among other entities, or it is an entity that reveals its "self" to man. It is doubtful that man can be both at the same time. The body "represents the individualization of my engagement in the world" (Sartre, 1956a, p. 310). This *identity* might well be an expression of all within the cosmos, an expression that allows man to encounter, maintain and create personal and special *meanings*. This is quite different from divorcing the body from men so that the body *becomes* what it is. As Sartre indicates in *Being and Nothingness*, there is a difference between the body as a *thing* and as a *possibility*.

As the long jumper stretches his limbs, at the point of "toeing" the board, he in no way conceives his body, in position or as a potential for quickness. Not even at the height of his jump, when the leg approaches full extension, does he conceptualize his *essence*. "In the fact of *my body* there is something which transcends what can be called its materiality, something which cannot be reduced to any of its objective qualities" (Marcel, 1952b, p. 315). The body, in the air, is not something the jumper *possesses* (object). In a larger sense it *is* indicative of personal identity. It tells the jumper who he *is*. *He exists and he is a body*. "I do not *make use of my body*, I am my body" (Marcel, 1952b, p. 333). Thus, the literature which implies that the body is an *instrument* of and for movement is herein refuted. The body is *not* an instrument, *as such*, for it (the body) is *who* (not what) it *is* (self).

The performer, understandably, *uses* his body to perceive as well as to experience a variety of other sensations. The jumper sees the pit as an element of space. As he incorporates his body to the situation the sport becomes a resolution of *object and distance*. The performer sees his body. Likewise the spectators see the body. Similarly, the space to be conquered is perceived. But there is a world of difference between the personal experiencing of the body *as is* and the more removed and impersonal evaluation of the crowd as the body as that *which is*. The former is *subject*, while the latter is *object*. When the body is perceived *as is*, reality of performance is more easily experienced. The body is now an *existent*, possessing extensive possibilities. It is open and accessible (*Existenz*).

Although the body is available to the person as that which is *personally* unique, an element of communal relationship is also of interest. The body is in constant interaction with other participants, spectators, officials, etc. "I apprehend my body in a communal context in which other selves are disclosed as already being there" (Marcel, 1952b, p. 333). Man thereby comes to know the body of others and secondly, his own body as perceived by others. The end of this analysis is to recognize that man knows his body *only* because of its relativeness to another.

In using his body man is able to relate to objects when indeed he deobjectifies his own body. The track and field performer, who hurls a thirty-five pound weight through the air, uses his body in and of itself, and not only to propel the object. There is a certain feeling that comes to the body through involvement in sport that is a sense of *being*. In the straining and alteration from normal pursuits, man *feels* his body as he never knew it before. "Pure activity becomes inertia to overcome the inertia of things" (Javet, 1961, p. 57). In this manner, all that man contacts develops a human dimension. The object is given *being* when man himself has *being*, indicating that the body is *live*. The sport object demands that man gives the self (not his freedom, but his sense of will) to the object. If man is not *available*, the object will remain a product of the instrument that produced it rather than a product of man who could have given it life.

Autonomy of existence can be achieved by the body *knowing* the object in a way that is not known by others or by the object. Through the process of transcendence he no longer perceives the self as is. The skin diver becomes part of the sea, the skier part of the mountain, and the hunter part of the woods. *In the body* and *by the body* man learns *existenz* in an exciting new way.

As we have seen, "our body is that which is most our *own* of all conceivable things, which is least opposed to us, least foreign and so least antagonistic" (Buytendijk, 1948, p. 218). As previously discussed the idea of one's body is not to be confused with the reality of same. Body image experimentation has indicated, rather conclusively, that man's body is often unrecognizable and alien to our perceptions given a specific set of conditions. But this is not to say that man is always specific to the condition.

Sartre, in a brilliant analysis, distinguishes three dimensions of the human body as they relate to sport. The kinesthesis of the body as both subject and object is stressed with the greatest of care. But perhaps what is more important is the emphasis on the body as a familiar entity to both mover and spectator. The body, despite this closeness, only becomes known as it moves. If sport provides no other function, this, in itself, would be sufficient. In this way the body, in sport, makes objects in the world accessible to man, thereby giving birth to all the body senses.

> The mountaineer who outlines his plans the day before and discusses his wish to reach a difficult top with his friends, destroys his intentions as soon as he takes his first step on the difficult ground. He no longer thinks of his shoes to which an hour ago he still gave such great attention, he "forgets" the stick that supports him while he climbs and with which he tests the reliability of a rock point, he "ignores" his body which he trained for days together beforehand with an eye to this trip . . . For only by forgetting, in a certain sense, his plans and his body, will he be able to devote himself to the laborious task that has to be formed. What there still is, psychologically speaking, is only the mountain. . . . Just because he forgets his body, this body can realize itself as a living body. The body (just as the plan) is realized as *landscape*. . . . The fatigue of his body shows itself in the first instance in the distance of the inaccessibility of the top. . . .
>
> The qualities of the body: its measurements, its ability, its efficiency and vulnerability can only become apparent when the body itself is forgotten, eliminated, passed over in silence. . . .
>
> The *second dimension* of the body comes into being under the eyes of his fellow-man. . . . we assume that the spectacle of mountaineer in his situation is watched by another, who remains unperceived. Seeing him climb I concentrate on the very thing that the mountaineer himself must forget for the sake of the work he is doing. *I see his body* and the whole landscape with which his body contends is centered in this moving living "object." This body is the pole from where the whole mountain and mountaineer is appreciated and understood. . . . the body there before me is governed by a center *in* his body.
>
> Also the mountaineer himself can constitute his body in the second dimension. This happens for instance when he tends the wound in his leg. The wounded place is examined and touched *in order to* cure it, or: *in order to be able* to continue on his way. And it may even occur that he considers his body as thing-body. . . .
>
> The third dimension of the body comes into being when the mountaineer becomes aware that I am regarding him. . . .
>
> He begins to feel hindered because he knows that the other sees . . . He feels vulnerable in an absolutely defenseless domain. (Van Den Berg, 1952, pp. 159–183)

As Van Den Berg points out there exists a look at another that changes the perception of the world (Van Den Berg, 1952). Athletes have long been aware of the effect of crowd behavior. It is most frequent for the plaudits of the crowd to motivate performers to new heights.

But this is not all. There must be room for the *appreciation* of the body . . . *a priori*. Performers are typically sensitive and appreciative of their arms, waist, "gastrics," etc. They cherish the immediate and the body is the most immediate of all. The body is of "primary familiarity." When injured or sore, it becomes known by the *total*. An athlete seldom admits to the loss of function of the *total*. He prefers to think in a segmented manner. "*The* reflexes are slower." "*The* wrists have lost *their* snap." Not only does he speak dualistically when he refers to the body but he no longer identifies the part of the body as belonging to him. It becomes an *object* of the *impersonal*. The use of the word "the" removes the part from the body that makes it belong to another. It is almost as if he has deserted it because it is not reacting properly. If the body is not sound the performer, putting so much "stock" into it, feels much like a jilted lover and personally escapes from the encompassing condition. Yet, this does not deny the appropriation of the body to its relationship with another.

The wrestler soon learns he has to work with his own body. But his success is determined not only *by* his opponent's body, but also by his *own* realization of *his* body in reference to that of the opponent's. Therefore, what *really* does exist for the participant is a factor of perceived relationships. Man's body becomes an entity of *other/self* and *object/subject* experiences, all of which become fused in time and space. For the wrestler, his opponent's body is a variable presented in the form of a barrier,* a tool (to be used), or as one of communicational receiver of awareness.

I think it is safe to say that man never knows the other's body—*as it is experienced by the other*. Of course, it is easy to measure or evaluate a displacement of the mass-body of another. But this is a segmented view which is not entirely valid. For man's body is "one" and all his expressions of movement are relevant

* Sartre uses the term "coefficient of adversity."

to the world of the individual. All one can do is *assimilate* the other as it *appears*. The emphasis, it appears, is one placed on the unification of movements within man. The other's body "appears within the limits of the situation as a synthetic totality of life and action" (Sartre, 1956a, p. 346). Isolation of the whole body, *from* man (mind/body), or segmentation of parts of the body (head, foot, fingers, etc.), is to make man less than what functions of a human life. Structures need to be revealed in *Gestalt;* all leading toward unity of the man. The wrestler can also be cited as an example here; he needs cognizance of all parts within the whole. To evaluate personal or opposing legs without consideration of the multi-correlations of the arms is to render an unrealistic appraisal of the "position" of man. One cannot deny the possibility of taking "advantage" of a certain *part* of man, but this needs to follow an appreciation of the totality if one is to succeed.

Initial evaluation tends to be body-oriented rather than *totality*-oriented. When looking at an athlete one is likely to remark about his "bigness." This is not solely a spectator reaction. The participant also makes this appraisal. Our reflections tend to be body-directed. And obviously our judgments tend to be subjectively and relatively determined. And this is the way it should be, for the perception of body is not absolute but a function of the relativity of the evaluator's experience.

In sport, man's body is frequently opposed rather than integrated with the other. At first glance one could attribute this to the quality of competition. However, upon closer analysis this element of "being against" is apparent, not only between opponents, but with one's own teammate. The "other's" body is thought of as a *thing* and is often maneuvered for the achievement of personal satisfaction. It is not unusual for players to sense this feeling in themselves and others and feel "guilty" about being *selfish*. Yet when one gets down to cases, sport is much like *survival*. In *life* cooperation *may* provide for *quality* but in survival man wants *just* to exist. Perhaps certain sport activities do combine both qualities of selfishness and altruism. But they are rare. One such exception, combining these aspects, might well be mountain climbing.

> Rock-climbing is also a sport I enjoy very much. I like the feel of the rope binding me to my comrades somewhere near the clouds. I like to feel the sensation of conquering the sky, although, in the final analysis, it always wins the victory over us. (Yevtushenko, 1966, p. 126)

Man does not climb mountains for material rewards. He climbs because he desires to climb. It is here that *actual* life or death is at stake. But one should not be easily misled. That is to say, to think that man cooperates *because* of survival is to beg the point that man enters the sport by choice. Although the Russian poet exclaims the virtue of nature, it is doubtful that man selects, as Sartre says, sport on the basis of the abstract over the concrete. I tend to think the climber climbs for basically one reason, because he climbs. If meaning, association, causality, etc. are to be attached to sport, this is fine, but this is not sport nor is it a personal priority. To assume anything less is to accept essence as prior to existence.

Sport often does request man to prostitute the *other's* body. One person often "sacrifices" one for another. As if this were not bad enough, we are also asked to become an "instrument" in the process of giant manipulations. This is done, by player and coach, despite our awareness that the reduction of man *into* another leads to destruction of the self. To see a world of this dimension is to admit the coldness of something that is less than human, and yet it is not so high as animal.

We must return to the discussion of the *body*. In few other activities of life is the body brought to such heightened awareness as in sport. Yet, in a way, the body is not recognizable. It is a tool that is used but, in many ways, it is that which is to be achieved. We know only too well the desire of man to "pump" up his body with the use of exercise. Frequently, when bored he turns to sport—hoping to "game-up" his weariness so that the body can be fortified.

To *take-in another's* body is normally done with respect to the image. "The other's body is perceived in a unique manner, not just as another object-tool, but as a synthetic totality of life and action" (Sartre, 1956a, p. 512). To assimilate this "total quality" is most important for any attainment of success in sport. Much as in social situations man is "ahead" if he can perceive the needs of another. So it is with sport situations if man can perceive the body. To be conscious of his body and the body of another allows man the advantage of the reality of *feelings*. In sport man attempts to master *bodies*. He attempts to constrain the obstacle or redirect its intentions. Yet, moreover than not, the *other's* body escapes me. It goes beyond my control. To realize the limits of the other body, as my own, is to *really* know the body. To actually control it may well be another matter. To admit the boxer causes my head to ache is to lose the importance of the body unless one actually realizes that it is the head itself that is *living* with this ache. The condition of my head might well have been *caused* by a punch from my opponent but my head is what I possess. It now harbors the reality of the consequence. It should be noted that I now know little about my head. What my head really reflects is my relative boxing ability as compared with another's. My head is real and its condition forms one part of the world which is now most immediate to me. It is my existence. ". . . The appearance of the body does not give us the body as it acts and perceives but only as it is acted on and perceived" (Sartre, 1956a, p. 358). In a word, the body is who I am. It is my existence.

In consideration of the mind/body problem one can see that an analysis of sport quickly offers a wholestic concept of the development of man. In sport, man *is* his body. No statement could be more inclusive. When one plays hole after hole on the golf course, or when one is hit by tackle after tackle, or when one soars through the air on his skis, there is the realization that the "I" and the "body" are indeed united. In some contexts the "I" is viewed specifically, while the "body" is an interactor. The "I" is the victim of a sprained ankle resulting from a tennis match. I hurt and I think about it with each movement; however, the sprain I am so *aware* of is situated within the soft matter of my ankle, inaccessible to my control. Certainly I can deactivate *it;* I can reduce the pain through medical treatment. Yet my *tie* to my ankle is both foreign and impersonal ("it") while at the same time it is *my* ankle. Injury, quickness, soundness, and strength *belong to me*, they are mine. They are not mental or physical as much as they express the *inward* abilities and limitations of my totality. Sport tells me that it is *I which is.*

But this is not the complete argument. For example, Descartes not only separates mind and body, but he separates sensation and emotion. I don't hear noises. I hear loud spectators. And I hear the crack of the bat.

To repeat the obvious, man *is* a totality. He not only *has* a body but he is a body! "Having a body includes the possession of one's own property within the world of creaturely nothingness" (Zuidema, 1957, p. 80). Sport does not allow man to escape from his two streams. On one hand he does possess the *being* of his body; yet on the other he possesses, as all humans, the element of *non-being*.

> [The surfers] were inarticulate until they got on their boards. Then they became almost eloquent. . . . They said the hell with the ordinary ways of making it, but they were left with nothing. Surfing seemed to them a *bodily* [italics mine] statement of what they feel. They are looking for the limits of control—the edge where you feel out of control but are really in control. Surfing put them in this position, but ultimately it didn't involve them in any statement about themselves. (Rogin, 1965, p. 106)

Sport provides man, within his body, an existence that is "happening" oriented. The situation occurs again and again; man is always being tested by that which we call sport. Perhaps this is what sport is. It is a drama of human life. To appreciate sport is to come to *know* the wholeism of existence. "I love sport because I love life and sport is one of the basic joys of life. Life is not very generous with its joys—they have to be seized by force. And to seize a thing by force, a sound mind and sound muscles are needed" (Yevtushenko, 1966, p. 128). Sport is a place for choice. Man chooses with *all* of him. He places himself in conflict with elements, thereby transcending the real world in a situation that is truly whole.

SPORT AND PURPOSE

To discuss something as abstract as *purpose*, applicable to sport, one must first consider the theoretical composite of the "real" of sport. We need to ask the following: What is sport *itself*? And what *meaning* is afforded to man through participation in this segment of life? After consideration of these concerns attention can be directed toward study of the *significance* of sport. Naively armed with the product of this contemplation, the attempt for philosophical *analysis*, not unity, becomes the summum bonum of this work.

This is not to infer that *a* meaning of sport is present and that the only necessity is for wise men of science and letters to arrive at the answer. Not only is this improbable, but it is also undesirable. Our task is to direct inquiry to the *conceptual* frame of *purpose*. Needless to say, we deal with relatives, uncertainties, vagueness, obscurities, perplexities and even paradox. However, inquiry into purpose might indicate directions for thought to contain, which ideally is *something other than itself*. Thus, we can come to recognize what sport "says" and *perhaps* means. To admit the interpretation of purpose in sport is difficult to attain, is to say less than the obvious; however, since its nature is *so* relative, the need for philosophical *analysis* becomes even more vital.

Initially, we can "define" purpose as that which elaborates a meaning, which possesses its own nature to constitute an object. In other words, the purpose of any happening is a result of that which occurs in sport *between* objects, between objects and man, *among* objects, and *among* objects and man. Basically it is one of *meaning*. Thus, it is *not* so much that the object, be it a ball, mask, puck, or whatever, be *real*, which it certainly must be, but that the basis of the purpose of the meaning that occurs to man through his *relationship* with the object be real. Real relationships exist both in present and non-present forms.

This reliance on reality and meaning carries with it a strong responsibility to what *is*, but more than that, what is meant, with purpose upon the completeness of man. For scholars of sport to understand *essence* of reality is not to escape the question of existence (the premise of dualistic-polarities is both naive and false) but rather to approach man's *being*. "It would be . . . to rediscover inseparably with the presence of myself to myself our presence to things into which we encounter completely" (de Waelhens, 1962, p. 5).

The application of man's will to sport is relatively meaningless if the sport activity is not to make man available (*open*) to higher levels of comprehension of self. In a word, it is the discovery of *being*. The knowledge man has of himself he carries to sport *without* choice. It is part of him. Interesting as it is, man might not be able to integrate this knowledge within the self. Sport, with its nature one of competition and movement, almost calls for man to reveal what he is to realize about himself. ". . . Knowing oneself and being a self are not to be kept apart" (Heschel, 1965, p. 7).

If knowledge of self and being are a separate entity within the sport situation, and *this* encounter is not actualized, then the endemic condition of non-being presents *itself*. Thus, internalization of man is avoided. Man is neither proprietor of sport nor of self.

Evidently, there is a difference between overt purpose, where *will* formulates the basis of our action, and covert purpose, where the basis for action may and may not be fully "willful" or comprehended by the individual. It seems that all my hunting experiences have faced me with this steady contradiction—to kill, and call it sport when I truly *can't* kill—even if I call it survival!

Characteristics of Sport

When I initially formulated the proposal for this work I was almost certain that I could define sport. Without being unnecessarily pedantic I could assume that baseball was a sport while sleeping was not. In my own mind, this book was to deal with activities such as football, race car driving, hunting, surfing, tennis, etc. It was not to consider board games such as Monopoly, checkers or even chess (which is often found within the general classification of sport). Somehow I *knew* what sport was but I did not know how to define it.

I began to ask questions of myself. What is this experience I call sport? What differentiates sport activities from other activities of life? When is an activity considered sport and when does it lose the qualities that make it sport? To be sure, these are searching questions of deceptive simplicity.

In attempting to respond to these queries one could easily "beg" the question. My first impulse was to rely on traditionally accepted classifications. When this became inappropriate, I turned my attention to "working definitions." But again this did not answer the fundamental problem. What *is* this book's concern? What are the characteristics of sport?

Certainly it is necessary to inform the reader what I am including and, of equal import, what I am excluding from the analysis. This is not an easy task. I am certain no formulation could encompass the many divergent activities commonly located within the province of sport. But my initial attempts had to follow the structure of deductive analysis. I asked myself what are the activities I consider as sport. Secondly, what identifying factors were inherent in these activities. No doubt this systematized attempt creates both errors of omission and commission; however, it allows the reader a scope within which meaningful discussion can be localized. Certainly the characteristics put forth are not meant to be definitive.

As previously indicated, my initial attempts were localized in the identification of factors inherent in sport. After repeated frustration I have come to realize that I can best describe sport by simple reference to theoretical constructs that are located within sport. Initial reaction by the reader, to this method of abstraction of traits, might appear unorthodox and perhaps even limiting. But, in truth, it provides a structure within which the reader can focus his attention. Thus, the stated theories are *not* meant to be (and certainly are not) all-inclusive elements found in *one* sport or localized in *all* sports. However, they are constructs that *are* located within that which I call the *spirit of the concept of sport.*

Contention of Interest. All activities so designated as *sport*, within this analysis, possess a quality which indicates that within the activity the participants, whether teams or individuals, contend differing interests and desires. Philosophically, those individuals writing in "game theory" have called this "conflict of interest." More commonly the term competition is used. However, the phrase *contention of interest* implies a *directed commitment* that is perhaps not as strongly implied in the term competition. In other words, in sport man overtly, through obvious thought, has an interest that is contended by either man, animal or nature. The participant may be able to regulate some of the variables in determination of outcome; however, he never, during the process or proceedings of the event, can manage to control the situation completely. Generally, it is easy to locate obvious preferences. Tennis player A desires to hit the ball to player B's side of the net. On the other hand B's contention of interest is to hit the ball to A's side of the net.

Outcomes are a direct extension of the theory of contention of interest. The desired results, accruing from "play," may be quite varied. Dependent upon the orientation of the activity, victory, reward, death are all "dictated" by the sport. In professional sports, the rules are such that they demand superior performance toward victory and assumed monetary rewards. Development of values such as sportsmanship is utterly naive and really not within the *real* rules of the game. Frequently, an "ethic" might be present but, more often than not, this is founded on "survival."

Thus, sport outcomes are in part based on *knowledge*. That is, each player must be completely aware of the *form* of the sport. He must know the rules and the interest of each player. He assumes, by social contract, the agreement of role contention—or else there is chaos.

Consistency of Role. A characteristic related to the construct of contention of interest is germane to potential "outcomes." It appears that toward the given "end," a consistent pattern of preferences is always maintained by the performers. The tennis player has a consistent and structured pattern relative to his "preferences." He always desires the same over-all end, and thus maintains a consistency of role expectation.

This characteristic carries with it the need for *choice*. The problem is placed in the forefront by the performer. What choice should I make in order that my partial influence over the outcomes benefits me the most (Luce, 1957, p. 6)? That is to say, given a specific set of conditions (that may or may not change), we could ascertain, one way or another, what choice the player should make. This point must be stressed. The dilemma of *individual decision making* is crucial to sport. Where this characteristic is not found—sport does not exist.

The thesis of decision-making, as applied to sport, must be conceived in two categories: (1) decisions made by the individual, and (2) decisions made by the group. However, if the decision of the group is one of complete agreement, it should really be thought of as an individual decision. Frequently, in so-called "team-sports" such as field hockey, football, basketball, etc., we assume the decision depicts *unitary* interest but, in truth, it might be little more than segmented groups' decisions. This could be a contributing factor in the apparent lack of consistency in predicting *outcomes*. We assume the team is making decisions as a group, with mutual interests, when in reality many individual decisions may be ones of conflicting interest. To achieve efficient "productivity" the individualized interests must be resolved or adjusted. So often this is the job of the coach or manager—to mold a group of individuals into a team.

Utilization-Actualization. This characteristic in sport is relevant to maximization of individual effort toward utilitarian ends. This point could be quickly misinterpreted if not clarified.

One could easily argue that in many sport events the participants participate without any overt attempts toward actualization. They might be engaging in "recreational" activity with no intent to better their ability. However, upon closer inspection, one will have to admit that if "sport" is the engagement, actualization might not be the intended purpose but it is always within the context of the media. Secondly, the participants perform with a utility function present. Utilization-Actualization theory does not imply an agreement with traditional ends, nor does it assume the participant knows the functions that others in the sport are attempting to fulfill. Although one has to admit this is usually general knowledge.

Variable Predictability. Related to the theory of contention of interests is the problem of variables. In the sport situation the variables which contribute to possible outcomes are *not* completely specified. It is possible to "program" all the possible "moves" in one given chess game. However, it is *not* possible *absolutely* to program all the chances that could occur in one tennis game. *Realistically* this might be possible, but absolutely it is not. It is this characteristic that, in part, eliminates all forms of dice games, roulette, bingo, etc., from sport. In each case it is potentially possible to predict the chance variability of a given situation. One cannot enter into a football contest with a mathematically determined coefficient of variable predictability. In games the controlling variables, hypothetically, can be predicted. In sport they cannot.

If this premise is accepted, we proceed to the next applied assumption; namely, that when the choices evolving from outcomes are based on knowledge, a specific player will select the choice yielding the most desirable result perceived. This might appear to be obvious; however, it is this premise, within the presented development of sport, that attempts to explain the difference in preferences relative to empirical results as opposed to non-rational preferences.

Perhaps the point can be better illustrated in the *game* of poker. The fascination in this game is the element of chance which, in turn, is interwoven by human decision. "Bluffing" is of course prevalent in many "sporting" events, but in poker this element is not "unique" as much as it is a basic skill and fundamental to the game. Poker is not so much a game of cards as it is a game of self-fulfillment. One can test his strength against his opponents. In the long run the cards are not important and thus man can make his own destiny. Poker involves *people.* It is inherently human. Perhaps this is one of the reasons it played such an important role in the settlement of our country, especially the west. Fortunes and territories were won and lost at the poker table. Unlike chess or even bridge, poker cannot be played against an IBM machine (Lukas, 1963, p. 57). The game has rules but they are so diversified that man has broad interpretational limits. This suits man just fine. For he has the security of boundary but also the excitement afforded by the presence of freedom. The *will of man* determines the rules and these rules are often changed, depending upon the specific conditions or the desire of the man in control. The dealer indeed does more than just hand out cards. He makes a prime choice. His choice of game indicates his perception of personal success.

The chance elements in sport and games are what appeals to modern man. In sport man pits himself against that which is fated. In a time of computer science and logical positivistic forms of analysis, the element of chance is all the more appealing to the man who would like to make room for emotion in a world that is perhaps a little too rational. Man has reason to hope. And after all there is always a chance the underdog will be victorious.

The western world often fuses thought and practice. Man's choice and will are believed predominant to the elements of *chance*. It is therefore not surprising that when man takes part in sport, especially when the activity is "recreative," his attentions turn to an activity that combines these elements. The "national pastime," baseball, is a case in point. It combines both skill and chance, with the emphasis on the latter.

Theoretically, the batter has one main purpose, namely, to hit the ball "where the opposition ain't." But in truth, the *prevailing* manner, even with the most skilled players, is to swing the bat in hopes of getting a "piece of the ball." To be sure, players try to "place" the ball; however, the majority of efforts can be described as a "swing and a hope." A hope, not only that the ball will hit the bat, but that it will *fortunately* avoid the glove of any of the nine opponents. The element of chance is great. To be certain the variables are so large that man must indeed be fortunate. Certainly, the element of chance operates in all sports. The basketball player might aim at the rim of the basket and score by hitting the backboard. The quarterback might complete a deflected pass. Or the soccer goalie might be saved not so much by his ability as by the goal post. Just a fraction of an inch will often make the difference between success and failure. It is difficult to avoid the element of chance; however, few sports possess the infinite and consistent elements of chance in the degree that is localized in baseball. It is not surprising that the "common" man, seeking some form of "hope," turns to baseball as an American pastime. It gives him a *chance*!

Sport: An Awareness of Human Action

To conceive of sport as simply games, activities, or even a value ("the sporting life"), is to say less than what is. To deny alterations in physical levels is for the most part to deny the truth; though, certainly, physiological change is only one incomplete segmentation of the resultant action. Obviously, much of what "happens" in sport does not lend itself to objective quantification. The physical scientist frequently enters this type of argument, indicating, not that sport occurrences cannot be measured, but rather that science has not, to date, developed the proper and suitable instrumentation for measurement. It would appear little exception could be taken to this type of "open ended" statement. Everything is possible . . . tomorrow. It assumes that the something to be measured maintains measurable characteristics. This may not be true. Perhaps this "happening" just does not lend itself to any form of measurement. The process, to which we affix the name sport, might well have mental expressions that are not directly observable. Or is man not this much of a dualist?

One could well ask, "Cannot the emotion of professional football be described?" Is the mood of the golfer amenable to analysis? Is the sensation of the javelin thrower determinable? No doubt behavioral scientists have made great strides in this area of human inquiry. Yet one wonders if there is not a little more. Are these perhaps philosophical situations, not proper for scientific study?

To this end the existential writers have talked of human awareness. In talking of the cosmos they have described authenticity of existence, will to power, despair and nothingness. Few would say the answer has been determined in the general battleground of life. Certainly it has not even been partially achieved in sport. Through the analysis of the work of formal philosophy, it becomes the task of the student of sport to develop a specific theoretical formulation. Certainly an inquiry centered around *human awareness* is most necessary.

Too much and too often sport is interpreted in some neo-Freudian manner. Is not the man's throwing of balls, discs, hammers, etc., examples of basic human drives? Is man sexually driven when he holds a baseball bat? Certainly, in this century we can recognize sport for what it is. Can we believe life is so accidental that it is nothing less than a product of the environmental forces? If man is not aware of his consciousness then he needs to work on the development of this facility, or suffer from making personal judgments that are really not his. "Consciousness is . . . a hole, a rent in the otherwise sturdy fabric of being" (Roberts, 1957, p. 199).

Sport is not all a cognitive process. It incorporates elements of desire, drive, love, care, feeling, etc. There is nothing purposeful, by natural law, in sport. To this end it could be said to possess no real direction or intention. Yet man does have purpose. He does assume direction. His reasons for action might be abstruse but they are present.

Operative Awareness in Sport. Most of sport experiences are controlled by man's feeling about a specific happening. The way a halfback decides to "cut" may well be based on the objective but the eventuation of the move is finalized on a subjective basis. He moves right or left, depending upon his "feel" of the situation. Although based upon the objective, his actions greatly reflect his emotional sensations. Frequently, emotions cloud awareness of the real more than they illuminate. This is neither good nor bad. It is the way it is. Man can't simply refuse to consider his emotions. To say "I will now be objective" is to refute the wholestic approach beyond reasonable certainty.

Our subjective being is truly united with our reason. It is merely for the convenience of expression that one can refer to the rational part of man. Man becomes aware of the presence of wholeness and thus proceeds to theorize about a segmentation of man. The awareness that is called for in sport is one of *operation.* Man needs to know how to react to a given situation. He must know how to operate, as situations are rarely identical; awareness of the whole becomes most necessary if any realm of transfer is to develop.

Perhaps the most practical type of awareness that is indigenous to sport is a form most normally disassociated with sport—namely, the theoretical. True, it might not yield results directly related to the specific sport event; yet, it does develop what some have called a philosophy of sport. In truth it is generally more of a *point of view* than a philosophy. But the difference is unimportant at this time. The thing that *is* important is what is happening. Generally, man is able to think beyond what is known and demonstrable. Concerned with operative awareness he theorizes and conceptualizes, processes only man has been able to achieve.

The reader should not be deceived into thinking that operative and theoretical awareness become fused in the man of sport. Evidence indicates quite the contrary. What the man of sport theorizes often remains quite far from practice. Perhaps it is this split and its immediate demonstration in the action of sport that gives the average man evidence for thinking of sport as little more than a fulfillment of pragmatic concerns.

It is obvious that theoretical awareness is much more than ideas "with their feet planted firmly in heaven." However, it does seek to develop conceptions based on subject/object relationships, in sport, that are unhampered by "the facts." In truth, the man of sport has not demonstrated great interest in much more than operational levels. The literary horizons have in certain isolated cases pushed beyond the "pragmatic" and "educational" and have attempted to assess sport as it is. It must not be forgotten that sport is a highly practical dimension of human life. Let this not be dismissed too lightly. It is in our awareness of what is operational in sport that we come to grips with basic existence. The need for theoretical measures is deemed of great importance by this writer (or else this book would not have been attempted). It must be kept in mind, though, that we are talking of extremely practical areas of the human dimension. The present stress on theory is not to suggest desirability, as much as the need to point to the "other side of the coin."

The fusion of theoretical and operative awareness needs something *more*. The performer can be as subjective as need be or, if desired, objectify each and every movement in the sport arena. He still remains *away* from sport as a central concern in the human dimension. How does man reach his fellow man in sport? What is the central concern of the human plight as it enters the sport field? What is the symbolic representation that man demands, in sport, to achieve personal existence? Searching and penetrating questions to say the least.

The present consideration is one of, for the lack of a better term, reality. In some way we must look at sport as a critical reflection of both man *and* existence. Thus, we need to differentiate between the *territory* of performance and the *symbol* of that performance. Semanticists have stated these concerns, of the *meaning* of what is, repeatedly; however, my interest is in more than denotations of sport. We must uncover what is involved in differentiating what *is* from what is *function*. Is the ritual involved with collegiate football really an indigenous part of the sport? Is sport purely object orientation beyond all else? Is sport an ontological mirror of life? Only the naive would expect direct answers. Nevertheless, through formalized systematic analysis, we would perhaps come a little closer to understanding this interesting form of human action.

What is being called for is the study of sport as it achieves human awareness. It has been more than hinted at that this is possible through an analysis of the meanings of sport. Traditionally formal philosophy has attempted similar projects through logical analysis. I refuse to yield to this temptation. Simply, life is not all rational and not all logical. What is needed is a formulation of *meaning*. What does the action *mean* to man? How does he complete his self in the act? How does man see sport? Does he perceive sport as a *crucial* part of his existence? Is sport more than an acceptable battlefield for release of basic desires? In a word, to what end does sport develop real human awareness? And, conversely, what is their *real* human awareness in sport?

It is difficult to believe that a theory of sport, as a *humane experience*, could even be attempted without answers to these vital questions. I think most of us readily agree that a structure, so developed, could not be based merely on *intentional* efforts. The importance of this task is, perhaps, not the answer to the questions, but rather the comprehension of the depth of the questions. To think there is a purpose, as a basic assumption, is to rob the argument of its beauty prior to analysis. The reality of the sport world is one thing, the symbolic representation of *it* (sport) or of *life* is another. Thus, a basic dilemma is one of *causality*. Does man run because of *cause* or does he just run? Does he say first, I need to run? I need fitness? I need exercise? I need release of tension? I need to involve myself with nature? I need a social relationship? It is here I must agree with Sartre. Man runs! Cause might or might not be present. The importance has been traditionally rested on *motivation*. Perhaps it is now time to become *aware* of the human element in sport. Motivation is important. But it is time we asked what *is* happening when man runs. A study of the *action* might well provide insights that *causation* would not.

This form of concern places man in a truly *humane* light. No longer do we study man as a lever, or a response. Man becomes more than a mechanistic bundle of nerve endings. We now look at *human* awareness. Man is more than the computer. In this new direction we consider his complexities, not because of relative importance or unimportance, but because of existence. We must first determine the humanity of man. Does he exist? How is this existence formulated in sport? And finally, why does he participate?

The end of this investigation will hopefully result in, not increased empirical data, but a fusion between man and the reality of what we call sport. We must locate the reality of sport in human awareness. If it is not there, it is nowhere.

Sport as a Situation

The situational context of sport *almost* cannot be generalized; however, that which is experienced, which is real, is experienced only because of the perceptions of the individual. If it were not a consequence of individual existence, sport could be thought of as a universal attribute. But this is not validated by experience.

The situation has some "consistents" that are usually present. The volleyball player is certain as to the height of the net and the size and weight of the ball, but not much else. Each situation, within the contest, is relative and as such is not completely known. How will the opposition "defense" the opponent? How will they "set"? The past affords a basis of judgment. But the future remains precarious. There is no beginning nor a perceivable end. The movements of sportsmen are undeterminable and undetermined.*

But where does man fit? What is his place within sport? Is it sufficient to say that man seeks gain? One does not come to "lose." But this demands an explanation of "gain." Is winning sufficient or is its relationship to self-fulfillment that which claims its importance?

It has been established that *within* the sport situation man searches for some kind of *being*, a being which, although affected by the transient situation of the event, needs some permanence. Science tells man of certain "constants." He can predict the bounce of the ball (with due respect to football). He is fairly reliable in predicting the "percentages" of the situation. He is even capable of making surprisingly reliable predictions relative to energy expenditure as related to each participated activity. However, this is all really quite superficial and relatively meaningless if one is attempting to provide humanity with solutions germane to *living*. "Man can achieve no greater goal than to become aware of what it means to be alive" (Arnheim, 1954, p. 23). Sport *does* possess the potential for unique views of man, but the value accruing from the activity can be no greater than man's introspection of the *things happening*—a view too often sacrificed to the demigods of victory, ego fulfillment and personal prowess.

Only *on self* can man rely for true security of self. Whether this is experienced *by* the sport situation, or developed because *of* sport, is of little concern at this point in the discussion. To be certain, it *is* an ingredient of sport. In unlocking a personal view of being of the self, through his involvement in the sport situation, man comes closer to discovery of his own variability. Within such a *revelation* (in its most mystical sense) men deduce their *own* characteristics. Again sport *affords* not guarantees this opportunity for authentic "realness" through that which is experienced in a perceptually sensitive manner. It can now be seen that man develops not by *the* situation, but by using *thought* to locate what truly *is*.

* For detailed discussion of this thesis see Jaspers, K. *Vernunft und Existenz*. Groningen, Batavia: Wolters, 1935.

Once it is established that man can identify the *I* in the sport situation, it is clear that the *relatives* of the specific situation need to be considered. Reality of *things* and of fellow *man* is thereby put through a type of metamorphosis for the individual. All within the sport situation cannot be determinable *in and of itself* but as relevant to the experienced *situation*. "Neither is the world . . . without me who knows it nor can I be without the world in which alone I am what I am. There is no world without me, nor am I without the world" (Jaspers, 1948, Vol. I, p. 64). The sport situation is the raw material for man to discover personal reality. Yet there is no *real* situation without man. Again we see the reciprocity between the cosmos and the individual.

Within each sport situation man does not achieve existence but the potential for existence. He is endowed with the capability of movement and of action—all of which brings him closer or further from fulfillment of personal being (here the polarity is truly *Being and Nothingness*). The direction is left up to man.

Perhaps this is what the sailor comes to realize. On the sea, as in many other environments, man frequently encounters prolonged *aloneness*. In this struggle with *and* against the forces of nature he finds "profound fulfillment" (Smith, J., 1965, p. 76). Perhaps man does not *know* what brings him to the sea or to the mountains or to the game. But he *is* there! When analyzed, fulfillment *might* appear to be achieved—yet man seeks again and again. Sport leads man in a kind of mystical relationship with the forces that compose and challenge him. Like the mountain climber, most men cannot tell you *why* they partake of the experience when "on the ground." But one *does* know once he is on top of the mountain.

Again, the discovery of self *is* specific to the situation. It is, in part, the *choice* that brings about self-realization. "Existence is real only as freedom . . . freedom is . . . the being of existence" (Jaspers, 1948, Vol. 2, p. 180). The sport performer comes to recognize himself through the specificity of the situation. He learns who he is. When confronted by the missed putt, the ensuing clash of the opposing lineman, or the flight of his *own* body away from the parallel bars, he comes to realize self. Through choice he recognizes true self. It is the dynamic nature of sport that insists upon the performer's decision, a decision involving certitude of personalized being, a being that comes about through the perception of the situation and thus the self. If freedom is *really* localized, the athlete has increased opportunity for achieving real selfhood. This cannot be dreamed, imagined, abstracted, or academic. The experience of sport is *true* only for the *performer*, for it is he that makes the choice in the situation. Therefore, only he has the responsibility to achieve *self*. The spectator may appreciate, emotionalize, or sense vicarious excitement. But the choice is not *in the actual*. It does not involve the kinesthetic elements so important for *feel*, the sense so necessary for the affirmation of existence.

Again, I need to stress, in the sport situation all is potentialized. The "molding" needs to be accomplished by the participant. At the heart of the process of actualization is the necessity of "freedom of choice." When this freedom is reduced, so is the potentiality for fulfillment. Thus, one has to question the place of sport, within this process, if this freedom is negated. The calling of plays by the football coach, instead of the quarterback, is an example of limiting the potential of each man. Let me not be guilty of complete naiveté. I am not confusing the ideal with the practical. It is obvious that American materialism calls for situations in which man is subdued in the process. Victory is paramount. To the victor goes the spoils; and in days of large gates and extensive commercial television markets the spoils are great. Yet one has to wonder if this process need start in "pee wee" football leagues. It appears that with each step on the ladder of competition—from community little leagues to high schools to collegiate and professional ventures—man gives up a little more of himself. To say it is *forced* upon us by the "evil" called *society* is to beg the question. Each man needs to look at himself. Each man needs to consider his own self. Each man needs to answer the penetrating questions of meaning and value. It is truly in personal choice that man differentiates himself from fellowman. "In choosing I am, and if I am not it is because of my failure to choose" (Jaspers, 1948, Vol. 2, p. 182).

Perhaps it is necessary to stress the awareness (consciousness) of the athlete. Participation in sport is not a guarantee of actualization of being. The self is *developed* through application of choice in keeping with internalized rules. Initial actions are not always results of conscious "ultimates." Science and the cosmos are not finalized. Yet man must act. The sport situation does not allow, by design, infinite thought. Man must act and move through selection of stimuli or else he *is not*. If man is interested in using the sport situation in an *educational* setting (and admittedly this is only one such place for sport), then man must have the opportunity to discover the self. This means every avenue for choice must be placed before the individual. Ultimate truths in sport are no doubt to be classified as "wishful thought," though not beyond the bounds of time. The "always" of the sport situation is manifested in the *completed moment*. The participant exists in the situation and simultaneously beyond the situation. In short, personhood is sought through a time realization of freedom within a specific situation.

Sport as an Immediate. For many men sport is both the "content" and the "object" of their consciousness (not to differentiate from the subconscious but rather to stress the act of the present and presence). It is in this experiential area where human existence is dramatized.

The baseball player swings a bat in an attempt to hit a thrown ball. The arc, force, level are all in accordance with the accumulation of variables as perceived by the conscious subject. Thus, mental sets affect not only our performance, but our *selves*. We *immediately* form a percept which ideally accounts for all the possible variables. It is of interest that our perception of the image is not affected by causation or result. Typically the object (*i.e.*, a baseball) maintains an objective nature which is independent of personal experience (except in the broadest sense of experience); whereas my experience of the variables, which will contribute to the actual swing, are quite *immediate*. Previous experience with the content of the bat may explain the immediate nature of its appearance, but this is not true if one considers the bat in its objective form.

The bat represents the physical object; however, my attitudes and feelings toward the object are rather private. My success with this instrument will depend greatly on my predictable observation. One must grant that initial attempts will indicate a high degree of skill prediction based upon technique. However, it will not be long before man goes beyond the "applied science." Success can now be described in terms of feel, touch, sensitivity and sensations. Perhaps the safest and most valid summary would indicate that the most successful hitters use techniques as a means, whereas the inexperienced and non-skilled often use technique as an end in and of itself.

It is I alone who feels the bat as I alone can sense it. It is I alone who "knows." The term I have selected to describe this experience is *immediate*. This experience between "my" bat and myself is *immediate*. It is close. It is uninterrupted and constant. It is present. For others this experience might well be an *indirect* experience and as such alienated from the total happening.

It can be now seen that the *content* of any sport experience is possibly a percept of a primary specific experience and thus the *object* of another.* No matter how alike an experience is, it is not the *immediate* one and not *the* one. Thus, what makes sport almost *so* immediate for many is that the objects are experienced or shared publicly. The immediate experiences are not shared, but the indirect experience is so frequent and so "close" that it appears to most vicariously. This one quality of sharing the immediate and indirect has always made "spectating" at sports such an important happening of most societies. Although the performer experiences immediately, the spectator shares similar experiences that are both public and private.

Sport as It Is

If nothing else, it can be said that sport is practical in that the goals, process and atmosphere *presumes* the pragmatic. Idealizers have discussed the "way to play the game," "the building of character," and every conceivable aspect of sportsmanship; however, the *action* is typically based on outcomes and not morality.

Empirical observation of sport has demonstrated that man is *much* more than just animal. He does not exist as *thingness* or simply a grouping of cell and tissue. The natural and behavioral

* For detailed discussion of related areas see Lemos, R.: Immediacy, Privacy, and Ineffability. Journal of Philosophy and Phenomenological Research, *25*, 500–515, 1965.

sciences have demonstrated their definite limitations in explaining the very existence of man much less an elucidation of the normative structure. Coaches and participants alike are fond of explaining away this phenomenon by talking of the psychologic "readiness," the "desire" to win, the ability to get "up," and other such evasive euphemisms. An example of this mystical language is found in the following interview with a collegiate football player. "We just hope we'll be up high enough for the game. The winner will be the team that wants to win it the most. . . . I think the emotional edge is in our favor. . . . We have great confidence" (Ziff, 1966, p. 3). If anything, such attitudes betray the conditioning that hampers a meaningful participation in sport. When does man speak for himself and not for the world?

Human Awareness in Sport. It seems that one of the great problems that confronts the world of sport revolves around the *self-awareness* of the participant. In a word, as a conscious *reactor* to the media, the performer by definition tends to lose *being*. Since he is primarily tied to *results* of action, the pragmatic nature of the sport world refutes *immediate* awareness. The best one can hope for is a type of *reflection*, which at best is delayed and involves all too much thought.

It is easy to see how Sartre admits both the presence and absence of conscience. "It has often been said that the reflective look alters the fact of consciousness on which it is directed" (Sartre, 1956a, p. 116). Sport, as an area of human involvement, produces immediate situations which could hypothetically be excellent media for *immediate awareness*. Typically, however, the performer reflects *upon* the *act* but at the same time *he* reflects on the involvement.

This, again, points to one of the constantly recurring themes of this work. Namely, the *duality* that exists in sport. Not only do we see the haunting mind/body problem but we are now faced with a split of existence. Sport cannot exist away from man. To estrange man from sport is to not have sport. Therefore, sport becomes possible, and indeed achieves a "higher" level, as man comes to be aware of his self.

This form of *reflective awareness* is certainly well beyond cognition, Awareness requires a unique concern that, in the end, is human.

Cognition brings on thingness. In sport thingness is *reflected* through mechanistic movements and rote motor performance. When sport *is as it is*, it achieves the dignity and grace of ecstasy. It *says* something meaningful to the performer. Its motivation comes from inner involvement. Perhaps it is this quality of awareness that differentiates the hunt from the kill. *Knowing* is simply not sufficient; sport requires *inner* authenticity. A quality of *emotion* rarely achieved.

When seen in this light sport maintains a *presence* of its own. In Sartrian language, sport is not what it is. In other words, the consciousness of sport, which as previously developed is the self of the performer, exists away from the situation. Man cannot *create* self in sport, although he can *develop* it. The performer needs to come to the activity with self (perhaps this is what the coaches mean when they talk of courage of an athlete). The aware self fuses with the sport situation to afford unity and, perhaps, in special spiritual moments, communion. In the language of the behavioral scientists, identity is achieved. Thus, it is evident that *being-in-itself* is refutable. What is called for is *presence*.

If one admits to the duality between consciousness and being, it is rather easy to perceive ways in which sport encourages the division. The very use of space and the demands of time reactions that occur in most sport activities tends to split the performer from the self. If man needs to shoot the ball through a basket or keep time to the music while spinning on ice-skates, it is questionable if he can really develop the inner self. Certainly all the stimuli tempt him to turn from his self to external object orientation. In a word, we have *non-being*. Here again we face a paradox; sport, by placing emphasis on the external, utilizes being to develop non-being.

Since sport only exists as it is, and its existence is partially determined by man, it becomes obvious that sport is what it is not! Namely, its basis is man. But man cannot achieve self in sport due to the duality of its structure; therefore, for sport to be what it is, man and sport will need to develop related foundations of existence. The grade-school football player might play at being a football player, but he is still a football player. If during the contest he were to play at being a dentist, he would not, in fact, be a dentist. The performer is what he is in authentic reality. Thus, the truth of self is partially determined by what man does in action. "Being-in-itself may ground its non-being, but not its being; in its decompression, it nihilates itself into a for-itself which becomes, as for-itself, its own foundation; but its contingency of being-in-itself remains out of reach" (Sartre, 1956a, p. 127).

Human awareness thus becomes a combination of reality and being. In sport it becomes a fusion of structure and action. Sport reveals itself as its component part, namely, the self of man, becomes actualized in movement experiences. Although the components *can* be separated, this act occurs only when sport breaks down. Somehow they seem to *implicate* each other.

Awareness of the Other. Consideration of sport leads one directly to the concern of individualization. Each performer, through self, delimits sport. The world of sport represents the participants. In sport, perhaps to a greater degree than most areas of human involvement, the self is externally perceivable through cognizance of the *complete* body. Thus, the awareness of one and a second person becomes a crucial consideration for analysis.

Unlike many traditional philosophical viewpoints, I am unable to see the role of man in sport as one of instrumentalism. Each participant, as well as each object, brings forth his own meaning. A tennis racquet assumes a different significance depending upon the performer who grips it. What might well occur in sport is both exciting and frightening. As man admits the awareness of one object or person to consciousness, he might well omit the other. However, the contrary could also occur. Namely, through awareness of what is, *the other* could be realized by its omission. Through the dynamic activity of sport, man might perceive the self as a dangerous involvement of motion. But this might not be true for the other. For man to be perceived, as is (and thus *is* sport), he needs to communicate to the other as one who will risk danger. "I can, no doubt, transcend myself *toward* the All, but I cannot establish myself within All to contemplate myself . . . and others. No logical . . . optimism then could bring an end to the plurality of consciousnesses" (Sartre, 1956a, p. 300).

This awareness of the other again demonstrates the sport performer as more than a collection of cells. He is indeed *human.* Each time he "participates" authentically, the world of sport conveys to him a specified significance; however, this significance is achieved through an involvement with *the other.*

Man selects a specific sport. No doubt he is attracted to a specific activity because of a variety of specified conditions. He selects "instruments" in keeping with the activity. He then organizes his body parts to cope with the intended action. Thus, he demonstrates supposed knowledge of the parameters of his body. He incorporates his many *tools* (his body as well as external objects) and proceeds to the dimensions of space location. He proceeds to participate. Does meaning accrue? Well, that depends. Basically man engages all these elements because he is drawn to participate. The concern of "meaningful significance" will be resolved dependent upon the awareness each man has of the *real* basic reasons he engaged in sport. However, part of the resolution must relate to man's awareness of the other. Thus, the *human reality* of sport is defined in terms of *being in* the situation *with* others (Heidegger).

Sport, as a world, reflects and/or reveals to us our own existence. Man is not alone in sport. He participates with others. Even if the sport is so-called "individual," man participates in competition with those who have scored par, or set a record, or will be involved in the future. Authentic human living is perhaps best illustrated by the *idealized* version of a crew team.

> It is intimately felt in the common rhythm of the rowers; each one of them feels within himself the same movement of transcendence toward a common goal, on the horizon of a common world, and feels it *with* the other rowers. In this conception, however, being *for* others has been replaced by being *with* others. It reveals the coexistence of consciousnesses without explaining it. (Salvan, 1962, p. 66)

This element of coexistence or relationship affords a feasible, although mystical, explanation of human *life.* It emphasizes the necessity of achieving deep personal relationships between societal components.

Life with Others. Individualism, as a philosophical doctrine, recognizes man solely in regard to personalized self. It is an existence divorced from the "team." On the other hand, collectivism views man only in relation to a societal aggregate. In consideration of sport we need to be aware that the situation itself is composed of individual persons. Yet a *collection* of individuals does not make a team. We must ask how man can locate a means by which he can *relate* to his fellow man without causing the individual to lose his own *being*.

Beyond the superficial attempt of man to win without winning, to compete without competing, and to conquer without really conquering, sport is *capable* of affording man an existence that escapes Sartre's *emptiness*. Sport need not be a futile experience diminishing intrinsic meaning. This is not to deny that the performer is burdened with the endless responsibility necessitated by freedom of choice; for indeed all men face this element of existential pain. However, in sport the involvement *can* be so "deep" as to accrue, what I call, a conception of *experiential mysticism*. This term is not to infer a quality of *love* that is so often used in philosophical and psychological literature. For I don't think *love*, as a true *giving*, is really possible in the sport situation. The emotion might be there, but the process is negated by the dominant theme of survival and conquest. But in one's sport experience, through use of perceptive reflection, one can experience a type of mysticism that is quiet, peak and flowing with *care*. But again I must stress the potential of this quality and not the actuality!

The aspect of sport that best exemplifies this point of experiential mysticism is best indicated by the mutual involvement between teammates. I am not referring to the process of teamwork and cooperation, but rather the expression that seems to develop *within* and *among* individuals in sport. Gabriel Marcel's *est coesse*—"to be is to be with others"—is most explanatory of this feeling. The emphasis is on an *openness* of individual to individual. I am convinced that some of the "better" (perhaps not the ones with the best win-loss percentage) teams I have *known* over the years, in a variety of sports, have possessed this feeling of warmth and empathy for each other.

The closeness that sport demands, on the part of its team participants, provides a full understanding and chance for the study and exploitation of the *single life.* When the performer lives his own life to maximum development, he encounters added meaning. Each and every experience becomes a "peak performance" revealing his own *being.* The more he can share this existence with those "close" to him, the more he fills his boundaries of the *very* human dimension. Two athletes who share this form of mysticism do actually unify their "bonds" with each other. Thus, human existence cultured on the battlefield of sport is *not* abstract but rather mystical, and yet not really a mystical extension of *being.* It is the *relations* between conscious performers that provides any meaning for being—if a reason is to exist.

I-thou. Martin Buber pleads for what he calls a true community composed of man with man. For Buber the world is centered around the importance of *relations* between persons. Traditionally man has overlooked this basic point as self evident, and thus neglected the real *humanistic* concern. Buber's emphasis on the importance of human life grows from his theory of communal relationship *Between Man and Man.* Thus the opposite of tyranny is community. If the performer is really to achieve *humanness,* he must develop relationships. Otherwise contacts are superficial. A man is truly saved from the "one" (the mass) not by separation but only by being bound in a genuine community.

Man lives in order to develop his *I.* However, the *I* can only exist as it relates *with* another being (*Thou*). The word *with* is crucial at this point, for it means a community of living rather than the encounter of two isolated individuals in a society. Life, therefore, and all that is real, is essentially a system of *intimate relationships.* One can only develop his *I* by relating to a *Thou.* Thus, a true communal feeling is achieved when individuals voluntarily concentrate on developing their own *I* and therefore, by definition, cause the betterment of the others (*thou*) in society.

It is important to note the use of the word *thou.* Buber does not ask to relate to a *you.* He does not use the impersonal second person singular. Instead he uses the word *thou.* He uses the personal or familiar form, a word meaning "loved-one." We can see a community is not composed of a *me* and a *you* (two isolated beings); but a community or a team involves a familiarity between two individuals relating to each other through the vehicle of *love*. Therefore, individuals develop their *I* by directing their own efforts toward a *love* of a *thou*. In this relationship we can understand the development and the enhancement of the self and at the same time the devotion to another. Each man's authenticity is achieved through genuine concern *with* a *thou*.

The *I-thou* concept stresses creative insights to the man of sport. Man is not merely an individual, and the team is not merely an athletic aggregate. Instead a person is one who genuinely *cares*.

I-it. I do not forget the man who plays *against* his *opponent*, the man who "plays to kill." The number of individuals in this category are too great to be ignored. I am well aware of their "realistic" world. These individuals, like their corporate brothers, cannot dispense with the institutions and impersonal forms of life. Buber calls this the world of *I-it*.

The *I-it* association is not one of evil. Man must live with organizations, he must rely on institutions, and he requires materialistic forms to facilitate his life. The world of *I-it* is a definite necessity. Also, the world of *I-thou* and *I-it* are not incompatible.

In man's freedom he can relate to anything or anyone as an *I-thou* or *I-it*. One would hope in a matter of personal concern, such as in a voluntary selection of sport participation, an *I-thou* relationship would be achieved between the individual and everything that would necessitate the maintenance of a meaningful existence.

To live one's life completely in the world of *I-it* is not authentic existence but rather pseudo-living. The real joy and greatness of sport participation comes in the development of *I-thou* relationships. Yet frequently man forsakes the *thou* for an *it*.

Buber's theory of relationship offers the man of sport one of the most sober proposals for the attainment of true *humanity*. Through the *thou* a man becomes *I*. Through the solution of problems man can achieve dignity. He comes closer to true existence.

If the theory of *oneness* is accepted, then man must reject *I-it*; for it is the *I-thou* which needs to be reached when attempting to achieve wholeness. Sport exists only when the individual is completely involved in the activity. He needs to be able to *respond* to the other. In this way sport becomes a *human* achievement. Perhaps this is what Charles de Gaulle meant when he spoke to France's greatest athletes. "Not only are you very likeable, you are examples of physical courage and character. Each time you appear you spread the good name and prestige of France in the *most human* of fields" (People, 1966, p. 64).

Sport as a Meeting Place. I believe it is clear that the human quality of sport is achieved through a personal "meeting" with one's fellow man. The sport performer needs to meet another, and indeed has the opportunity, not in usual ways, but absorbing all of the *other* he participates with. When he loses himself in the meeting, sport becomes secondary and life becomes primary. "When *Thou* is spoken, the speaker . . . takes his stand in relation to the immediate relationship to the other, and by his experience he is enabled to confirm: All real living is meeting" (Buber, 1953, p. 4). For sport *to be what it is*, man *must be*. This demands involvement—a type of *presence* calling voluntary *thereness*, a quality not possible unless there is a *real* meeting.

Sport provides man an environment for two distinct forms of meeting. The first, *the intuitive*, provides for all the "felt" experiences that man cannot seem to symbolize adequately. Yet they are there. It is in the *I-thou* relationship that man *transcends* the actual happening. Indeed, can man *say* what occurs when he skis? How does one express the feeling of excitement prior to entering a contest? Has any one *adequately* expressed the real feeling of tension that comes to the angler at the time of the big hit? I think not. But it is there. It is felt. Man knows it to be related to the meeting. The intuitive becomes very real.

The second form of meeting might well be related to the inner response of man which is potentially demonstrable. It is here that *essence* becomes the fulfillment of the meeting. It is the concrete. But let this not fool the reader. Sport is initially viewed as existence. Man looks and, perhaps, reacts to the composite. When facing an opposing player, man sees him as he is. He perceives a tennis player, a baseball pitcher, or a soccer player. He is perceived in basic existence. It is not until a process of detailed segmentation is initiated that man begins to consider the essences of sport. One does not see arms, strong legs, big hands and massive musculature. One sees man! He is there in his wholeness. To focus in on essence is to admit thingness and the emphasis upon *I-it*. To admit existence is the raw material for humanity and to stress *I-thou*. Yet it is curious how often we hear of references to the strong arm of the quarterback, the good foot of the soccer player, the "headiness" of the pitcher, and the eye of the basketball player. It is almost unique and kind of an exception when one hears of man in his entirety!

> Just as the melody is not made up of notes nor the verse of words... so with the man to whom I say *Thou*. I can take out from him the colour of his hair, . . . his speech, or his goodness. But each time I do it he ceases to be *Thou*. (Buber, 1953, p. 89)

Sport demands instantaneous knowledge of the other. It stresses flexibility of process and admission of the composite.

Sport as a Little More than a Human Achievement. To most participants the *Thou* has been experienced if not expressed. To those who have taken part in this *meeting* it appears to be a little more than a human achievement. Many of us have been in sport situations "where nothing seemed to happen." Yet the same environment, at another time, produced a significantly meaningful experience. It appears that man might well attempt a *meeting*, with all earnestness, but *feel* and *know* nothing of the *Thou* experience. It seems that no matter how hard we try, no matter how honest the encounter, no matter how authentic our intentions, we can not reach what the situation potentially reveals to us. Thus, it is obvious there is something beyond the *will*. To a certain degree we *volunteer* for the meeting; and to a degree we are selected. "The *Thou* meets me. But I step into direct relation with it. Hence the relation means being chosen and choosing" (Buber, 1953, p. 11). Indeed it is more than a human achievement.

Perhaps this is what is meant by "playing for the breaks," the *real* breaks. We continue to try. We tackle, we strive, we hit the shots, we slide hard, we charge the boards—all with the hope, and not the assurance, that we will achieve the meeting. Perhaps in all honesty it can be said that the sport performer does this more with hopes of game-victory than for actualization of humanity.

There is in this analysis a subtle reminder of the relationship between cause and effect. One does not simply *wait* for the "breaks." One makes them! However, the making does not insure the result. The *I-Thou* relationship calls for *action*. It says to man, meet your fellowman. One cannot *make* the self understand the beauty of a gymnastic routine. No one can bring the meeting to man. Yet the association with the other might well yield the meaning of the gymnast's movements. The experience is necessary. Man must be *present*. And yet there must be more.

Sport as a Subjective Experience. The encounters in sport involve man in practical and, to a degree, objective experiences. The gymnast must "practically" be able to perform a variety of movements so that he can "achieve" in his desired activity. He has nothing if he does not perform in the *presence* of a *Thou*. In this case, *Thou* might well be non-human; however, it is not an object or thing. It is a *Thou*. Thus, in his *presence* he lives in the *present;* thereby *living* a life. It is important to recognize that the *Thou* emphasizes the determination to live, to be, and to exist. It stresses the present time. Man is not preparing to live. Nor is he living in the past. In his movement experience, he is what he is *now*.

The sport activity, perceived as a *Thou*, facilitates man's living. To be sure, this is not a measurable dimension of life. But like life, gymnastics might well be artificially objectified by man; however, the real is much beyond quantification. To go through the gymnastic "routine" in a mechanistic fashion is to admit the *it*. To score each movement, numerically, is to indicate the sublime. To think of each turn or twist in an objective realm is to avoid life. All of this fosters the world of *It*. But again the necessity of It needs to be pointed out. Life could not be organized and effectively developed with the *It*. On the other hand, to treat the experiences of life as *It* is to diminish *real life.* "Without *It* man cannot live. But he who lives with *It* alone is not a man" (Buber, 1953, p. 12).

When a gymnast confronts his "movements" he, potentially, meets a *Thou.* He is *open* and available to his act. And the act opens to him. Man comes to really *know* himself. By performing the movements he *encounters* his reality. At the same time he meets his "move," the move, indeed, takes on a personality. It too develops life. Perhaps this is what is meant by a *self-testing activity.* Certainly the self is more than *me.* It is the *I-Thou.*

Man emerges from the experience with a new self. He learns who we are, as a specific and a generality. Man is more than a gymnast. But the gymnast is never more than the man. For this transference to occur man must be *accessible* when he enters sport. He must approach the meeting with a readiness for relationship.

The gymnastic routine might be "styled." The kip, turn-table, giant swing, thief vault, etc., all have their "rightness" in the heavens of the ideal. Yet each man must give "style" to the movements. To a degree, it brings both unique "self" and awareness of "other" to realization. To look at the movement objectively, is to divorce the performance from the man. This type of dualism leads to isolation of man from his self. What is needed is relationship between man and his movements. The gymnast and the movement *meet* each other. To "judge" another becomes a process of knowing another's existence. To determine man's emotion, to feel a man's sensations, to share the "betweenness" of the movement are necessary before man *scores* man. Can this be an objective process? I think not.

Sport as It Is—in Retrospect. To say what is potentially feasible is one thing. To say what *is* is another. Sport has frequently suffered as much from its advocates as from its enemies. The former claim all the world's treasures, while the latter admit no riches. Like the Hollywood adaptations of good and bad "guys," their fantasy role is too far from reality to afford meaningful discourse.

I must admit that I am not overly optimistic about the role of sport in development of the "humanness" of man. I have discussed the development of *I-Thou* and *I-It* relationships as basic to the fulfillment of life. Both constructions are involved in the life process. Both are necessary; however, life exists only *between* the *I and Thou*. Thus, the question is one of priority.

Does sport foster the *Thou* or the *It*? I think present emphasis is unquestionably on the *It*. The *Thou* takes time. The *It* can be "rushed." The *Thou* takes *patience*. The *It* "feeds on" discontent. The *Thou* is synonymous with warmth. The *It* germinates in coldness. The *Thou* requires personhood. The *It* is fostered by aloofness. The *Thou* is desiring of care. The *It* is too impersonal to care.

One must ask what is the emphasis of sport. Is sport a process of duration, warmth, love, personhood, and care? Perhaps it is, in the potential; but it is not in the actuality. Sport as it is is cold, impersonal, objective, hard, and remote. The child playing sand-lot football learns he must be "tough." The prep school basketball player soon learns Darwin's laws. The hunter is frequently more killer than sportsman.

However, all is not lost. Sport does provide a *meeting* place. It does allow man to *relate* with fellow man. Depending upon the specifics, certain activities do lead man to transcend the actual. This experience, normally reserved for theological encounters, enters the halls of the "everyday" as revealed through sport. Man does learn to experience the self, to test his humanity, and to face his real self—success or failure. In this way sport provides man with a comparative yardstick. It says to man, determine your individuality as a *one* or as a collection. Both have their place in the parade of humanity. It is for man to choose. It is man that *needs* to locate the *Thou*.

Togetherness: As a Potential

The individual, as an entity, and the team, as a collective, are frequently viewed as a functional unit working toward *oneness*. Each element of the team is thought of as possessing *being-in-itself* and revealing "substance" as basic to this modality. As individuals, with distinct personhoods, they are "locatable" in the sport situation and thereby, because of *their responsibility* for their encompassment, are in a real sense *present beings*.

Most individuals who have participated in sport realize there is more to the "team" than substance. It is easily seen that the substance of the team lies in the existence of *each* of the performers. However, these substances are not always formed as one would desire and therefore the term *chance* must be introduced to explain the *presentation* of *substances* into *forms*. In turn each substance is given *purpose*. This point must be emphasized. Man gives direction to the team since it is man who has the team within his self. When one thinks of the ramifications of this thesis, it is difficult to understand how man gives up this freedom, in fact *allows* it to be stolen from him, to become an instrument of the mass. This is especially unusual when one considers that man has no fixed nature, as such, but evolves his existence according to the choices he makes.

This is not to infer that the individual is *completely* altered as much as his own *form* is standardized within the total harmony of the desired presentation. In certain ways the team becomes an attribute of personal form. One refers to the Chicago Bears as being "rough," the Los Angeles Dodgers as "quick," and the 1927 Yankees as "powerful." The purpose and characteristic of the team become diffused to signify a symbol for collective being.

One could argue that it is the individual on the team that gives the unit its being. But in all truth, "with being . . . depends upon other substantial foundations of being" (Brugger, 1957, p. 23). Sport personifies this principle. The team has its *own* being. It can maintain its own identity. Like a compound, composed of elements, the team might and might not display the characteristics of its constituents. Men are sacrificed. Others are used as decoys. The team has "rights" *over* the individual members. It is this quality that differentiates a *true* team from an accidental combination of individuals. Integrally related to *team being* are values associated with the individual's effort, to be unmistakably related with that element of *teamhood*. The resultant manifestation is an *intentional* desire to communicate with each other, but to rarely go beyond this level of responsibility.

Traditionally, *togetherness* has been conceived, in sport literature, as a derivative of teamwork. This proposition, as naive as it may sound, purports that the sport situation encourages the individual to relegate himself to the good of the whole. He blocks, sacrifices, and works for the good of the team. Naive? Yes! Because all the norms of our competitive world discourage such altruism. Why should sport be different? And indeed it is not! Man does *cooperate.* But he does so *mainly* to the degree that it affords personal achievement. There is little that separates the man in the grey flannel banker's suit from the man in the grey flannel baseball suit except a heightened degree of sophistication by the former and a heightened degree of compulsive urgency by the latter.

Man is not directed toward togetherness from *without*, yet this is what the team is asking. A move toward another must be internally motivated. It must not be forced. But this is what "team spirit" has come to mean. "Do it for the good of the team." This, in essence, is asking man to be what he is not. If man wants to "do it," it will be done as a result of an appreciation of the vitality of the *other.* If he does do *for* the other, he is reacting contrary to authentic destiny. This type of understanding or misunderstanding, as the case may be, has been developed in direct contradiction of basic cultural truths. These descriptions paint the picture of man as a unit *of* the whole. He is not! The unit is of man. A typical symptom, accruing from this oversimplification, is a cry for the individual to rise above the mass. Typically, this plea is not adequate because it makes no allowances for any description that fails to view substance and chance as factors in opposition. In sport this is clearly not the case. In order for the individual to exist "in the other" does not *necessarily* mean he must exist "in an other *one.*" He might as well exist *within* many. Man can retain his own being as it is in or relates with others. Of course, this means the individual does not necessarily identify with *the team* as much as with *individuals on the team.*

The quality of existence that best describes the relationship of the individual to other individuals on the team is *with being.* This term assumes a *sharing* by team members, but indicates a dependence on chance and a relative independence of the environment in the facing of difficult times. One can hold up "his end" of the team responsibility although the rest of the aggregate is getting defeated. This *with-being* aspect also affords a unification that *embraces* and *incorporates* others, but it does not *fuse* individuals. There is an atmosphere of the present time, but *maybe* not future time.

Because of *with-being* a team may and may not be *determined* to succeed *as a unit*. Members might well be *joined* together but because of a lack of unification they could well participate toward diversified ends, although always being aware of the common good. For a team to be all that it is, requires *form*. *With-being*, in this cause, must develop toward *one-being* if true teamwork is to be attained. Perhaps this is the quality that is often recognized when one senses that a specific group of individuals personify *teamness*. The *being* of individuals is *formed* toward a single objective. By molding substance and chance into form it proceeds within the frame of *single purpose*. While this theory does not lead to the idealistic conception of a team, we can well comprehend herein the internal relations of any given unit.

The being of the individual is common to all parts, thus manifesting the development of *team-being*. The whole is representative of *with-being*, not as a *mixture* of individuals but rather a unifying composite.

Perhaps this is the quality leading to what we might consider an acceptable concept of *team spirit*. None are separated from their existence. Using reason and free will, man chooses the value of life that matures into a form of mystical relation and interdependence *between and within* one another. "... Through spiritual actions, (individuals) establish a special kind of association, they receive a new kind of being: being-one-with-one-another" (Brugger, 1957, p. 24). Sport maintains the potential to unify form that actualizes real team potential. Of course this is quite different from saying man subordinates himself for the good of the whole—a thesis, I trust, that is not contingent on man's purpose and therefore does not exist at all!

It becomes apparent that if *with-being* is to be employed, as a realistic interpretation of teamwork, a strategy for the development of this *form* must include the element of personal *care* as a responsibility of each member of the unit. This process is an abstraction if it is centered exclusively around mere interest or fascination. Its mark of authentic validity is that it is grounded in a type of deep concern.

Caring, in sport, takes on a variety of *forms*. The "comradeship" between teammates, the "relationship" between coach and players, the "empathy" of one opponent for another, and the "responsiveness" of the spectator can all be inclusive of caring. In the dynamic world of sport, caring takes the form of a sensitized internal emotion that brings alteration to the cared for and he who is caring.

The team experience provides for a millennium of factors which afford the opportunity for man to experience *another* as *distinct* and, at the same time, as one of a *unification structure*. In a way this expresses the "home town" feeling that is so identified with sport. Every spectator can identify with *his* team, for in a sense he too is part of the oneness. After all he does demonstrate his care by "supporting" *his* team. It is significant to note, however, that while strong identifications are developed (*e.g.*, *our* Dodgers), the individual generally demonstrates his separation from the team. There is both an identity and a separation. This is the way it "should" be, for this is almost the definition of a team.

Caring involves a knowledge and loyalty. It incorporates a commitment that can easily be replaced. The idea of *constancy*, no matter how much of a pipe dream, is considered to be a vital part of the sportsman's "caring." What makes caring so difficult for the average man of sport is not the commitment. Caring requires emphasis on the *process* and not the *results*. Since sport is primarily an *end*-obsessed aspect of life, it finds difficulty in justification of anything that is not goal-oriented. For one performer to *really* care for another—with all that is implied—appears rather remote. At best we might say that a potential is recognized, but caring as a factor in sport tends to be superficial. This process of maturation is just not feasible in a culture emphasizing extreme competition. For this reason it is obvious that certain real problems develop when one considers the concept of teamwork.

Sport provides its devotees a *charted* voyage upon an unkown sea. Unlike life itself, it provides a shore that is reachable from which man can take a breath and gaze out upon the world. For some, sport is the whole and all that is real; and life becomes recognizable as man reaches the boundaries and limits of the sea. But for most, sport makes man face his problems as immediate. Hence, man has to submit or counter the forces which attempt to determine the outcomes of existence.

The concept of the "team" appears to be one of interlocked human gears, each trying to move so that the whole can progress. Upon closer inspection one comes to appreciate the need for a highly intricate mechanism for integrating independent choices, operating by will, for man's self projection. Each of the voluntary drives collaborate to reverse conflict and increase efficiency. The place of the individual is suggestive as the concept of the team becomes definitive.

Whatever else is involved in teamwork, it is futile to deny the dimension of the *humane*. To the idealistic spectator this involvement might be thought of as an *I-thou* relationship; however, the commitment to mutuality is not so easily achieved. "I become through my relations with the *Thou* as I become I, I say *thou*" (Buber, 1953, p. 11).

This concept of association not only affirms the autonomy of the team, but stresses the autonomy of relationship between teammate and teammate, as opposed to the autonomy of the individual. "Each, considered by itself, is a mighty abstraction. The individual is a fact of existence insofar as he steps into a living relation with other individuals" (Buber, 1961, p. 203). In revealing his care for the other, if this is possible, he reveals his self. Attention is normally drawn to the *act* of caring, but it is the process that makes us and our object *more* than object.

Realistically, however, one has to ask if *mutuality* is not too much to expect among teammates. If it is, how then can we expect *co-existence* between man and man? In sports where partners may be called for, such as handball, tennis and badminton, one might concede the possibility of the development of such a relationship, as doubtful as it might be. However, in team sports, especially contact activities, where man tends to get lost in the mass, it is beyond the *plausibility* of man (some say instinct) to expect this continuous form of creative action. We are asking for man to reflect clearly—as if he were uniformly unthreatened—when all the time we require him to survive on the battlefields of the stadiums and gymnasia.

It could be argued that footballers, as an example, cooperate—and they do. But their involvement is not authentic mutuality in that it is not an act of volition. It might be said they are occupied in a form of *with-thereness*. They move in order to accomplish what needs to be done. Man does not truly act in *mutuality*. His actions are selfishly motivated and because of established *patterns*, a common good is the product. As each performer attempts to personally profit, impetus and direction is given to the whole. Perhaps the best we can say for the *I-thou* relationship, as a reality for sport, is that it is within the potential. But then that is saying what is given: all is within man's existence. However, to *reveal* this relational structure to existence, *as it now is*, belongs to men such as Don Quixote. Again, we cannot be surprised by this finding. Within a society that fosters personal gain through competition, and where cooperation is pursued as far as it is necessary, it is not surprising that man's *will* fosters a *Superman* cult. Sport, as a mecca for man's competitive nature, cannot suddenly become a palace for mutual sharing. Man is simply not a fountain. He cannot be turned on and off at will.

A second problem in the concept of teamwork is that it assumes a priority upon *responsibility*. In most situations the athlete is responsible in the sense of fulfilling an assignment; however, in the deeper sense of responsibility, being freely aware and available, to care for fellowman, is beyond the realistic theory of sport. Responsibility is not a function of human existence as much as a sense of team urgency and necessity. Thus, a *true* construct of responsibility would demonstrate the athlete to be one who not only plays within the rules, but *responds* within the rules to another in such a way that it exhibits real reflection and concern with others' needs. "Responsibility presupposes one who addresses me primarily, that is, from a realm independent of myself, and to whom I am answerable" (Buber, 1961, p. 45). Man is present when he is *on* the team. But he is *ever-present* when he is viewed as *of* the team. In this sense he is not only relational but potent.

It is easy to see that if one couples the idea of *mutuality* and *responsibility* a deep sense of ethic is produced. It is suspect if teamwork brings about or even fosters such "high" levels of concern. In the utilitarian and competitive realm of sport man seldom can think beyond the limits of perceivable results. In man's actual participation the "game" is made significant by a selection of values not in any way ethically related (nor for that matter not related, just unrelated). Man cannot always modify his situation through rational process; however, in his responsibility he can take no refuge from the comprehensiveness of his choice. The ethic is developed, not given, from man as he faces the world. It is reasonable to assume he will select "the rules" he finds most comfortable. And these are not necessarily the rules of the church. They are the rules of war. Mutuality is simply not the way to play the game. Not if one wants to win. And if one does not want to win, why play the game?

In a deeper sense, *mutuality* leads to further complications for the actualization of teamwork. If one assumes that performers *relate* to each other, one must immediately concede the development of a *Thou*. One must allow for the type of personal deliberation that is conducive to apprehending not only man but inner man. "The *inborn Thou* is realized in the lived relations with that which meets it" (Buber, 1961, p. 88). Thus, by means of deduction we are faced with *mutuality*, of all things, giving rise to *dualism*. (This should have been obvious prior to this point.) The very discussion of authenticity commits us to the necessity of actions that do not always reflect our total. That is, the athlete has his inner *Thou* as well as possessing a *total Thou*. Therefore, any relationship between teammates is a problem in *location*. What is revealed? What does the discourse mean? Each self of the unit presents *varied* forms for others to relate towards. When the quarterback returns to the huddle and discusses the previous play with *his* end (note the possessive, not mutuality), is this characteristic of teamwork? Obviously not. Man presents only part of the *Thou*, if any at all. If each person is a possession and therefore little more than an instrument for the other, is it possible to achieve mutuality? Does man seek relationship or conquest? Does he desire communication or isolation? Perhaps Buber gives us part of the solution by saying that "instinct is something greater than the believers in the 'libido' realize: it is a longing for the word to become present to us as a person, which goes out to us as we do it, which chooses and recognizes us as we do it, which is confirmed in us as we in it" (Buber, 1949, p. 88). In truth then we cannot call man dualistic but *pluralistic.* Man is many dimensional and to assume polarities might simplify the issue but does little to clarify the existence of man. Indeed, he is pluralistic. And this is what his relationship to *others* on the team demonstrates. The athlete is not solely involved in himself, but neither is he just an identifiable segment of the team. He is, and represents, much more than a two-headed coin. "Individualism sees man only in relation to himself, but collectivism does not see man at all, it sees only 'society.' With the former, man's face is distorted, with the latter it is mashed" (Buber, 1961, p. 200). The team is neither *I* nor *Thou* nor is it really *I-Thou.* A more proper category, which I trust would be in keeping with Buber's categorical imperative is *We.* The linemen and the backs on a football team don't really *relate*, *respond*, *care*, *trust* and *participate* in any depth of mutuality. They are not *one* as much as *We.* Rather than a *true* societal structure, a team can best be described as a *collection* of isolated individuals unified by a common *interest.* The term *We* is quite descriptive. For it represents "the plurality of human beings through the grammatical form of the first person plural" (Rotenstreich, 1959, p. 155). The *team* is truly not *I-Thou* as much as it is an extension of segmented parts. Not that each member is, in itself, separated from the self, as much as one is separate from the other. In reality, a team is composed of individuals in existence as opposed to a mutuality of interpersonal relations.

The existence of team performance, thus defined, does not afford a breadth and depth for individual exploration and meaning as related to the consciousness of the act. This is not the way I would "like" it but it is the way I see it. My only defense is to indicate that I see a great deal of value in studying, analyzing and eventually appreciating sport, as it exists rather than the way I would wish it to be. The existence of the team environment *creates* the personal setting for the performer, while his transfer to a state of becoming is highly possible within the *We* context of sport. Team situations in sport transpose *Its* into *We's*; however, *Thou's*, by definition of sport as it presently exists, are rarely achievable.

Thus, a serious criticism of team sports must be put forth; namely, the development of authentic actions, on the part of the participant, is most difficult to achieve. Reality, as we have come to experience it, is an outcome of *relationships*—specifically, that which occurs between the *I and Thou*. "Real existence, that is real man in his relation to his being, is comprehensible only in connection with the nature of the being to which he stands in relation" (Rotenstreich, 1959, p. 155). The team encourages a *We* development which symbolizes and signifies man's plurality and de-emphasizes his dualistic determination.

In this way the team member can be viewed as associated and non-associated with other members. In discussing his responsibility to himself and his mates, Sandy Koufax said:

> . . . If I could look back . . . and see how it cost me a ball game, I'd be disturbed with myself. I'd be wrong for myself and I'd be wrong for twenty-four other guys, because I wouldn't be capable of doing the best I can, I'd be ashamed of myself. (Koufax, 1965, p. 36)

Perhaps it was this strong feeling of responsibility for the self *and* the *we* that precipitated Koufax to announce a rather premature retirement from baseball.

"Life is not lived by my playing the enigmatic game on a board by myself, but by my being placed in the presence of a being with whom I have agreed on no rules for the game and with whom no rules can be agreed on" (Buber, 1957, p. 102). It is the *individual* who is the focus. He brings realization to his own self. Life and sport are both played with "others." The concept of teamwork demands each member of the unit to be *aware* of the other; but that is quite different from placing oneself *within* another. The team player, when it is all said and done, is concerned with personal existence and its relevance to personal being.

This is not to infer that there is an out-and-out contradiction, specifically involving the relation to oneself and to one's teammates. All that is being said here is simply that they are not *identical*. The point is simple. Team sports promote priority of the *I* (not the "island onto itself") over and beyond that of a relationship. Sport is not any less because of this development. If nothing else, it provides a *meeting* place for man and man. Teamwork, as a workable concept, has problems but they are no more than bridging the gap between collectivism and mutuality. All man can do is to be aware of the process and the action of sport and in this way work toward the end that seems best suited to the individual.

Realization of the Self

If nothing else has been demonstrated to the reader, it should be evident that sport presents a diversified arena for worthy scholastic inquiry. How is man to achieve personhood within the milieu of diverse events? Are there standards of action which facilitate unification of man and the environment? What are the dimensions and parameters of sport which afford opportunities for self realization? Obviously, these are questions without simple answers; however, they are appropriate questions for philosophic study. Certainly the literature is filled with glib responses based upon superficial reactions. It remains for the philosopher of sport to unify the personal aspects of sport.

The sport scene apparently places emphasis on the individualization of man. On the other hand, one cannot ignore the stress of socialization. Togetherness, teamwork, and "unit" terminology are present all too frequently in the annals of sport. Yet, it is evident to most, that the man of sport performs within a *personalized*, if not individualistic, frame of reference. The world of sport provides development *within* self as well as *for* self. The performer recognizes his responsibility to himself (this, of course does not negate his relationship to others), and develops an evaluation scheme based upon self-development. This is quite unlike the *social* man who perceives of his worth relative to the societal whole. Although sport lays claim to this latter form of socialization, the critical mind must doubt the validity of this assertion. Men of idealized virtue might well claim "they are part of the team," or they may claim they do not care how much they score "just as long as the team is victorious." Yet the astute critic must wonder if such highly competitive activity could yield such altruistic truths. Is it not possible these words are designed as self-camouflaging? In truth, for the team to be really successful, if it were considered to be a social unit, the individual performer would need to submerge his self into the collective self. This is no different from community structures, large business, or any other social organization demands. Yet it is not *really* accurate to think of team performance as a process of desensitization in favor of the unified composite. The most one could hope for is the development of the "team player." This term alone depicts a performer who has gone "above and beyond the call of duty" in his attempt to be *useful* to the unit. It is, by mention, the exception who is accorded this almost "goody-goody" honor.

More often than not, sport provides for actualization through self-extension. The media encourages man to test his raw abilities. Each day he needs to prove again, not with words, but with action, that he remains capable. Few areas of human concern require such demanding feedback. The youngster learns early in life that on the sports field "blue-blood" does not count. Man cannot count on status or social position or previously achieved excellence. He is never granted tenure. He accepts and thrives on the endless chain of uncertainty. To this end, he is a man who seeks freedom to express his humanity.

For man, truly "taken" by sport, the human encounters are always mixtures of thought and feeling so expressed through the movement of the activity. Neither the intellect nor man's other qualities is paramount. Man, in engaging in sport, lives approaching authenticity. Therefore, it is really the will that is a determining influence in man's life. One need go further than Nietzsche to understand that human action is indeed left to the supremacy of the will. Again, one can make the superficial, but perhaps valid transfer, of the value of *desire* to each performance. It is common for all who have been touched by sport to appreciate one man's complete affirmation, while another never approaches his potential.

In its *moments* sport presents a phenomenon that man seeks, and hopefully attains, only rarely. Yet each sport situation provides the atmosphere, within limited boundaries, for such attainment. I speak, specifically, of a "happening" that makes man available for self-realization. Man looks for "proof" of affirmation and sport, trite as the experience may be, brings to man a sense of *that which he is*. In a way sport says to man that his life is *not* absurd—it is that which it is "meant" to be.

And still man realizes that sport is, to a degree, compensative. This paradox is especially true in activities that seek more and more of the individual. However, more is not defined in terms of development and refinement of skill as much as larger obstacles to overcome. Fred Van Dyke, a prominent "big wave" surfer, gives a clue to this senselessness.

> Guys ride big waves for ego support, to compensate for something that is lacking in their lives. . . . They have an underlying feeling that they're not doing anything with meaning. Man needs an outlet that's ego-gratifying. Surfing gives you a feeling of accomplishment. But the feeling is gone in four seconds, and then you have to start all over again.
>
> Surfing should be fun. It's not fun. It's absolute terror. Big-wave riders are scared people. They have to go out there to prove they're not afraid. . . . Once I broke my board in half . . . I knew I hit the ultimate . . . Then I realized what a complete farce it was. I still surf, because I'm a victim of my culture. I can't transcend it. (Rogin, 1965, p. 104)

Van Dyke's use of words such as compensate, meaning, terror, ultimate, and transcend are not accidental. They are the words of a man who has carefully analyzed his sport behavior relative to his purpose in life. He can't escape and yet surfing is no more meaningful than are his other experiences of life. For Van Dyke and so many others, surfing is an attempt at liberation. An attempt that is doomed by the absurdity of the totality of life.

In *living*, man can't hope to continue, continue and continue. The aspiration is defined as locating a *reason* for life or a philosophy of life or even a basis for living. This is academic gobbledegook! A meaningful life cannot be synthesized and produced artificially. Sport, if it is to be meaningful, must be authentic. It must be what it *is*. Nothing more and nothing less. It can only be revealed through personal experience at an almost mystical level. Sport does not avail itself to just any form of empiricism. If it is personal then it may be meaningful. If it is not—it cannot.

Sport has a basic place in most of our lives. It is present; therefore, it assumes a reality that is significant and theoretically has meaning. We hope it will make us open (existenz) and available to meaning of life. When in truth it provides most men with little more than *comfort.*

But let us not stop here. For sport, by its nature, requires a type of completeness. If one pleases, a form of loyalty toward involvement. This is the saving grace. The experiences of sport and the commitments by man to the sport situation form a "wholeness." This unification of man and environment is a measure of unity, a step toward *universality*. "I think of immersion as a mode of living in the present with complete absorption; one has the sense of being comprehended and sustained in a universal situation" (Bugbee, 1960, p. 265).

Sport does not lend itself to a process of generalization; the *happening* itself is what is meaningful. For man truly to attain self-realization he must divorce *motive* from action in the true act. This does not mean that a reason does not exist, as much as that motivation is not complete in and of itself.

SPORT AND MEANING

A football season is a lot like life in microcosm. The season begins with warm and sunny days filled with optimism and hope. As the season progresses, the sunshine wanes, the warmth diminishes, and optimistic hope is qualified by the hard, lifelike realities of fierce competition, unexpected injuries and the innate difficulty of sustained human effort. The days grow colder, the rains come and optimistic vision becomes more realistic. It is always easier to declare the top position in anything than to reach it. While hope perdures, ultimate victory is again a fickle lady, ever to be wooed with all one's might, but never in this life to be securely or forever won. Each week is a new encounter; each season a new challenge. Life is like that, too, because it is spent in time, amid all the vicissitudes of *personal trials and existential difficulties* [italics mine]. Anyone who thinks otherwise lives in a dream world, where reality has been entirely replaced by fantasy. But a football season, like life, is *authentic and real* [italics mine], as well as somewhat fantastic . . . the football season is indeed worthwhile. The noise is ephemeral and does die away. The display, the spectacle, the color, the excitement linger only in the memory. But the spirit, the will to excel and the will to win perdure. These human qualities are larger and much more important than the passing events that occasion them, just as the ebb and flow of all our daily efforts add up to something greater and more enduring if they create within each one of us a person who grows, who understands, who really lives, who does not merely survive, but who prevails for a larger, more meaningful victory in time and, hopefully, in eternity as well. (Hesburgh, 1966, pp. 56–57)

There is a great deal of truth in what Father Hesburgh, President of Notre Dame, says. Sport does begin anew with each event. The mistakes of the past are quickly forgotten *if* man can now succeed. As man attempts to meet the test he does go through a process of existential pain. It is the anguish of his own existence. Yet one has to wonder if Father Hesburgh, one of the greatest leaders of our time, is not being a bit "inspirational" when he believes sport takes man *beyond* survival. The meaning of life is wherever man authentically applies himself to this end. It is wondered if sport indeed does *really* provide this amplitude of human involvement. Most of us would *wish* it did. But *does* it?

In reality, human existence can be reduced to meaning. The problem is one of *purpose* and not value. But in the case of sport it is difficult if not impossible to separate one from the other. The nature of the activity is so directed to encourage competition and minimize cooperation. No matter how "Christian" the purpose, it is suspect if it leaves the realm of the reality of our modern world, a reality which fosters material and pragmatic ends. "For what we will be cannot be affirmed as meaningful if what we are cannot be called meaningful" (Kwant, 1965, p. 223). Thus, if man is to *be*, he must do more than follow or repeat standardized actions—he *must experience* the meaning of each and every situation. For how could there be a tomorrow in sport if there is a meaningless today?

To speak of "eternity" might well be within the realm of the spirit. But one must wonder if it is truly in the sport we now experience. Every performer I have known is "tuned" to the present. He is obsessed with *today's* action. How good will he be in today's meet? How strong will he be *right now*? As Father Hesburgh indicates, each event is a new *encounter;* the performer knows no other *meeting* except the one he is now involved in. The new encounter says to man, time and again, *this is it.* Man "plays them one at a time." As he experiences the new engagement (it is interesting that the world of sport frequently uses the word "meet" to describe this encounter), he must experience *each* one in a fresh and spontaneous way. It does not matter how humdrum or repetitious the event really is. If he does not get "up" for the meet, he faces defeat, both on the field and within the man. Therefore, we again face an interesting realization relative to dualism. We are able to conceive of *duration* of meaning. That is to say we cannot think of the past, present and future as if they are separate entities. We have developed the concept of *whole time* in sport. That is to say, there is *no future meaning* if there is *no meaning now*, in the present. The performer is being naive if he believes he can have an experience tomorrow that *will become* meaningful if he "fakes" the experience that *is*. This is not meant to imply an endless regression based upon original "sin." However, the problem for many men in the modern world is how to *suddenly* develop meaningful experiences. In other words, once man becomes committed to the unauthentic, it requires great awareness and effort to achieve a new *now*.

> Any schematic relationship between experiences implies units. . . . Theories of time, moments, before and after, and so on are schematic relationships of units, into which experience can be specified. (Gendlin, 1962, p. 155)

Sport involves this form of *time-meaning*. The limitations of each event are circumscribed by rather vigorous time boundaries. To realize that each time sequence relates to another is a rather horrifying thought. It means that the performer is continuously united to previous experience. If man is to attain meaning, this experience must be *felt* by him. To deny this *necessity* is to refute man's experiences as being schematically related. To imply a goal of human existence, based on relations, is to commit man to the future when he well might not be there. Existence is *not* clear. We don't even really know ourselves, yet we are asked to know others. We don't know our present, yet we are asked to relate to the future (the assumption is made that we are *sure* of our past—what trickery!). No wonder man enters sport with rather superficial and easy goals. Winning and losing become an escape for facing the realities of the world. Even if man loses in sport he still *knows*. On a short-term basis this might well be justifiable. At least he avoids the dilemma of knowing that there must be *more* of a *purpose* than fitness or victory. Yet to admit a *value* that is *real* requires *meaning*. And meaning is not easy to come by. Thus, man selects *one* goal and/or value that *is* real.

Generally, it is victory. Whether it be *defeat* of an opponent, or the *killing* of an animal, or the *catching* of a fish, or the *conquering* of nature, it is victory. Is it not interesting that man thinks *he wins* by defeating, slaying or conquering? Is it not odd that the highest level of animal needs is to push the "other" down in order to elevate the self? How funny it is that man thinks he will attain *meaning* in the *future* by substituting *value* (generally concretely limited) for meaning in the *present*! When will man realize he needs to *involve* himself in the present? The very *greatness* of sport is what he is denying. Namely, it is an arena of the *now*. We receive immediate and involved experience that afford the basis for *meaning*. Are we so insecure that we need to look for the values in the future? In so doing, we perhaps hope that we can avoid a confrontation with the now. And of course it is always easier to talk of what *will* or *could* be than to speak of what is. Tomorrow's world could be anything the idealist dreams it to be. Today's world is real. It is present. This is not to refute the future. It is just to emphasize that *reality is now*—let us deal with it.

Man's existence is a question of the present. Sport speaks to man's present, if only man will hear it. The area of culture might matter to some degree, but in all truth it is man that is responsible for his existence. Perhaps music is different from art which in turn is different from sport. But as Jesus said of the sower, the results depend upon the soil. How rocky, shallow or rich is man? What is the meaning man attaches to the world of sport? To see it as is, is to recognize existence. Certainly, the experience can be changed at a later time, but for the present the experience must be turned into a *sensed* meaning.

In the present of sport, *as it is now*, as it appears in existence, it possesses a quality of *likeness or fitting*. In itself it is. But it also unites man to *whole-time*. Somehow it says to man that the meaning derived in sport is *related* to future man and to another man of the present. Therefore, when man says sport *means* something to him, he is admitting its present quality as it is, but also recognizing its tomorrow quality as something more than it is. It is this quality of sport, if not prostituted by the "seekers of the perfect world," that can make sport so inherently human. It says to man the activity *transcends* time as well as form! It allows man to reach out and understand a world he *knows* but has not come to recognize. It brings all of existence *to* man because of the *likeness* quality that is in part a definition of meaning. Sport speaks to him. He has never heard this sound before. It might well have been there; but for him it did not exist. Sport as a meaningful experience is more than sport. It is more than what each man experiences. And yet it is not more than man.

The Meaning of I

The more scientific and mechanized our life becomes, the more the individual is neglected. In medicine he becomes a "case," in politics a "citizen," and in athletics a "horse." Man becomes a particle in the great and total formula. As we have seen, *truth*, in sport, exists only as the individual *himself* produces it in action. In sport it is for man to shape his own destiny and in so doing develop the *I*. "Do not think as a thinker . . . think as a living, real being. Think in existence" (Tillich, 1944, p. 68). To be a real man one needs, first, to avoid becoming an object in a vast industrial and political world. Existence is best achieved by a process which enables the individual to *realize* what he possesses. But this is not all. In order to discover the *meaning* of the I, and not simply the I, it becomes necessary to locate the dynamics of the sport situation and translate them into meaningful forms.

When man partakes in sport, he does so for many reasons. But certainly one of the deeper "drives" is ontological in nature. Who am I? What is the meaning of my participation in this life? As most men he is seeking identification of the true nature of man as basically resolved in the psychological and social aspects of sport.

Early analysis of the participant in sport was directly patterned after Freudian psychology. Sport was conceived as an avenue of release of aggressive tendencies. The little boy was "channeled" into throwing a baseball rather than a rock. As he advanced in age he substituted a bowling ball for a baseball. Freudian psychoanalytic theory assumes man will in his actions, in part, attempt to gratify the libido and other aggressive drives. Thus, sport becomes a medium where man can mediate between his instinctual needs and the requirement of social living. Modern psychology has altered its direction so that concerns have not been directed to *illness* as much as *personal irresponsibility*.

In this context the behavior of the athlete may be "inappropriate" or "unethical" but rarely indicative of illness. Behavior is evaluated in terms of social criteria, whereas sport standards tend to be rather broad in limitations. If the football player is penalized for a "personal foul" (as if other fouls are not personal!), the type of behavior is nothing but "inappropriate learning and living." The behavior is simply not appropriate relative to the "rules of the game." The choice, of course, was voluntary (there is no recognition of any priority over man, such as the subconscious), made in freedom, so man must live with the responsibility of his choice.

Now, the sport performer is no longer viewed as an animal imperative but rather as a social being whose fulfillment is directly relative to the *human* content. This requires complete interpersonal commitment between athlete and athlete. In this way, man escapes *nothingness* and attains his own completion. He finds the I and he knows who he is. He is no longer a possibility. He is his existence.

Man can now say, "I am." But really, who is he? The expressed contributions that sport makes to man's life are often glib and trite. From the scientific explanations to psychological analysis sport has been credited with doing everything from increasing longevity to the diffusion of sexual guilt. Whatever the approach, the existence of man is often misused and ruined. Sport does contribute to human existence but in such a way that almost defies description; for a lack of a better term, I might say that man *transcends* himself and may potentially emerge with a discovery of the self.

Through constant questioning, endless doubt, and ever persistent uncertainty man locates an inner *being*. Sport affirms more than his existence. It gives being certainty.

> (through surfing) . . . I sought a meaning for life and found it when I ventured helplessly among the towering waves of Makaha. I was no match for their awesome power but, with courage and the confidence that comes from overcoming one's fear and ineptitude, I got a brief glimpse of glory. (Quinn, 1965, p. 82)

Man no longer is a meaningless question. Surfing has transmitted meaning, not of the sport but *of* the man. He now has a locus in the world. Being can be affirmed. Factual existence is presented with its own *being*. And the existence of surfing is the existence of man. I now can know my I.

But sport goes *beyond* affirmation. For man can find a haven of refuge in the rules, order and logic of sport; yet simultaneously, he can escape what he encompasses. This is a lot to offer man. But it is true that in sport man both escapes and becomes one of the crowd. He can select sport activities yielding loneliness (*i.e.*, surfing) or he can subject himself to the spectator and allow his existence to be transmitted, partially determined by another. This is not to infer a "nature" of sport but only to recognize certain "generalized" qualities of the specific. In a way, man derives protection from himself through the externality of another. But if he *truly* engages in sport, he transcends rather than protects.

Sport says to man that he can find out who he is, but this should not be a structure of knowing *where* he is. Sport places man out of "that which is" to "that which is for now." It provides a place to locate the man by coming into contact, and perhaps even communion, with the elements. But this is always within the situation I experience for myself. "I sought beauty and found it in the fascinating perfection of breaking a wave . . . I sought harmony and found it when I joined together with a curling wave" (Quinn, 1965, p. 82). Through the freedom of the sport, man experiences his I as he never before experienced the self. Constantly on the edge of being, and confronted by his existence, he potentially can locate the *meaning* of the *I*.

Man is *in* the world. He is in the world of sport. But unlike an object, man does not maintain a place in space. Rather he uses space to achieve his human desires. If meaning is not activated, then the involvement of sport becomes a cold process of moving objects in space. Only, man becomes the object. In this he loses his freedom and loses contact with the world of *his touch*. He goes further from meaning and closer to nothingness. Obviously, the determining factor is not sport but man. He must approach the immediate, and just as he cannot *use* his self he cannot *use* sport. He must *involve* himself in the act and inquire into the self during the dynamics of the experience. To sense a little of this strange technique is to come a little closer to the achievement of personal meaning and a little further from a sense of self as an instrument.

Sport: Relation and Meaning

Sport reveals man's basic existence. One does not need to be a behavioral scientist to realize that, perhaps, for many, sport *becomes* (not *is*) an arena for psychological solutions to conflicts. But to say this *is* sport is to demean man's efforts as basically *and* uniquely animal. On the other hand, to say sport is not animal is, equally, not to see sport as it is. When the athletic team performs, it incorporates both animal and other levels of existence. The aspects of man are welded together to reach a common purpose. Yet, as we have seen, a purpose does not necessitate a meaning. But without the *collective*, no matter what the individual purposes *are*, no total character could be developed. Thus, to this degree, the total purpose *and* meaning must be *related* if there is to be any sense to the athletic performance.

The sport situation therefore attempts to harmonize the *fittings*. The meaning of each performer, in some way, must be *like* the meaning of each other performer. If not, the result will certainly be chaos. Perhaps they win on the court but they lose in the world (when meaning is experienced, in essence, it gives rise to other meanings). Thus, the world of sport becomes a *correlative* between the meanings of each performer. In sport we have truly a group of individualized meanings operating in *mutuality*. Thus, the experience of sport is one of *interinvolvement of meanings*. But one thing must be made clear. While the team's performance might well be *meaningful*, it in no way is in direct proportion to the total of individualized efforts. In truth, the meaningful team performance might well greatly differ from the meaning each man attaches to a given action. Meaning of the group is beyond the meaning that each man holds. Therefore, one could conclude there is present a *collective character of meaning*. In this way it can be seen that the necessitated multiple relationships of society are a result of the amplification of the meanings that are inherent in individualization.

When man looks at most sport situations, he can easily view the constituents which are functioning. The performer experiences a chance for a meaning of fame. A second sees the meaning of societal approval. Another sees riches as *in* the experience. While still another participates because he sees the religious functions of life being met in sport. Meaning is sensed in sport, and man directs his energy to achieve what is there. To be sure, the meanings are exact and generally quite comprehensible to the conscious. But to participate in sport is to be *contacted* with the whole of sport. Thus, man might well enter sport to achieve one end and shortly be involved with other meanings. Some close their eyes to these meanings. They do not want to be threatened. Or perhaps they see their immediate purpose being deterred if they *do* become involved with other aspects of life. But some do "open" themselves to the immediate. What *was* sensed is *now* beckoned. Man becomes aware of the "many" meanings and he relates *to them* as well as each to each other. As the performer seeks fame (and this is found on the sandlots as well as in the stadiums), he may recognize the mystical qualities that are revealed to him in sport. He sees human movement as a *means* to achieve fame. But he sees it as more than means. He recognizes the application of movement, as it is, to the mystical. *Likeness* is seen *in* the activity and between meanings. It is truly, in the words of the statistician, an intercorrelation. "A given felt meaning can be called forth by symbols, situations, or objects. These could 'call forth' other felt meanings, which in turn could select other symbols" (Gendlin, 1962, p. 161). It is most probable that the man of sport does not really identify many of the "felt meanings" that are available to him. But this does not demean the sport as much as it does humanity. Sport cannot really be perceived, as it is, divorced from man. Yet, if sport is more than cognition, man will need to "release" himself from the bondage of *specified meanings* in order to encounter the range of the *many* interwoven meanings. To say this is possible is to admit the promising. But to look at sport, in the present, is to be dejected. Certainly the most idealistic dreamers among us would not admit that this end has been achieved. On the other hand, to admit it to be within the province of the human is to recognize that perhaps it is not altogether a human achievement.

The interactions of human meanings are simply not possible if initiated *directly*. Our world *does* function indirectly, in a symbolic manner. Again, man reacts not to the territory but to the map. To understand the interaction between man's experiences and the existing symbols he uses, we arrive closer to comprehending the multitude of *meaning* man admits to his world. In understanding the creation of meaning for the man of sport, we need to grasp the impact and importance that symbols possess in the development of a meaningful existence.

Sport and the Symbol

It is not possible to consider sport unless we consider man. A consideration of man, as a unique animal, leads one directly to our prior discussion relative to the *needs* of the individual. As was demonstrated, a consideration of primary human tendencies toward *relations and meaning* indicate a quality that is so subtle it is almost forgotten. Namely, the athlete cannot perform *any* operation unless he *thinks*. (The reader will note this is contrary to the popular caricature of the football player doing little more than reacting to a given stimuli *without* thinking.)

It is common to consider *thinking* as an adaptation to life rather than as a gratification of a *need*. However, this does not account for the prolific nature of thought processes, and the unceasing activity of transforming the world into meaningful symbolic forms. The individual of sport needs an active and alert mind. He constantly needs to solve problems, adjust to new situations, hypothesize about what will or will not work, and be able to transform input of information into meaningful patterns of action. No quarterback, pitcher, sprinter, or boxer could *exist* in a significantly meaningful manner without this quality. There is an endless attempt to transform everything into meaning. One can attempt to explain this in a more sophisticated form of those animal responses which are part of the instinctual apparatus and working in the service of *survival;* the amazing world of imagination which man has created can presumably be regarded as a more complex version of the conditioned reflex.

Susanne Langer has criticized the zoological model of human intelligence as merely a more complex form of those utilitarian neurological capacities which animals demonstrate. She points out how human mental activity is always in great excess of any purpose it might serve, and that the whole world of thought and imagination serves no purpose as far as the satisfaction of man's instinctual needs are concerned, and is more likely an actual handicap. Sport, like art, religion, poetry, and music, really does not serve an essential or primary form for gratification. Sport is more than mere animal. In fact, the athlete who attempts to destroy as a barbarian, or fulfill basal animal instincts, will no doubt hinder his performance. The words of Langer are quite appropriate to sport. Unless man in some way *restricts* his basic needs, he will hinder his performance rather than facilitate it. It is therefore not necessary to pose the usual conflict between biology and culture, an argument I have tried to avoid, but rather to consider the possibility that the *need* to attain *meaning* is as important as those other needs which are traditionally biological.

> The basic need, which certainly is obvious only in man, is the need of symbolization. The symbol-making function is one of man's primary activities like eating, looking or moving about. It is the fundamental process of his mind, and goes on all the time. Sometimes we are aware of it, sometimes we merely find its results, and realize that certain experiences have passed through our brains and have been digested there. In every mind there is an enormous store of symbolic materials, which is put to different uses or perhaps to even no use at all—a mere result of spontaneous brain activity, a reserve fund of conceptions, a surplus of mental wealth. (Langer, 1948, p. 72)

The individual of sport can never really rest. His mind needs constantly to produce ideas and new patterns of relationships. The following view of symbolic transformation is essential to the needs of all men, but especially vital to the sport participant.

> . . . (The mind) goes right on manufacturing ideas, streams and deluges of ideas that the sleeper is not using to think about anything. But the brain is following its own laws; it is actively translating experiences into symbols in fulfillment of a basic need to do so. It carries on a constant process of ideation. As all registered experience tends to terminate in action, it is only natural that a typically human function should require a typically human form of overt activity; and that is just what we find in the sheer expression of ideas. This is the activity of which beasts appear to have no need. And it accounts for just those traits in man which he does not hold in common with other animals—ritual, art, laughter, weeping, speech, superstition and scientific genius. (Langer, 1948, p. 73)

Sport is just the type of *overt activity* that does express man's inner thoughts. This is where the action is. The animal kingdom might well play, fight or even battle, but it is not capable of sport as known by man. The complexities of human involvement are carried through in the complexity of sport. Man deceives, schemes, excels and plans, in life and in sport. The process of symbolization is developed as a core experience in life and thus becomes integrated in sport. *Thought* is an essential process in the attainment of meaningful forms of movement which eventually comprise the *form* of sport. The relationship between the symbol and the experience needs to be meaningful if man is to actualize his potential.

If man fails in his attempt to achieve meaningful forms of sport, he loses the "biggest game of all." I refer to the attempt of the failure to achieve authenticity, a failure to *relate* meaningfully to the subtle and complex relations of the thinker to his thoughts. A defeat here and the individual is no longer a man of sport. He is nothing but an animal or a human machine. Both *can think;* but they cannot *relate* to their thoughts. There is no meaning. It takes man, *a real man*, to develop meaning.

In sport the participant *feels* meaning to the degree that he is aware of the implications of the symbol. His direct experiences in sport provide an immediate foundation for the sensation of meaning. Too often the sport performer, focusing on the material and the immediate, will mistake the symbol for the reality and it will not be viewed in its "symbiotic" function of assisting in the "mutual growth" of a *relationship*.

Acceptance of the postulation stated above assumes that meaning cannot and does not operate in a situation where man divorces himself from his fellowman. Therefore, the *real* place of the process of symbolization, in any media where highly competitive functions tend to divide the relationship, is suspect. As soon as one mentions the general category "sport," or even the specific activity, such as basketball, a sensation of meaning is released which does "something" to the relationship between man and the activity. This reaction is no doubt part of the perceptual field and therefore greatly influenced by experience. What basketball *means* to each man becomes a function, in part, of the experiences. It immediately calls forth what Buber would call the "living bonds." Even if one were not this poetic, it would be difficult to deny the *connections* between man and his *milieu*. It can be seen that any meaning of sport that is maintained by a given individual is directly influenced by his ability to *relate*. Therefore, a sport happening is a symbolic occurrence. Each and every time man sees, performs, and/or hears anything related to basketball he associates the stimuli into an experience. This then may evolve into a "feeling" about basketball. He might not be able to differentiate between the various forms of "input" of the senses, thereby explaining his thoughts of the *total* experience. In any sport, man lives on the edge of human experience. The thrill of movement and sense of competition keeps man *attentive* as he precariously balances on this edge of the totality of experiences. This dynamic aspect of sport might well be intriguing but it might also hinder the development of clear perceptions, which need to be based on clear evidence of the experience.

The imperative question for the critic of sport might well be the following: How does sport relate, as a symbol, to the sensed meaning of man? It can be seen that sport, or at least the process of sport, implies a relationship between the elements of sport. The very factor of sport being whole or complete allows and, in fact, facilitates the symbolic process as one of *totality*. Therefore, the meaning of sport, as a symbol, is always relative to the whole of personal existence.

It should not be forgotten that sport provokes, by its very nature, an *emotional* meaning. Its existence is one of dynamics and excitement. Its physical form of symbolization is not a picture, as it is for the artist, or words, as it is for the writer, but rather a combination of movement forces and patterns. It depends, to a great amount, on the physical objects, body and environment. The meaning that is sensed is one of *being*. Man communicates his being through an expression of action. Certainly this is a valid concept for the sport performer.

In this way sport performance *gives* meaning to man. But man must be ready through the initiating of awareness. If the sport experience is going to be meaningful, then the *action* (performance) must in the words of Husserl be *intentional*. If man is not aware of the purpose of his act, the symbol, in the concrete might well *appear* to be identical with the meaningful form;

however, it is no more than mere coincidence. The concrete image is not what determines meaning. Rather emotion is the identifiable factor. Emotion cannot occur accidentally. Too much is *involved.* It must be intentional. It is this form of recognition of the action for what it is that creates meaning out of the sport experience.

It is necessary to reiterate that the concern of this discussion is with the *concept* of the *process* of sport. As such, the experience of sport must be considered in its relationship with other aspects of the total environment. The individual might well be directly relating to sport; but, at the same time, might well be establishing relationships with other experiences. Sport, as a *process* is something that is happening at many different points and places of human existence. Therefore, the meaning of sport is inclusive of not *only* sport but all *related* experiences. It is easy to see the *effect* sport has on the multitude of dimensions of life. The meaning that sport experiences is germane to other aspects of the process of existence. Its only distinction relates to the *aspects* of emphasis that in some way differentiates it from another element of existence.

Subject and Object. Sport as a form of human movement is most assuredly more than a rote process but, as an experience, it is deeply rooted in the heart of human existence. Analysis of human movement has generally been complicated by the dualistic arguments of man as an object (material being) and as a subjective (mind) force.

Frequently, man becomes confused by what *is* and what *appears.* "We have of the universe but formless visions, fragmentary, and which we complete with associations of arbitrary ideas, creating dangerous suggestions" (Proust, 1943, p. 19). If we assume the *object* is that which *exists*, all that is not an object is *nothing*. For example, there is no symbol that can communicate what a football really *is*, save a football. It could be described in texture, touch, smell and appearance. To the man of sport the football, in its universal *whole*, is to be thrown, kicked, run with, and advanced. What brings about these phenomena is *nothing*. As Sartre indicates the way of handing *it* its usefulness is nowhere to be discerned. Man, in a meaningful activity (a sport contest), transmits this *nothing* into the world. "The nothing is at the very heart of the being, in its core like a worm"

(Sartre, 1956a, p. 474). Thus, the *object* is transformed to *being*. It is given *life*.

This is the same point that I have made formally (Van Den Berg, 1952), namely, the object *is*. The football is always something. One can think of the football as nothing but leather and laces but, by design, one needs to conceive of the football as something more than it *is*. For it is no more than leather and laces in essence but not in existence. The football is an object but through man's involvement it has been tranformed to a vitalized reality. This one little "insignificant" football not only encompasses the objective world but also the human world.

This single word, football, might well connote in the time of year, formations of clouds, spirit of spectators, brilliant colors, and cocktail parties. But this is all a process of *human* association. The objective is human, because man interprets himself in what he sees around him. The football is never, in reality, relationless. It is *nothing* (transference of the abstract object to the fullness of human existence). For different individuals *the* football has different meanings, although its properties are the same. To the manufacturer it is a product, to a fullback an object to be carried, to the referee an object to be placed, and to the ball boy an object to be wiped dry. It is most difficult to describe the object's existence since it is dependent upon man. "For man is not coiled up within himself, but is outside himself" (Sartre, 1947, p. 291).

As the participant moves, he must be always aware of the importance of giving, what Buber would call, the *It*, life. Man does move *what* he is doing. It is more than mere shifts, turns and twists. They are the movements of the whole man as he encounters his immediate environment. If this man is to have life, then the object must have life. If the object is lifeless, then this will be the plight of man. The player may have to forget the movements of the self in order to move but he best not forget which is subject and which is object.

Meaning in the Perceived Reality

The participant involved in sport assumes a *perspective*. This is but one view within the total world. By choice, man creates an existence for himself. His movements and reactions become a projection of the self as he sees himself in accordance with established patterns.

The sport situation, itself, possesses a present that can be perceptually determined. Presented with, what might be called, an automatic focal point the sport participant radiates from the self to his *existenz*. In so doing he perceives all that exists. The roll of the wave, the flight of the duck, the motion of man all yield themselves to his perception.

The milieu of events that are available in sport provide the raw material for meaning. However, it is the development of conscious perception *of* and *in* elements that yield available meanings. The projection of relational modes results in determination of the extent and intimacy of each act of sport.

It is in sport that one is immediately presented with the *real.* The middle line backer is real. He possesses an immediate relation to others that is not a dream. The water is a real force to the swimmer and boatsman alike; and likewise the ball is a real object to be hit, kicked, shot or thrown. Yet for different men the same reality might well appear different. "We need not ask ourselves whether we perceive the world really. We must, on the contrary, say that the world is that which we perceive" (Merleau-Ponty, 1945, p. 11).

To talk of meaning in sport we need to relate to *what* is revealed to each man. Existence of that which is real is a dimension of the existence of man, but concomitantly the existence of man is partially a determinant of that which he is aware of as real. In discussing the 1965 National Football League Championship game, the Green Bay Packer quarterback, Bart Starr, more than demonstrated his feeling of the necessity of perceptual awareness. "We wanted to make them *aware* . . . Their defense played a fine game, but *we* created the right climate in *their* defense thinking, and it was time to take advantage of it" (Maule, 1966, p. 17). Once man perceives the conscious awareness of the act, relative to a given situation, meaning becomes apparent and he can make significantly meaningful decisions. His conceptions must be immersed and linked to the motions of the environment, for if not, reality is not present. However, without distinctive perceptions man cannot move in a meaningful manner.

Realistically, essences *appear* first. Man sees colors, sizes, shapes, etc. Then matter forms patterns. We see the changing color of the speared fish or the blueness of the water. "They (perceptual stimuli) penetrate to and stimulate within one a certain 'apparatus' which makes me belong to the world and point myself in its direction" (De Waelhens, 1959, p. 60). The participant turns to his world, at first without vigor or even excitement, but all the time what he perceives draws him *into* the world. It becomes a part of him; therefore, feeling the security of approaching oneness, he coordinates his existence with the self. Soon the essences of the world, previously external but now internalized, are now *available* to the newly aware. The elements of sport have place, substance, presence and relationship to each other and to the man of sport. Simply, they are now *meaningful.*

The participant's initial concerns are not with complete "knowing," for, at this junction, little is available to him but the awareness of what is to be known. Obviously, at this rather primitive state, the performer's meaning is far from complete. That which he perceives, by smell, sight, taste is exclusive of other perceptual fields. Meaning must be *specific* to the situation. It must relate the existent to that which exists. This statement might appear to be self-evident; however, senses always take form in the real world of the performer. Thus, what man can sense is within the world and likewise the world is what man can sense. What is available to man in the media of sport might appear superficially similar to all other domains, but it is not. Transfer of *meaning* is a naive dream. Man must experience in the situation all visible horizons. All of life is reducible to *an* action and meaning which in some way is related to *that* specific *knowing*. Sport is no different. It is not necessary as a way of life. We *really* don't derive our survival fitness levels from sport. Nor do we *really* learn the lessons of the "real" world from sport. But we do learn what makes itself apparent in sport. We do learn about sport. Anything else is a bonus for the perceptive. This is about all man can ask from any of life's endeavors.

To look to sport for a *form* of uniqueness is to recognize the performer's *existenz* as it reveals meaning in the *operation* of the event. The man must, by definition, concern himself with reality. What is really occurring becomes of paramount importance to the performer. If nothing else, sport provides for a complete and true experience of what does exist.

The sport experience is a simple and direct confrontation attempting to approach "reality by the individual existent functioning as a totality" (Mihalich, 1960, p. 41). Here the individual harmonizes cognitive and emotional elements which are often perceived as separate. The emotional element is often expressed as drive, spirit, morale, "being-up," etc. When in truth man is a *total* composite of his experience and therefore the perceived world.

One could argue that nothing actually exists in sport, therefore allowing no knowledge of one's being. Because at the same time, "being is and is not nothing" (Heidegger, 1949, pp. 352–392). When one is involved with putting a ball into a hole, he subtracts himself from the immediate situation, therein causing *nothing* to become the negation of the total golf situation. In order to achieve this temporary detachment one has to maintain complete *sensation* of the total situation—the speed of the green, the lie of the ball, the break of the green, and the touch of the body. The golfer then gives up individual contact with the situation. Suddenly he is there and yet not there. He becomes *fused* into the wholeness of the totality, the reality.

Any individual who has participated in a sport such as football can recount the apparent inconsistency in what Heidegger refers to as *mood*. The crowd is roaring. The player looks toward the stands. But none can be identified. There is only a furor of colors and a rash of forms. All of this gives the *feeling* of excitement. As the participant enters the huddle, he listens to the call of the play. There is almost no attempt at recollection of "his part" in the play. He attempts to concentrate, yet all that might be immediately visualized is a sudden blade of grass, a dirt spot on the uniform of a teammate, or a reflection of the sun. Suddenly, they break from the huddle. Each man goes to his assigned position through a combination of partial awareness and semi-partial habit. The performer is there but not really. He is submerged, as an individual, into the formless and faceless totality of nothingness. He is *there* but nothing more.

His perceptual senses give him feeling more than a knowledge of the known. He sacrifices personal identity (to his *one*) in favor of *thereness*. It is not, as Heidegger indicates, a "mood of boredom," as much as an expression of submission. He is involved and encompassed by the reality he perceives. His sense of specificity is present but in a real sense his individuality is lost. In a way, he has transcended his self. His enmeshment in what is totally *real* takes on a form of *meaning*.

Varied sensations come to man. Happiness, fear, despair, are all part of the emotion of reality. No longer are emotions divorced from the participants; they are experienced and as such the quality of *thereness* is present. Since the participant is now part of *what-is*, he plays "hard" because this is what is called for within the total process. Nothing is *really* revealed. Man goes through a type of *play-acting*. He approaches reality, almost as if he really believed the character he was playing. In this sense the player is approaching the realm of nothingness. In the game *that is*, many a football player experiences the trembling and nausea the existential writers point to. The vital point, as I recall my own thoughts, is that these sensations are nonconceptual experiences which facilitate personal performance. The reality of the game situation is somehow "co-existing," but not integrating with the perceived emotion.

Perhaps it is this expression of mood that Sartre refers to as a constant theme in his works. In *Nausea*, Roquentin discovers his meaning of existence through the acceptance of mood and emotion as cognitive expressions of the human experience. In this sense the performer is *asking* for the "drive" or "reason," for the continuation of the experience. The view toward the stands, the hardness of the bench, the dirt that seems to be in the way of each blade of grass, the unevenness of the white yard lines, the perspiration marks on the uniforms, all become somewhat part of the *perceived* sport. All of this makes man ponder the reason and determination for being. After years of unconscious awareness of the acceptance of things, the individual soon realizes *meaning* in the sport as well as in man himself. There is no reason for the perceived experiences, beyond their existence. They just *are*—that is all there is to reality.

Somehow involvement brings a resignation which leads to sustained acceptance. One leaves the field with a sense of having been "done." Somehow one realizes that there is eternal meaning in the empty stands, the muddied field and what one "recalls" as the echo of the crowd. In a way, the glory, the victory and the sense of being *in-it* is not meaningless. One can't really explain it, but somehow it seems to leave a satisfaction that indicates it is justified—or at least almost justified.

The lessons one gleans for life are not the ones mentioned by coaches and commentators in their trivial after-dinner speeches on the "value of sport." Rather than "learning to get off the ground," there is a sensation of the *justification of existence*, if one needs such. Perhaps this could be "transferred" to another, but since it is specific to the experience it would no doubt lack meaning. Certainly man transfers mood and emotion. He could constructively involve himself in other elements of life. He, no doubt, could endure the short-termed tortures of life. Perhaps he could find reason. Somehow it really matters not. The person is integrated through human experience. His experiences in sport tell him what he might have "sensed" all along. Namely, the verdict is not on the scoreboard, but in the reality of a *meaningful* existence. To achieve this end, man must confront reality through his actions. Thus, awareness of reality is imperative; yet if the happening is to have meaning, it must *transcend* itself.

It is simultaneously *specific* and *beyond specificity*. Assuming objectivity is present, *meaning* becomes a dimension of subjective necessity. Yet real value needs to come from release of meaning. Allowing meaning to be propelled from the "inner self," the individual now has a *why* for action. So does his fellowman. "There is in fact no perception which is not the recognition of an object that another has already invested with meaning" (De Waelhens, 1959, p. 62).

The performer can now communicate with those of similar experiences, and yet he cannot. There is a passing-on, but yet not a triangle, of meanings that are grounded in the esthetics, kinesthetics and just plain sensation of movement. Meaning is established because it becomes known. And man knows only what he has brought into his awareness.

Although sport operates within a framework of meaning, it can be determined that within this framework is a structure of reality which is centered in real time and space. It is not the *same* time and space of the outside world but it is *real*. In a sense time and space are both "essentials" for the operation of sport. Sport does not use "world-time or space" but it does assume temporal relations that are *related* to world conditions. But the very fact that sport allows for the "stoppage of time" and the artificial controls of space indicates a distinctive character that is projected on man's *reality*. The events are not operated within "indefinite and infinite" conditions. Thus man can structure his action in a way that does not duplicate the reality of living in an *open-ended* existence.

As man is freed from the bounds of nature, through use of the "superimposed," the multitude of choices and potentials, with the opportunity for instant feedback, provides man the opportunity to evaluate *his* reality. In sport he is free to create the patterns necessary to accomplish goals. His movements are limited by the totality of ingredients composing skill and the limitations of space, times and regulations. But never is he free to become what is meaningful to him. The individual symbolically attempts to realize his meaning of life through the totality of his experience. He attains a powerful force of integrating all in the environment as an intentional modification of what is potentially perceived.

> . . . play is a symbolic act of representation, in which human life interprets itself. The most ancient games are magical rites, the principal liturgical cultures of primitive man, expressing his being-in-the-world, in which he represents his destiny, commemorates the events of birth and death, weddings, war, the chase and work. (Fink, 1960, p. 105)

Sport, more than play, is reality itself. It is the truth of human life in all its relations. When engaged in sport we live within it. We reflect ourselves as a mirror sends forth its image. It is not part of the mirror, but of that which confronts the mirror. "Human play is the symbolic action which puts us in the presence of the meaning of the world and of life" (Fink, 1960, p. 108).

Sport makes one "available" to existence. It opens the individual so he is receptive to this creative and novel experience. Perhaps the relationship of sport to existence and being is best summarized by Rilke.

> In merely catching your own casting all's
> mere cleverness and indecisive winning:—
> only when all at once you're catching balls
> an everlasting partner hurtles spinning
> into your very centre, with trajecture
> exactly calculated, curvingly
> recalling God's stupendous pontifecture,—
> only then catching's capability,
> not yours, a world's. And if, not resting here,
> you'd strength and will to throw them back again,—
> no,—wonderfullier!—forgot all that, and then
> found you'd already thrown . . . (as, twice a year,
> the flocking birds are thrown, the birds that wander,
> thrown from an older to a younger, yonder,
> ultramarine warmth),—in that mood of sheer
> abandon you'd be equal to the game.
> Both ease and difficulty would disappear:
> you'd simply throw. A meteor would flame
> out of your hands and tear through its own spaces . . .
>
> (Rilke, 1960, p. 328)

Sport has a meaning that encompasses the human sphere. Whether one relates to self or God, it is perhaps true that lived existence is broader than any given instance of sport. Yet each instance does mantain relation to the total appetites and tendencies of identity with reality. The sport action shows man what is, both in the world and in himself. I am almost tempted to say that man is whole only when he engages in sport.

Man's imagination and will drives him to sport and in so doing brings him to a meaning of existence. Potentially sport provides not so much an outlet for drives, as an avenue through which man attempts to perfect himself in light of self-discovered meaning. To many, sport with its infinite structure through the rules and regulations is a symbol of the rather restrictive life man leads and which brings about a precariousness of man's existence due to externally imposed values. As man suffers in his immersion (Heidegger uses the term *geworfenheit* to explain man being thrown into the situation), he must make meaningful and authentic choices if he is to do more than survive. Of course, the unauthentic select the patterns of the "other." In many ways an analogy may be drawn with the way light rays shed light on themselves. By their very existence, they illuminate themselves as something both distinct from and related to their environment. Sport also reflects the "revealedness" of human existence. It provides an awareness and avenue for being by its own existence and its association with man. Likewise, man is both clarified and expanded as he involves himself in the process. The individual's perception of reality in sport may well reveal things and events that formulate meaningful concepts of the dynamics of existence.

Sport as a Human Absurdity

In literature, architecture, music, dance, sculpture, and painting as well as other forms of human expression man centers his efforts on the *creation* of the new. His manipulation of time, force, and mass is an attempt, in part, to break away from *the known* images of the culture. I don't think this could be said about sport. Influenced by the material culture sport serves to *preserve* the present. The attempts of the baseball player, golfer, hockey player and rower, are to *repeat* the conventional. Obviously the attempt is for greater skill and precision. But ultimately sport is an instrument of maintenance of the *status quo.* Its temper is conservative rather than liberal. Its process is the structured rather than the unstructured. Its product is maintenance of form rather than creation. Its instrument is the rational rather than the emotional. Pascal might well have been discussing the plight of sport when he said, "The last proceeding of reason is to recognize that there is an infinity of things which are beyond it. It is but feeble if it does not see so far as to know this" (Pascal, 1962, p. 76). It would seem that any human activity, sport included, could not operate as if *reason* was to solve all of man's problems. To recognize the unknown is to be *reasonable* if not rational. To not admit to the human, *as he is,* is to be irrational. To participate in activities that foster the rational at the exclusion of all—and to thereby limit itself to the known rather than the unknown—is absurd.

In constant affirmation of the human relationship, and paradoxically attempting to conquer, the sport participant operates within a *rational context*. But he is performing realistically to *irrational* concepts. His desire to achieve the arduous is mixed with feelings of the heroic and all of this is eventually reducible to the sublime.

To insure meaning and examine existence, the athlete pursues herculean tasks demonstrating strenuous prowess. The distance runner trains through exhaustive powers of the will. The weight-lifter experiences a seemingly endless number of *repetitive* exercises (well termed "reps"). And the swimmer submits himself to lap after lap of agonizing immersion in the water. The self is presented to the world as if there is *reason* to the sport perspective. More often than not the athlete finds himself, as an object, rebelling from the realness of order. The conflict is disguised through a highly disciplined act by, typically, the most *undisciplined*. The hard is made soft and the soft appears hard. The athlete is both tough and tender, free and other-directed, fated and free-willed, personally concerned and other-interested. Sport, like life, includes relatives. There are not one or two truths but innumerable alternatives. This, in itself, becomes *absurd*.

It can be seen that contradiction in sport, in its variety of forms —from strategy to choice of imperatives, unlike the arts and music—is not a point of departure but is the *infinite answer*. When the athlete must decide (*really* decide) for the good of the self or the team, he reaches into being and throws it open to existenz (not *dasein*), reconciling the dilemma in terms of nothingness. The *realness* of sport and simultaneously its make-believe quality ("it's only a game") causes most situations to indeed be absurd. Unlike many other avenues of life, sport does not afford opportunities that allow man to exist. There is not enough time to sulk and less opportunity for people to realize that escape is being attempted. To reach despair is assumed to be a quality of defeat rather than a recognition of the *death of futile hopes*. Of course, suicide, either figuratively *or* literally, is taken as plain "bad sport." The performer simply *accepts* the absurd as the condition of existence. It is real. He performs within it and responds to it. This is called "good sport."

The performer, accepting the absurdity of the sport situation, has achieved partial victory. He has recognized and triumphed the contradiction of the situation with free will. In accomplishing this feat he directly alters the structure of the value system. What is "right" on the field might not be accepted as the thing to do off the field. The responsibility of the act might well be different as the situation calls for varied commitments. Frequently, in praising the sport performer, we demonstrate a remarkable admission of the absurdity of sport. For example, one might say of an athlete, "He is an All-American both on and off the field." This statement is earnestly made as if it were possible to be in one place and not the other. In truth we come to recognize the varied aspects of man but we don't come to know man as he authentically exists.

As a form of the absurd, sport frequently demonstrates a concern with the truth. In the presentation of "problems," one must be concerned with the genuineness of the solutions. However, in essence, the solving of one truth only provides man with another problem in the progressive search. Once the quarterback unlocks one door another appears. Perhaps this is what makes sport so exciting to man. Being rational, sport provides immediate problems which when pursued with reason (strategy) afford immediate feedback. Since the horizon of sport is unlimited (one never *can* bowl a *perfect* game—although he may score 300), the problems are unlimited. Knowing he can never attain *the* truth, he engages in the absurd; hopefully, he can solve the immediate and return another day to pursue answers to further problems. *Unperfected perfection* might be what is responsible for keeping our golf courses crowded.

From the *absurd* it is easy to see how sport is reducible to what Sartre calls *nothingness*. The athlete, with all his being, can surpass *himself* when he considers the sport situation as one that belongs to him for his utilization. The paradox is obvious. As the gymnast engages in movement, the apparatus and all that *is* is used for-itself; thereby arriving at *being* from *non-being*. *Being-in-itself* is not produced by *being-for-itself*. By being conscious of his acts, the performer uses all media for what he *and* it is intended. In so doing man gives meaning and value to the inanimates of the world.

Nothingness, which in-itself is non-being, is so conceived as more than space for man's movements in sport. Nothingness is *all-over*, it exceeds even the emptiness of time and space, a concern more truly imperative for the dancer than the sportsman. Nothingness *has* dimension; although not limiting nor definable, it affords man the opportunity of space and *feel* and almost endless opportunities for achieving *being*. Nothingness both refutes and affirms what *is*. The activity of sport is beyond the self of the performer. It is at the basis of transcendence. "Nothingness can be concerned neither outside of being, nor as a complementary, abstract notion, nor as an infinite milieu where being is suspended" (Sartre, 1956a, p. 85).

The gymnast performs in nothingness. This is his arena for action. The realness of *his* world is established through the apprehension of nothingness. In a word, it is the *place* for all that is real and all that is to be realized. All of his possible "moves" are part of the infinite choices of realities that he must experience. Through the function and structure of the movements, the *human condition* appears to the performer as if he were looking through a key-hole. His movements, with a potential for all levels of expression, form a type of concealed or shaded image of reality. It is there but it is nothing. As he swings on the high bar or vaults over the side horse, the apparatus *itself* has a nature of nothingness and thus *for-itself* it is destined to a role of what it is not. At the identical instance it is not what it is. The gymnast creates these dimensions as he comes to *use* nothingness for-itself and in-itself. Within the spectrums of sport, nothingness is characterized by "being what it is not and not being what it is" (Sartre, 1956a, p. lxviii). The being of nothingness is thus seen as a function of the *action*. The efficacy of the reality is crucial to the inner structure of sport. In a sense this is what sport is all about. It is central to action. The performer, as he moves, transforms non-being into being in the world of nothingness. What is evident is the distinguishing characteristic of the performance in which man does not perceive himself, as man, as being important. The performance is marked by the presence of the necessity of *human* expectation. In this latter dimension man comes to realize his existence in sport activity.

It can be seen that nothingness is that which allows and/or disallows actualization. In short, the specific "move" might be difficult (internalized negation) for the gymnast. Concomitantly, the "horse" might not be appropriate for the performance (externalized negation). Thus, nothingness leaves one in direct conflict with forces of *existence*. The feeling of emptiness comes to the performer in forms of anguish and fear. If anything, sport performance tells man about the "not-quite" quality of life. To contemplate this element of our world is to embrace nothingness.

Man must recognize, what he already knows, that he does not understand all within his environment. To limit himself therefore to his cultural forms is to segment life. It is time we altered Descartes' thoughts, *Cogito ergo sum*—I think, therefore I am—to read, *Est, ergo cogito*—I am, therefore I think. Thought is *one* part of man. It is not a panacea. We cannot answer all of life's questions through objective means. To suppose that sport will provide the "full experience" is highly remote. As a maintainer of the culture it must work to maintain *all* of the culture. And certainly the creation of form is one exciting dimension of humanity. To maintain the present is to limit the human horizon.

Why is man on earth? Why does he live? Why does he select sport as a segment of his activity? Obviously the answers are not yet known to man in their entirety. To answer these queries is to admit the personal as divine. But how can we continue to live in sport without participating in some search for the solution to these penetrating human concerns? How can we talk of *meaningful* sport participation until we delve into the question of "why"?

It should be clear that in this setting I do not deny the rightful place of empiricism, factual data and the validity of certain aspects of sport. It is inconceivable to deny the relationship between rational thought in man and sport. My specific objection is aimed at the *exclusiveness* of this thought. It is simply *unreasonable* to assume that all of life's activities do not possess the potential for something *beyond the reasonable*. In this manner sport could well open itself up. It could become more available to the recognition of the *transcendental* aspects of existence. In this light, if sport is an absurdity, then an extensive opportunity is provided to man. An opportunity to discover the potential for a greater and perhaps more intense meaning.

Although I would be the first to admit sport reflects the culture and thus is often limited by its "mimic" character, I would like to submit that sport is more than a demonstration of existing movement patterns. Knowledge of the variables assists man in his involvement; but unlike science, sport goes beyond the empirical. Somehow we cannot explain all the forces that are an intricate part of sport. Does anyone really know what is meant by the "spirit" of a team? What is involved with getting a team "up"? How can we explain the "peak performances" that by definition are so very infrequent? How do we explain the irregular performance? What is involved with man's "feel" for a specific activity? How do you explain the sudden rapture of a sport thrill, such as gliding down a ski trail or capturing the board as you ride the wave?

Strongly based in an objective world we tend to say these "elements" are part of our existence and they are brought to our awareness. Perhaps this is so. But is it possible—in our transcendence—that these feelings come from *no where*? Irrational? Yes! But remember we do need to go beyond our objective shells to understand what objectivity does not allow us to comprehend. To go *beyond* our human experiences is perhaps the most *human* experience we can have. This does not mean we *accept* or believe each and every input that is not reasonable. Rather we admit that objectivity is but *one* system and we will employ other systems in a continuing, searching concern to discover the truth of human existence. To do less would be inhuman; to do more would not be human.

The sports performer goes beyond assuming responsibility for personal choices. Learning well from the thin-lipped naturalist Emile, the pole vaulter defies gravity, the sprinter explodes through resistance, and the swimmer dares massive forces and load, all see that the sport *movement* must be in keeping with the *essence* of nature. Thus, *control* over self and environment becomes a higher priority than freedom. It is this element, among others, that makes *discipline* such a very important part of the sport experience. Many would like to think of the man of sport as being *freed* by nature; in truth his restrictions are personal *and* natural. Let us, individuals with an interest in sport, not forget that a wide gap *might* well exist between what is natural and what is nature. The former is no doubt almost a replica of the latter. A most *unnatural* point to remember.

Yet it is the restriction of the *natural man* that is a factor in the dehumanization of man which has become such a popular theme in modern literature. As we witness the increase in mechanical and technical "assistance"—such as electric timers, replay machines, exercise "gadgets"—one can hardly wonder if we are increasing our "efficiency" at the cost of de-humanizing mankind. Personally, I cherish my modern conveniences and greatly enjoy the superior performances of the latter half of the twentieth century. But I must wonder if this is what sport is all about. Does man need *hide* from himself and his fellowman in order to escape his personal commitment? If so, I question the place of sport in the development of a strong culture. Materialistically successful but not strong—this is the plight of man. Like society sport crumbles from a disease of dehumanization.

If we are to view sport as anything more than "play time," then we must understand the irrational as a part of human experience. The immediate reaction to such a proposal might well be a scream of "ridiculous!" Does this not mean that sport may well be absurd? The answer is an unequivocal yes. Sport *may* well be absurd. To see man attempt artificially to control internalized and externalized nature may well be absurd. To see man be encapsulated by determined stimuli, under the most adverse conditions, may well be absurd. And for man to estrange himself deliberately from his brother might, indeed, be absurd. To understand the value and meaning attached to sport is to begin to appreciate, if not comprehend, man.

It is no wonder, with all the opportunities for choice that confronts the performer, he often demonstrates overt signs of displeasure. Faced, and in fact condemned to, infinite freedom, man finds it difficult and often frustrating to make a choice. Anguish can be seen as a result of the threat of the present. And sport is focused on the present. Man knows almost immediately with the act if he is achieving or not. Entering the game, committed to all that is involved, he is "forced" within a frame of near anguish. When the situation becomes too absurd, when he is faced with too much tension, the hopelessness of the situation brings reality to him in the form of concrete existence. It is unlikely this awareness diminishes man's performance; on the contrary, sport flourishes when anxiety is increased within acceptable limitations. It is almost as if the performer recognizes "what counts" cannot be achieved and rather than continue in the futile search for a meaningful existence, he "cashes in" on the obvious prize—victory.

At this stage it should be pointed out that sport is not the only area of human life that may be touched by the absurd. Contemporary art has fostered this quality as a direct challenge to mankind. To rid itself of "copy" and to increase man's potential to assimilate and embrace existence is but one part of the intentions and achievements of sport.

How could any area of human involvement be considered as providing meaningful experiences to man and then be confined only to the rational. To do this is to assume man is a unity *of* reason. An extension of this thesis is one, I trust, man could hardly accept. Sport *does* provide an experience of mystical dimension. Man communicates with himself and others (and perhaps *the* other) when he "cracks" man. Speaking as a participant of a "contact" sport, I found when I tackled a man that there was *more* than the hit. To say it was satisfaction is true. To say it was a feeling of security is true. To say it was a cathartic experience might well be true. But it was more. It is more. To say I understood it, or understand now, would be to admit the absurd is accessible through reason.

There is, to be sure, a certain degree of *completion* in sport. The player on skates attempts to perfect movement. The routine of the gymnast is complete. Each participant attempts to cover "the holes." But truly this is a function of self-communication. The performer sees himself in the world; and as such sport provides a connective link for structured expression. To the degree that the self and surroundings are understood is the degree man achieves meaning in sport. To assume this is not a function of self-exploration and awareness is to convey apathy to human existence.

> ... my invisible self, my personality ... a world which has true infinity, but which is traceable only by the understanding ... a countless multitude of worlds annihilates as it were my importance as an animal creature, which after it has been for a short time provided with vital power, one knows not how, must again give back the matter of which it was formed to the planet it inhabits. (Kant, 1889, p. 1)

Sport as much as any area of human involvement points to the impossibility of offering a *reasonable* explanation between the inner and outer world of man. To assume that we know why man takes part in sport is presumptuous—no matter what the behavioral sciences might indicate. Again, human action cannot be accounted for by demonstration of empirical data. Man, in his freedom, is basically non-prophetic. To ask even this much from the man of sport is to demand he be a "sooth-sayer."

It is rather odd that in man's attempt to *be* human he needs to seek the transcendental, which is beyond humanity. But this really is not *too* strange, for great men of all civilizations—Socrates, Christ, to mention a couple—reached beyond their own time to achieve that special touch of humanity. But *it is strange* that, as the very area of human life which stresses the development of the *whole man*, sport must admit to a dualistic quality. This is not the typical split of mind—body and reason—emotion but it touches on an equal dimension, if not one of greater depth, namely, sport "pays a premium" to the man who transcends the real. As a "recognizer" of both *what is* and *more than is* sport establishes a strong conflict. Is this any way *to be* absurd? "You bet it is!"

Sport *is* so very popular because it can and does cater to all of mankind. Its raw brutality greatly appeals to the animal in man; while its rhythm and grace appeal to the aesthetic in man. It is no wonder we get confused by categorically assigning rugby and figure skating the same name, sport. At best the classification is most artificial. Yet both fuse the dualistic segments of man's existence. But there is more, much more. In both activities man conclusively demonstrates his desire for nature, romantic as it might be. It is in the sport experience that man can receive tangible evidence of his efforts. The "feed-back" is direct and immediate. There are few places in life where man can "keep score" with such facility. It is not unlike man to think he can achieve meaning by determining the facts. As he remains prey to his material culture he still believes the more he "collects," the more he will *possess*. Absurd? Who knows? He is still playing the game. And *some* say he is winning.

As the performer attains recognition he becomes what Nietzsche would call a *Superman*. He wins. He achieves. He defeats. But man is not *all* animal. Man needs more. Soon the athlete looks to the social and the spiritual phenomena of life. It is *here* sport becomes absurd. The demands of competition, victory and personal achievement do not readily afford *real* amity and symmetry between man and man and/or man and nature. Romantic literature might well speak of this idealization but in truth it is *not* present. The very structure of sport argues against *this* form of transcendence as a general happening. Man cannot be turned on and off much like a water fountain. If sent out to conquer or defeat, he will do so. But to turn from killer to lover, at the happen-chance demands of the idealists, is just not what *is*.

Sport as an Absurd Dehumanizer. To ask what exists in sport is to inquire into the nature of sport. To be sure, sport develops its heroes. But in truth these noble images are not *of themselves*. Instead their individuality conforms to the mass of society. "His body is the carcass lived in by the masses" (Wolf, 1966, p. 2). To a degree the man of sport becomes anonymous. He loses his freedom as he becomes "a member of the team," or "the unsung hero." Who has not heard a coach say, almost as an afterthought, "Let's not forget our line"? This type of felt "necessity," by the coach or backfield men in football is communicated to me as a projection of guilt. A guilt of *using* fellow man as an *instrument* to achieve an end. The "instrument" might well reach worldly success, but he never does reach personal truth. A feeling that goes beyond the roar of the crowd and the touch of gold coins. He loses his humanity; for he really is little more than a "puppet" doing little more than *acting* as a mimic of the objective world.

Sport is marked by its involvement with the *numerous*. In the world, the participant deals with "many faces" of both known and unknown dimensions. The problem is not *the activity* which demands contact with the *mass*, but the constrictions that are placed on man's efforts. To think of man as an individual *in* his own right, and not an instrument of victory or defeat, is the dilemma of sport. "The individual is in the truth even if he should happen to be thus related to what is not true" (Kierkegaard, 1944, p. 178).

This is the crux of the problem. Man risks his basic existence when he enters sport. Is he to be himself or is he to assume the character of the group? Again, we come to the importance of freedom as a function of the "authentic" in sport. If sport is to react against absurdity, then it must provide a truly human experience. Man cannot be forgotten as a grain of sand on the beach. He needs to be *considered.* Man faces, all around him, overwhelming threats to this personhood. The social emphasis upon technology and mechanization indicates man will be nothing but a by-product of advancement. Instead of limiting the thought of man by demanding he conform to established patterns of movement, sport has the *potential* of providing the environment for actualization. It is on the field man *could* be what he is. But this is *more* than skill development; rather, it is development of the self. It is man saying I am more than the culmination. It is man convinced that truth is to be found in the real experience. To be a winner or champion is not necessarily to be man.

> There is a view of life which says that where the masses are, there too is truth, that there is an urge in truth itself to have the masses on its side. There is another view of life which says that wherever the masses are is untruth, so that although every individual, each for himself silently possessed the truth, if they all came together (in such a way however that the many acquired any decisive importance whatsoever noisy and loud), then untruth would immediately be present. (Kierkegaard, 1938, p. 179)

How man uses his freedom in sport will be the determining factor of the truth which is found in sport. To look for anything less would, indeed, be absurd. Man must keep his own style. He must maintain his own individual character. To settle for less is what Sartre would call the "stealing of freedom."

The man of sport knows this only too well. The athlete meets another man. *In* the self the football player is proud he is what he is. He honestly believes he is worthy. Fellow man conveys a negative reaction to the athlete; although, not knowing why, the player feels guilty for being an athlete. In a word, he has let the societal man *steal his freedom.* He is robbed of what he is. Now he is that much less. Authenticity can never be attained if the individual prevents himself from *being.* Only he knows the truth of his own human existence. To prevent submission is possible because of the unique *action* of sport. But to bring this potentiality to reality is a mission that is apparently slipping away from man.

Sport encourages man to give up his freedom. On the field and off the field the stress is not individuality but adaptability. Truth does not come to man only through the sport action experience. It must be brought to awareness. The importance of *absurdity* is in the recognition. The recognition that man is constantly fighting to maintain *being;* yet he is willing to trade it for the first hint of calm. Ironically, sport is the place for the violent.

The excitement of sport is not only directly related to the *events* themselves but, as has been indicated, can be specifically attributed to unusual defiance of reason. Baseball managers "play the percentages" and football coaches stay "close to the book"; but these admission in themselves indicate the high proportion of instances where rational deduction is not applicable. In this way, among others, sport avoids a sterile direction toward prediction. The players, coaches, and spectators are all engrossed with the unknown, if not the absurd. For years the trademark of the "Brooklyn Bums" baseball team was the unexpected. "It could only happen in Brooklyn" became a national slogan. But in truth "it" happened with great frequency everywhere sport was played. Wherever men of sport convened, the "unbelievable" become quite believable. The pragmatic control of objects and men is both plausible and impossible when it comes to sport.

The analyst of sport is left with no choice but to reduce the game to its elements and circumstances. To a degree this explains the almost neurotic preoccupation with some coaching staffs for projection rooms, "area-frequency" charts and their narcissist-like manner of observing and recording each trait and ability of a "prospect." With little desire, and perhaps ability, to transcend into the abstract, personnel have "guessed" incorrectly as frequently as they have made the correct evaluation of future athletic talents. In attempting to describe the elusive qualities that go into making the composite of an athlete, which cannot be measured by a tape or stop watch, individuals have attempted to express their thought through such clichés as "He gives that extra something"; or "he just seems to come through in the clutch."

What has not been clearly admitted is that the human potential is unified. It is the whole man through his sensations, intellect, will, and *all* his "content" who affords any form of causation. It is the cognitive experiences which must be totally evaluated since it reflects the totality of being. This in no way indicates that the specific elements of the sport cannot be vitally and accurately evaluated. One could not argue that man in sport could be stripped of basic essence, but by the same token I must insist that he be given the efficacy of his emotions.

In sport man is plunged into his own existence with concomitant tensions. Existence, for the participant, is not only important but vital to his technical advances as well as to his true significance of purpose. Sport turns man to himself by making existence a personal matter and causing him to "face up" to each crisis as it unfolds. Existence transcends beyond the individual's subjectivity and speculation. There is no logical way in which man can express his desire to strike at a ball, "rack-up" another human, run the lonely track or follow a little ball for hole after hole. These are experiences which possess the potential for personal feelings—so personal that at times we don't care to reveal them to anyone including ourselves and, therefore, certainly cannot be translated into universalities.

It is clear that not all occurrences can be made available to rational explanation. It is in this domain that sport is both limiting and challenging. As we have seen, we do not make sport more real simply by measuring the concrete. Somehow it needs to be something more than just "absurd." Through study and analysis, insights into personal being must be achieved in order to afford meaning to what could be an *it* world. The authenticity of sport rests ultimately in its recognition of the human reality for each of those who hope to attain oneness. Thus, existence is grounded not in the mode but in the being himself.

Looking at sport this way, as it exists, we could see that which *is occurring*, as a sport entity, is that which is of value. Every phenomenon, as it relates to man's participation in sport, is a human fact and therefore, by definition, it is significant. For the runner leaving the "blocks," the swimmer making her "touch," the golfer gripping his club and coxswain beating the count to his crew, the *objectivity* of the phenomenon is what is important. It is what *is* as it appears. Take it out of its context and the meaning is altered. It is this that makes sport what it is. The value, the importance, the significance of the sport act, are both *all and none*. If one desires to speak as naively as indicating its "novel" contribution, then the act, whatever it be, is *in* sport; and as such is of great import, for the sport is of import. Thus, to criticize the scholar of sport by making reference to the fact that similar phenomena occur in other areas of human endeavor is simply to demonstrate ignorance of the value of *the* phenomenon in *the* context. A phenomenon cannot exist in a vacuum and thus its importance lies in its *existence*. In this case it is in sport.

SPORT AND THE RELIGIOUS

At first impression it would normally be assumed there is little, if any, relationship between sport and religion. Sport is a competitive, dynamic, and, to a great degree, individualistic activity. Religion is a non-competitive process founded upon deliberation and commonality of social organization.

Upon further investigation and analysis it can be realized both are areas of human activity expressing a strong desire to formulate a value structure in keeping with the "common good." Both sport and religion employ intricate rituals which attempt to place events in traditional and orderly view. Although both are rather emphatic about the demanded intellectual involvement, one cannot help but wonder if this trait has not been greatly exaggerated. One has to doubt whether intellect is not overshadowed by what the religionist calls "belief" and the athlete calls spirit. To put it another way, is there a great deal of difference between the *mystical* elements in sport and religion? Both realms weave extensive laws and rules around the activities and participants. Although often given logical explanations, relative to this form of externalized regulation, more often than not the basis is in traditional truths which may or may not have modern reasons for support of the order.

Another interesting parallel between sport and religion is in the area of *justice*. In religion God is *just;* while in sport the credo is "may the best man win." Somewhere, in both sport and religion, there is realization of the unjust or the unfortunate, but likewise, theoretically, it is ignored. God *is* just. And the best man *will* win.

Although both sport and religion are concerned with *justice*, it might be in error to assume both realms of human activity draw upon *truth* as the foundation for *rightness*. However, it is equally erroneous to assume truth is not a segment of both sport and religion. Although truth is dealt with in other sections of this work, it is important to look at this concern in relation to sport and religion. This is necessitated by the frequent observation that religious truth is fundamentally different from other categorizations of truth. This analysis will demonstrate the existence of areas of equivalence.

Literature is filled with the truths of statements. Scientists know well that they need be *amoral*. They might well formulate and *test* a hypothesis; however, to attempt to prove it to be true is simply not to be a scientist. The scientist must remain objective and "above" morality. Thus, truth is an impartial outcome. On the other hand, religious truth is a product of personalization. It is derived frequently from a system of beliefs, a process of extended morality with extreme personalized concerns.

I contend that religious truth is one often used in sport. While it may be clever logic to state that propositions in sport, as in religion, demand careful scrutiny because of the complexity of the task (truth *is* more than victory), it simply is not "the way the game is played." Evidence is forgotten, facts are reduced, tentative conclusions are founded upon the present and most often the expedient. Sandy Koufax, in a recent article, hinted at this type of truth as one when the *given* does not work: "truth" becomes anything as long as it spells victory. "When you have your stuff, you *should* win. . . . when you can end up winning not on . . . your arm, which is, after all, a gift, but on the strength of your brains and your experience and your knowledge, it is a victory that you feel *belongs peculiarly to yourself* [*italics mine*]" (Koufax, 1966, p. 91). On the surface, one could say this is most unlike religious truth. Certainly, religious truth is beyond mere "I pray to gain" philosophy. However, in reality Koufax is indicating something much beyond *the pragmatic*. Is he, by saying "it is a victory that you feel belongs peculiarly to yourself," indicating a personalization of *true* religious involvement? This is not *just* a God-given victory. This is truly a religious experience of personhood.

The apparent non-religious perceptions of the truth of and/or sport are derived from the mistaken attempt to relate religious truth with either the natural or humanistic concerns. In reality the athlete needs to sponsor a personal search. Truth becomes a religious commitment. A type of personal "sentence" to locate truth through a process that Tillich might call doubt and faith.

Doubt, Faith and Concern. To locate the truth of a situation the man of sport must *free* himself to question, to inquire, to doubt. Doubting, as a process, is what makes man really human. It is in a sense, his mechanism to reach and fulfill human dignity. The sport situation not only provides this opportunity for the performer, it demands it. Each movement is subject to personal doubt. Is this one most efficient? Do I act now? How might I increase performance? It would indeed be rare for an athlete not to question his own worth and value each and every time he enters the sport situation.

At first glance the opportunity to doubt might well appear to be a great temptation. Given this freedom that is provided in sport, will man not doubt to excess? And secondly, will not the process of doubting bring about increased anxiety? The answer to both questions is unequivocally negative.

First, doubting must be recognized as a process of externalizing that which is already internal. Man does not and cannot doubt something that he does not possess as a prior awareness. That is to say, the sportsman cannot doubt if his act of hunting is really a desire for "game" as opposed to a desire to kill, unless he already has this question *within* his self. A doubt is simply not manufactured. It is an expression of uncertainty due to a prior condition. Therefore, if a doubt is present it must be responded to. There is no question of excess since the doubt represents an area of human dilemma requiring additional information and communication.

The question of increasing anxiety is still with us. It is almost as if man were completely Zen. Do we really believe that when man is thinking he is showing signs of illness? I think not. Anxiety is increased, not when the doubt is considered, but when the doubt is not dispelled. Bury a doubt, stop a doubt, hide it, refuse to seek the truth and one might reach short term "peace" but not a deeper peace that only the truth can achieve.

Indoctrination and external censureship is something that man is constantly facing. To be stopped from the outside is bad enough, but to deceive the self by a type of self-indoctrination is still worse. Man must face his doubts. He must turn to them with an honest attempt to solve them. And to accomplish this he must employ real *concern*.

As the man of sport enters into meaningful thought about his activity, there are at least three major categories of doubt that must be answered by concern. First, he must encounter the *scientific* doubt. Will what I am doing "hold up" under the same conditions? Secondly, and usually a primary doubt for the sportsman, is the *pragmatic* doubt. Will what I am doing work? And finally we have the *existential* doubt. What is the meaning of this activity for me as an individual? Why do I participate? Who am I when I perform? It is this latter doubt that is basically the concern of this book. Namely, what is the role of sport in man's existence? The existential doubt can only be answered by deep concern of the individual. He cannot run away from the doubt. For if he does, the doubt will not disappear; rather it will increase the *felt* anxiety. The way to dissipate doubt is to demonstrate structured concern. Through the search, and perhaps the answer, man will achieve real life, a life that would be denied if man were to continue to live with the anxieties of doubt.

It has been my experience that sport has the potential to assist man in a demonstration of a meaningful concern relative to the existential doubt. In the awareness of human movement man could well come to develop a sensitivity of his own self that would be most rewarding. Perhaps some do. But in honesty most do not. In fact, sport is frequently *used* as a place to escape the existential doubt. "I will hit a little harder." "I will work a little more." "I will be a little tougher." "I will stay with it a little longer." In the fierceness of sport man tends to lose any form of existential concern. It is rare indeed when man enters sport with the desire to explore the self rather than defeat the other. Parenthetically, I might add that at times sport works in spite of the individual, and awareness is brought home without an extended concern.

Perhaps this is one of the most important dimensions of sport. In this *special* media of time of space, unlike the real world, man can use *concern* to arrive at a solution for his doubts. Certainly, he learns the realistic limits of his physical capacity. More frequently than not he comes to realize how much preparation he needs for a given event in life. And about this there can be little negative comment. But does he come to know himself? Does he learn the *real* lessons in life, and not the typical naive concept of "getting off the ground"? The application of concern takes time, real time. It requires man to analyze his own worth, and to question his own dignity. At the minimum it asks man to be committed to the search for truth of the self. It is truly a moral and religious process that goes beyond cognition. Again, we must ask if man truly takes the time necessary in sport or does he take the expedient road and *involve* himself so deeply in the *activity* of sport that he "shuts out" the potential for concern and ultimately a meaningful existence.

To employ concern is more than taking the time for reflection. As has been indicated, it is the embellishment in a truly religious situation. Concern would be directionless if it did not incorporate an element of *faith*, a faith that is *more* than *belief*. In typical theology, belief is a statement of probability. That is, if one says, "I believe we will win the game," he is expressing a statement of probability. He is saying, "We probably will win." If the coach says, "I have faith we will win the game," he is expressing a statement quite *beyond* an expression of probability. He is not asking for blind acceptance. Rather the statement of faith is one of concern, deep concern. His *faith* is an indication he is not going to sit back and "let the chips fall where they may." But rather, through *faith*, his deep concern will cause him to work, study and re-evaluate. To answer the doubt which belief shuts the doors to further learning. Probability, by definition, indicates there is no real reason to do anything more in life. One must take his chances. Belief (probability) will cause man to accept the fortunes in answering his doubt, a most unsatisfactory method for locating authentic existence. Conversely, constant concern, causing increasing searching, brings man to a new and open *existenz*. He now is able to come closer to an authentic answer to the prevailing doubt. Now, through the use of doubt and concern, he comes to recognize the truth of sport as applicable to the person. He comes to know himself, not as a thing, but as a person operating in a realm of existence that provides him with some partial solutions to very basic elements of life.

He has recognized the doubt. He has opened his self to it. He has employed concern, via faith, to reduce anxiety and to arrive closer to the truth. He is closer to the authentic life through his perceptive involvement in sport. He is more than what he was. Because of this religious experience in sport, is man now a "happy" person?

This question cannot be answered in either the affirmative or negative. The employment of faith to answer one's doubts does not guarantee any form of "perfect happiness." And yet man is truly better if this sport participation includes spiritual awareness. Perhaps the answer to this problem is given best by Paul Tillich in his work, *The Courage to Be*.

The use of faith to attempt to resolve man's doubts takes a great deal of *courage*. It is in faith that man *risks* what he considers to be valuable and important to him. When the man of sport inquires, of himself, about the *true* reason he hunts, he might very well find out he is not motivated by the altruistic desires he was allowing himself to believe. In risking to find the true answer, man might well lose what he desires most. This indeed takes *courage*. It is easier to live in ignorance. It is easier to dogmatically shout down the doubt prior to the use of faith. Certainly it is easier to fire the gun or hit the man next to you than to ask, "why"? Why do I do the things I do?

Of course the reward of faith—if there is one—is that it brings man closer to authenticity. It allows him to know what is truly so. He risks. He might lose. But he also might win. In fact he always wins, through faith. How can man be less than a victor when he relates his sport activity to the self in a manner that constitutes a reflection of authentic personal existence, an existence that is predicated not on tradition but on the situation as it now presents itself, free *from* an unaware life and free *for* existential completeness—a life of *meaning*.

The Religious Meaning of Sport. If conceptual work on sport is to be fruitful, somewhere it must concern itself with the meaning sport has for man. In this way the sport experience can be viewed as a potential for reality rather than an abstraction.

Sport is real. It is very real. Its systematic position, with its emphasis on the contribution of physical things in their existential structure, illuminates the extremes of reality. Its events and phenomena occur in life and give rise to the indispensable synthesis of *personal* existence. The gymnast must consider the objectivity of science, the quiet of the aesthetic, and the instance of emotion. All are meshed into the total product. The gymnast, *in* his movement, means *all* that he can realize. In the language of the religionist, he culminates his personal life with a transcendence that is more than *mere* human.

Athletes, in general (or at least those that are judged good beyond their mechanization), at some point in time, come to realize that there is something beyond *all* that is mortal, *all* that is comprehensible by the human mind. Within the movements of the athlete a wonderful mystery of life is present, a mystical experience that is too close to the religious to call it anything else. The meaning of life arrives in the culmination of the possibilities.

In this, experiencing of the mystical, the athlete becomes aware of that which is *beyond* reality. To *the* athlete this is a personal sensation. It is more than *fascination* or *interest*. It is a form of dynamic voluntarism that extends man *beyond* the powers of rational mind and physical body. It is truly a wonder that the gymnast feels—he knows, in fact he *more* than knows, that he can *truly* express his own "state" in motion. He transcends the actual, and as most mystics, he performs so that *he is now available to the performance* in a way that is not completely understood by performer *or* spectator.

Like religion, sport offers its "followers" a grouping of myths, symbols and rituals that facilitate the total experience. It must be understood that basically religion makes life easier. It places life into an orderly sphere. The spirit of man, in sport and religion, is an exercise of personal venture into the scientifically unknown. The arenas and coliseums are little more than shrines for *spiritual* activity. They allow man to escape the boredom of everyday life and reach out to a larger existence.

> Through bodily activities subjected to the control of the will, energy and courage are sustained, and the individual seeking contact with nature draws nearer to the elemental forces of the universe. (Jaspers, 1957, p. 68)

Man transcends the daily life and even the sport itself. He goes beyond reality, nature and even imagination to a location for the self. "The one who experiences it knows that it is important for him; it concerns the *meaning of his existence*" [italics mine] (Guardini, 1962, p. 90). Suddenly, the athlete, in his movement through space, senses a quality of *allness*, a form of complete unification.

The performer becomes sensitized to life. He becomes responsive to his alliance with *another*. He cannot reduce spirit to function—a constant demand of the "real" world of sport—but he can transform the functional to make it *more* than real. The gymnast uses *nature* to defy it. As he is suspended from his "rings," he experiences a sense of the *unusual*. His *real* existence is precarious. One slip, one miss, one moment of loss of concentration and *all* is defeated. In a *whole moment* he instantaneously and simultaneously concentrates on the action but at the same time *detaches* himself from the real. He is in this world and yet another.

Man's wholeness (spirit, mind and body) is integrated in sport. The mystical element of sport attempts to clarify certain aspects that are not, in other ways, understood; yet the paradox is also true; it makes sport more difficult to comprehend. Man becomes intimate with himself and is now ready and available to others. He comes to learn what it is to be an individual, but in a rather distinctive way he learns imminent responsibility for the collective. (This is especially valid in "team sports.") *Others* are allowed in; fellowman becomes one through the mystery of sport involvement.

Sport, like religion, assists the participant in developing an idea of his self. Through the dependence on authority (rules and officials) and at the expense of personal determinism, man attains personhood. Of course in giving up his freedom, a rather expensive price for one to pay, he receives a commodity in exchange; namely, the security of personhood. In the game he *knows* what he is to do. He is to *win*. Regardless of the level of the competition he knows he is to win. He is told to advance the ball, enjoy himself, etc. Whatever the "directive" he knows well the "name of the game." It is *win*. It is rare that man's goals in life are so clearly defined.

As in religion, the athlete must place great importance on the worth of his fellowman. He needs to *recognize* "him" not as an aid to his transcendence as much as an awareness of a *reason for being*. But this in itself might well be a contradiction since it has not been established that man does have a reason for anything, much less sport. This *compulsion* for purpose is best translated as leading a life in a meaningful direction. Thus, sport as religion *gives* man a reason for his *being* and thereby really discovers its own significance in man's existence.

In the new and freshly rediscovered cosmos of each sportsman lies a *personal* approach to transcendence. Just as no valid claim can be made for any specific religion to have the *only* path to a deity, similarly for a specific sport to assume it best contributes to man's existence is nothing but presumption.

Sport, as religion, is a form of *symbolic* representation of meaningful realities. To be religious is to provide spirit to the symbols of the mystical. In religion man admits his dependence on the *non-rational*. So it is in sport. Much time is spent scouting an opponent and scientifically devising game plans. This type of activity will no doubt continue as man attempts to reduce empirically his degree of error through scientific validation. But when it is all done, the reasons for victory are frequently explained in mystical terms. "They *wanted* the game more than we did." "They had heart." "They showed great spirit and desire." We continue to *try* but admit life is *really* impossible to plan. We accept the compromise that reality forces upon us, or at least reveals to us.

To understand personhood is to comprehend truth. To insist on a proof for the truth of religion is to mistake the absolute for the known. Sport provides the truth of performance. The fact that truth is personal and subject to the situation is to say no more than that it is not universal. There is no one way to play the game. The performer must select a personal pattern, suited to himself and/or the team. He attains his truth and worth through the limitations of these confines. Once he has made the original choice of participation, he is condemned to act in accordance with established patterns, or else the contest is absurd.

There is a purpose to religion and sport that is located in the minds of man. It is meaning. In both realms man determines the limitations as he adapts his own disposition to the realm of the *almost* impossible. To comply with the dream of betterment, the religious and sporting both turn to metaphysical realities in an attempt to locate the finite and real. It is not surprising therefore that sport, like religion, employs an extensive ritualistic dimension to its relative activities.

Ritual

Religion has been a constant force in the history of man. For some religion has formed a path to absolute thought; while for others it has expressed relativity of expression. However, regardless of personalized expression, the tradition, ceremany and rituals of religious life have traditionally given *order* to mon's existence. In truth, whatever else religion is—and it is many things to many people—it is a media affording persons relatively stable ways of attaining the security necessary to live in a dynamically accelerated and changing world. To be sure, to understand religious life is to go beyond the obvious organizational doctrines. One has to be sensitive to the internalized and subtle relationships found within all of living. One has to *feel* the mystic to *really* understand. Yet the rituals of religious life are not to be considered superficially.

A similar relationship exists in sport. In and by itself sport provides man with a range of personalized meaning. Like religion sport situations are filled with ritual. This is not to say that one can understand sport by simply relating to ritual. Just as in religion, full appreciation depends on an awareness of what is not always obvious. Yet one can hardly ignore the place of ritual in modern sport.

The evolution of man has demonstrated a constant and prevailing need for ritual. Modern man's *need* for ritual continues. But to a greater degree than ever before, religion, and the associated rituals, plays less of a role in man's life than perhaps at any other point in history. With the reduction of ritual in religion, it is not surprising man turns to other "rites" to again see some form of quasi-order to his life. For many, sport fulfills this function.

Example after example could be utilized to illustrate the parallel in ritual between sport and religion. Perhaps two will suffice. In religious life *morality* is the *summum bonum.* To live as one *should* is to be valued. If one cannot lead the perfect way (and few of us do), there are established rituals ranging from confession to renunciation. In sport man is to play according to the rules. When he does not, he too faces "rituals" ranging from warnings to removal from the activity. One has to wonder if there is any relationship between the confessional "box" in church and the "penalty" box in ice hockey.

Any football "widow" can tell you that one of the first events of any football game is the "traditional" flip of the coin, a ritual determining who will kick-off, who will receive and who will defend which goal. Not too long ago this act was the *real thing*. However, today's game of football requires such intricate planning that the "flip of the coin" is *really* performed much before game time. This of course enables both teams to make extensive strategic plans. But the *ritual* continues. Prior to each contest the "captains" (an interesting ritualistic word in itself) go through this bit of acting. All for the sake of keeping *order* in the life of the spectator—and the television camera!

This discussion is not intended to develop a negative concept of rituals. Often rituals bring about "higher" outcomes for people than perhaps were originally intended by the participants. The man of sport like the man of religion must always ask, "What does one desire when he enters into the sport situation?" Frequently, the conscious benefits of victory, acclaim and monetary factors are re-evaluated by true appreciation of the value inherent in the activity.

A concomitant outcome associated with ritual in sport, which is frequently taken for granted, relates to the rather strong allegiance achieved through the various and sundry rites. As in religion, sport has maintained the interest of the populace by observation of rituals ranging from ingestion of specific foods (peanuts and hot dogs are as much a part of baseball as is home plate) to the recognition of special events (doubleheaders are normally played on July Fourth and Labor Day).

The codes of the hunter and fisherman, specifically related to *means*, perhaps are what differentiate the sportsman from the killer. The rituals of limits, bait, and test of line are as much an attempt to preserve the ideal of the spirit of sport as they are a realistic precaution to preservation of wild life. The rituals afford the average sportsman a *reason* to participate, a reason more noble than "just catching something to eat." Soon he becomes extensively involved in the *sport* situation and achieves strength through the associated values.

Festivities related to sport events, from the All-Star baseball game to the friendly golf game at the local club, include rituals which deepen and strengthen the impressiveness of the activity. Can a baseball game *really* start if each man were to just take the field when he was ready? I think not. The team must be *led* by the captain on to the field. In golf the player with the lowest score on the previous hole has *honors* on the next hole. Thus, he hits first. Although this ritual often slows up the golf game, the custom continues (generally the person with the highest score would be the shortest hitter and therefore could tee-off when a strong driver would need to wait). Nevertheless, the rite continues—each man aware of the *honor* and tradition.

Examples are almost endless. The huddle with players and coach with interwoven hands and arms prior to taking the basketball court; the traditional handshake between rival football players after the contest; the touching of the gloves by boxers at the start of the match; the tossing out of the baseball for the first game by a dignitary; touching *each* base when the ball is hit *out* of the baseball park; the seventh inning stretch; the meeting of umpires and representatives of each baseball team prior to *each* game—all of this does something to enshrine devotion to "societal values." I think it is more than coincidence that baseball, perhaps more than any other sport, appears filled with ritual. Could this be what we mean when we say it is the "national pastime"?

From the fields and streams to the sandlots, rituals attempt to unite man to the activity. The ritual in the church and the ritual on the field are both remnants of the actual. To a degree they are symbols attempting to communicate meaning to man in his activity. For this, modern man has desperate need. To many, sport *becomes* what religion *was*—it serves as the prevailing attempt to keep order and loyalty.

This, of course, is not to say that the meaning in sport is the same as one received in religion. The *real* ideal is too far removed. However, the ritual is there for those who need and want the necessary symbolization.

Again it is the ritual in sport, just as it is in religion, that plays a part in the unification of the participants. Through systematized forms, rules, commands, and prohibitions man is united with his fellow man. It is of interest that baseball, again, often makes use of religious terms to express the giving up of oneself for the good of the whole. The "sacrifice" shows man is *really* one of a team or group. This is in keeping with the earliest of religious rites. Sacrifice is of great import to the sport scene and let no one be naive in believing it does not appeal to the "religious in man."

I think it is fair to generalize to the point of saying that ritual maintains both a real and important role in sport and religion. Although it often might be outdated, sublime and unpractical, the ritual remains. In sport there is great action. Frequently, the ritual turns man away from the inward self and brings pressure to accept externalized stimulations. This external nature of sport is the facet that makes many sensitive individuals deplore the role of sport in our culture. For in itself it threatens to take the *sporting* aspects out of sport; and to replace it with superficial pomp and rite. In a word, it threatens to make all sport a "spectacle" and vocational, if not professional. This is frequently difficult to see because the rituals *themselves*, for the most part, appear to be joyous and festive.

Sport as a Religious Symbol

Sport as a symbol of human involvement reflects a sensitivity to spirit. Man's intensity of participation and his commitment to movement, as *more than he knows it to mean*, is descriptive of the type of subjective sensitivity, at times identified with a religious religious structure. Certainly, on the surface, it appears that man's *symbolic movement* and religious symbolism are polarities. Sport is obvious, distinct, goal oriented and almost crude. Religion is mystical, supple, process centered and almost elegantly pure. But for one who sees beyond the surface there is more. Sport *is* a religious symbol in the sense that it does not *really* relate to a cosmos of *things* and *objects* but an expression of a meaningful reality of man as an *inner whole*.

In this sense, sport is *more* than a symbolic "set" eventuating into a genetic theory. Sport is more than an avenue for release of aggression. Its form extends beyond a *mechanism* for socialization. If any *one* thing (and certainly sport is beyond a single entity), sport endorses Nietzsche's "will to power." But again the symbolic figuration of sport is more than the expression of the definite.

Sport, as religion and, for that matter, politics, evolves into a symbolically developed *ideology*. Sport becomes both what it is and a declaration of the culture. If one needs objective evidence, he need look no further than the Americanization of sport in keeping with the technological and materialistic values of our society. Fencing, once a sport of beauty and grace, is now "aided" by electrical "gadgetry," all done so that we can better *judge* man. Collegiate athletics, personified by "big time football" is an accepted prostitution of mankind. In institutions espousing all the high-sounding ethics of mankind, faculty and administration "look the other way" so the "mighty buck" continues to roll through the gates. Thus, the creed of *play* is replaced by a *work-out*. Contrast the western world of goals with the eastern emphasis on process in sport. Herrigel demonstrates clearly that archery is a *within*, and deeply religious experience. To a certain degree, one could say that the sport phenomenon possesses a potential for the *immediate* which is only actualized when a process of transcendence occurs within the participant. In reality, one must admit this is rarely achieved on the American sport scene. Again, the materialistic cult to which we pay honor places a competitive premium on sport. The soul of the culture and the soul of man is typified by the often referred to quotation, "nice guys finish last."

If we leave sport, as empirically determined in the modern western world, and turn our attention to its transcendent quality, then again it is possible to perceive the religious symbol. Sport, played as is, may still express a "soul" to man. It is possible to appreciate a basically religious symbol if man can *extend* to beyond the empirical nature of the symbol. Thus, sport can be viewed as a symbolic force of religious dimension.

To say sport is symbolically significant is not sufficient. The truth that symbols are empirically representative of the culture indicates, to a degree, the *problem* of the sport-religious position. That is to say, transcendence must go beyond the societal imagery. It is this dimension that makes *meaning* a possibility. However, none of this is possible unless there is recognition of the sport symbol as *valid* in its own right, in its *existence.* The specific phenomenon, be it an olympic performance or part of a junior high school track meet, has a potential for being-in-itself. One need do no more than look into the soul of the performer to recognize the religious association, one of depth, sensitivity, faith and tenderness. Listen to the words of Buddy Edelen, one of the great marathon runners of the United States, when he was asked, due to his long training regimen, when he has time to go to church. "I was closer to God out there on those roads than most people get to Him in a lifetime." Probably only Mr. Edelen *really knows* what he *means.*

Perhaps, at this point in the discussion, it is necessary to differentiate between two different types of symbols analogous to both sport and religion. First, there is the empirical symbol, one which establishes validity of sport and religion. Second, the symbol of transcendence, which goes beyond the actual.

In the first category, religionists are apt to place symbols that relate to divine beings. Religious symbols are representative of the eventuation of the mystical process. Although many examples can be given on this level to parallel religion, it is important to recognize that the present concern is with sport as a religious symbol and *not* the symbols contributing to religious and sporting life. Thus, many sport experiences actually form religious symbolization in that they signify a God-like concept. For many the experience is *ultimate* and, at the same time, potentialized with religious qualities.

The transcendence symbol is one that goes beyond the present. It is a concept which incorporates all of *life.* To objectify the conceptualization might be to demonstrate reality, but in no way does it represent the true feeling of the act. The sport performer accepts the elements, even if not as a believer, and becomes *aware* of the world. Although his specific act, as a sport occurrence, might not be religiously intended, it maintains the *potential* for true awareness through the conscious. How true this act *really* is is a function of the *inner man.*

Sport and Religion—As Institutions

An initial inquiry into sport and religion indicates the institutionalization of both facets of human life. The splendor of institutional religious life symbolized by clergy, temples, laws, and literature is comparable to commissioners, stadiums and arenas, rules of the game and an extensive heritage of truth and folklore.

Modern day sport has become institutionalized at almost all levels. Few youngsters can enjoy the feeling of playing a "pick-up" game. Interests of socialization initially led to specified customs. The higher the level of organization, the greater the psychic and financial involvement demanded by the institutionalizer. All of this has made serious impressions upon the participant.

Firmly established as a secular activity, sport has become a function of communal involvement. One cheers for the Green Bay Packers, the Los Angeles Dodgers (one is still tempted to say Brooklyn Dodgers) or the American Olympic team. In truth these designations are most artificial. In recent years baseball teams have changed city allegiance and basketball teams are "gypsy" in the way they leave one city for another. Who could ever believe the Brooklyn "Bums" would move to "hip" Los Angeles? But it did happen. The institution is there in name but not in roots. Nevertheless man identifies with *his* representative.

The paradox of this activity, of appearing change, is relative to internal and external alteration. In religion, the church edifice might alter its appearance or even move to another locale; perhaps clergy will even be reassigned. But the structure always remains constant with the basic ideology and purposes of the institution. So it is in sport. Man and facilities are altered but the basic purpose remains constant. The sport participant comes to recognize the "character" of the institution and identifies with the *meaning* of the institution. The New York Yankees capitalized on the "what it means to be a Yankee" attitude for years. Players who were "washed-up" were traded into near greatness when they joined the Yankees (John Mize, John Sain, and John Hoppe were just a few who learned to play "like Yankees"). The cry to "break-up" the Yankees was indeed a cry to *de*institutionalize.

Similar to religious institutions, the world of sport is slow to make internal alterations. Major league baseball remained in two leagues with a total of sixteen teams for roughly half a century. Weight classifications in boxing have not been considerably altered in recent years, despite changing conditions directly related to increased size of the human. Rules, although they undergo minor alterations, really are quite static (tennis is still scored with the traditional love, deuce, etc.), which in truth makes little sense and leads to a great amount of confusion.

Attached to the image of institutions, especially true in religion, is the idea that they are so large, and thereby secure, that they tend to be moral. Yet ethical conduct, in truth, is the last consideration of most institutionalized sports. Witness, if you may, the example of recruiting collegiate athletes or the "baby-sitting" system established during the wars between the National Football League and the American Football League. All of this is supposedly forgotten now that they have met on the field with the traditional handshake. Much like the "purification ceremonies intended to remove the effects of broken taboo," the sport scene attempts to demonstrate its morality for the world (Coe, 1916, p. 114).

The image of sport that confronts the populace is one that reflects, not the institution, but the spirit and vitality of that which should be sport. Frequently, it is little more than a symbol. From this form new and live meanings are derived. Thus, like the bowing at public worship, man's standing for the seventh inning stretch becomes a part of the image.

This is not to assume that the derived meaning presently held from sport in some way reflects the heritage of the symbolic form. Sport is more flexible than most institutions. Since the ideal is not *really* idealized virtue, a type of pragmatic loyalty develops, a legion to the ego of the institutional directors.

It is of interest to view the rather dynamic change (comparatively) in institutionalized sport during the latter half of the twentieth century. Although private organizations, mainly out for the *goal* (whether it be a Stanley Cup or the Little League Championship), support the institutionalization of sport, there is growing evidence that humanistic concerns can emerge. One example is the Stokes Benefit Game. This annual affair sees some of the greatest basketball players of all time volunteer their services for a charitable cause. Perhaps the tasks of sport are not all impersonalized. But yet one wonders if this, like the Shriner's East-West Football Classic, is not an example of the "exception that proves the rule."

A Pursuit Worthy of Itself

Many are chained to the thought that both religion and sport are little more than cultural devices affording man an arena to fulfill egocentric drives in an eternally secure fashion. To be sure, both sport and religion are populated by many such individuals.

To many sport participants the activity is there solely for man's selfish exploitation of himself and others. As a player he is frequently capable of solving basic problems on the field or court. For some, they are of a psychological basis. Unable to fulfill basic needs at home, many a young athlete has found the demands of the coach, the expectations of the crowd and the concerns of "followers" to be suitable masochistic substitutes. For others it might be an attempt to test personal discipline; while still others build security through conquering. When the playing days are over, the needs, only superficially met through participation, are channeled through other means. As the coach says, whether *his* team wins or loses, *my* boys (although he might be talking about twenty-one-year-old college *men*) are playing well. Thus, the same needs become personalized in the players and the vicious cycle continues. While this pattern is true for only too many, it certainly does not represent the complete story.

It is true that because of emotional and materialistic factors man has frequently *exploited* the sport situation. This is not, in itself, an indictment against sport as much as a concern for what *man does* with sport. Man might well be attracted to sport *because* of specific needs. However, this is not to say that *sport exists as an effect.* Psychological needs might very well contribute to man's readiness for sport. But certainly these feelings are not what *created* sport. *Sport is . . . for itself.*

So it is for religion. Man might enter the "order" for the feeling of absolute security and to possess the proverbial "crutch." Again, this sensation might well make man "available" to religion. But certainly this feeling, and others like it, is not responsible for the creation of religion. The parallel between religion and sport is only too obvious.

The authentic foundation of sport does *not* rest in the fulfillment of man's drives and desires. To think of sport, or for that matter religion, paramountly existing as an avenue for man's fulfillment is not to say it is some form of panacea. If man continually views sport and/or religion as a stadium for personal gratification, he moves away from sport, and religion, *as it is.* The further man can divorce himself from egocentric needs, the closer he will come to the location of the *real* value. Unfortunately, the American obsesssion with *ends* and *goals*, to the almost complete avoidance of *means* and *process*, has caused us to miss the *real* of sport and focus on *outcomes* as the *human* answer. It is that *process*, and not the results, which is the mark of *true* humanity!

Sport and religion are not mere conveniences for man. To involve oneself in the *real* of sport is to engage in the process. To look *within* ourselves and to ask questions of *process* is to recognize the basis of sport.

Frequently this explanation is not sufficient for man conditioned by empiricism. He still asks, "What does one mean by process?" To those seeking scientifically *significant* answers to philosophical questions . . . well, shall we just say you are in the wrong pew. To locate the *real*, man must look for it with open perceptions. But these perceptions are a function, not as much of our eyes, as they are properties of our sensitivities. As has been repeatedly demonstrated sport is more than an instrument. It *is* something *itself.* As in many experiences of life we look at what we desire to see. Thus, frequently we recognize football as catharsis, "Saturday's Hero," large crowds, excitement and pomp. In a word, we recall the sport*ing* and never see the sport. This is no different from what is done in religion. "To understand religion through the analysis of the sentiments it instills is to miss its essence" (Heschel, 1951, p. 236). Sport must be understood by an involvement of emotions as well as by its inner worth.

To sense the *real* of sport as *itself* is to demonstrate concern in its existence. One must be *aware* of the *total* situation. This leads to futher inquiry plus realization of the process. Sport is a *human* event. Its basis is *within* man. The use of the body transcends this *inward* sensation into time and space orientation. In the *awareness* of the act man's existence stands before him. While performing, during the phenomenon, man both has and does not possess all that drew him to sport. But these things are not *really* necessary. For sport, when *felt and valued*, goes deep into and beyond man. To say this form of transcendence in sport is not a religious encounter is to refute what is.

Sport and Spirit. Sport suffers because of the obvious "overshadowing" of that which is not apparent. The aggression, speed, action and general "loudness" of sport cause many to miss some of the more serene aspects of the situation. Again, as in religion, man's attention turns to the glorified. "The strident caterwaul of the animal fills the air, while the still small voice of the spirit is heard only in the rare hours" (Heschel, 1951, p. 239). Simply, we see the force of the kicked ball, the serenity of the sailing boat, the grace of ice skater and the strength of the gymnast. But we must go deeper for the *spirit* of sport.

Certainly by spirit I do not refer to the post-adolescence emotion associated with collegiate participants. Nor do I refer to the *esprit-de-corps* espoused by some professional teams (football dynasties often refer to this element) as if they were some group of boy scouts all trying to be good *together*. Rather, my reference is to the *quiet*. It is the quality the athlete *knows* is present yet he can't touch or explain. If one needs to name it, call it mysticism and color it *deep and sure*. Words only serve to hide the feeling. "Apparents" only distort what is *real*. But each man who has *really* been involved in sport knows the spirit well. It is too much like religion not to be associated with the mystic. Something of faith, something of peace, a touch of power, a feeling of right, a sense of the precarious—all of these and more is what *real spirit* of sport *is*. The man of sport lives in realms of time and space. But he also lives within himself. All that he does tells him who he is. To rephrase Heschel, all existence is personal. The world of sport provides us with time and space situations. But it is man in his interaction with himself who derives meaning from the dimensions afforded by sport.

When all is said and done, sport itself has a *being* which is developed by the *typical* "acts" of man as a participant. To say this, however, is not only to admit to the humanistic dimension of sport, but to emphasize its imperative *nature*. Man is the focus for and of the *act;* and therefore is the foundation for inquiry into *being*. Sport is more than a "road" to travel, it is also a *way* of traveling. What occurs is a type of involvement that may well possess a quality of the ideal, or the naive or even the "ultimate." In a sense it might be called mystical. As man transcends from personal being to the being of the sport he brings his own image to the new creation, a birth of the sporting man.

In many ways this process is most similar to a traditional religious experience. Simply, the soul transcends to the spirit. With the newly found spirit the soul is in *existenz*. It is available to all of being. The parallel between religion and sport might not be so far fetched as one might think. As a result of mystical commitments, sport and religion open man towards the acceptance and actualization of being. A partial answer is now uncovered to our obvious difficulty in *defining* sport. Basically, sport, like religion defies definition. In a manner it goes beyond definitive terminology. Neither has substance which can be identified. In a sense both sport and religion are beyond essence.

To *have* sport, within, and not to *know* sport, is to really *be* sport. When man encounters sport, he is not to *conquer* the presence of sport as much as fulfill one's own soul. In speaking of bullfighting, Steinbeck says, ". . . there was also that moment of what they call truth, as sublimity, a halo of the invincible human spirit and unspeakable, beautiful courage" (Steinbeck, 1965, p. 102). The bull is little more than an *object*. Certainly it is an object possessing great potential danger to man. But in its danger is its beauty, for an object it is symbolically placed before man for him to transcend. In this manner the "human spirit" is truly born. As the symbol of nature, the bull, with all its brutality and, at the same time, beauty, charges the grace and dignity of man. To say this is not a truly religious encounter is to not indicate what is presented.

Existence of Sport and Religion: A Conceptual Dilemma. In using the word "sport" it is frequently a temptation to apply it to usual activities of life. Generally, it is taken on face value. But I have certain apprehensions in both the definition and semantics of the word and it might be best to inquire as to what is sport's existence.

We could submit the thesis that sport's existence (if there is such a "thing," and I contend there is) depends upon personal encounters. This theory is equally applicable to religion. The encounter is of a mystical nature unlike anything "human." Both sport and religion can be experienced. Although this "meeting" is not always on a conscious level, it is *present.* To paraphrase Kierkegaard, sport is a *concept*, not a name.

The implication is clear. Sport is perceived in a manner which has its own character. To say we learn from the examples of sport is not to refute the argument of specificity as much as to theorize relative to transfer—a generalization I fear to be grossly simplified. To identify the "personality" of sport is again a religious act. One can't simply say sport or religion is omnipotent, divine or eternal. To admit this is to deny the individual and his perception of the real.

Through depth of *experiencing*, man, in sport and religion, goes beyond the empirical and the known. When this transcendence is in process, man comes closer to a form of conceptualization—be it God or sport. To admit to the relativity of this concept, *between* man and man and *within* man, is to distinguish between absolute logic and personal validity, a distinction which has formed the foundation for action, and thus value structure, for many men. The man of sport must go beyond the factual to the conceptual. Like the man of religion, who looks to God as the creator of the real world, the man of sport has to play the game as he finds it. Neither the man of religion nor of sport need concern himself with the creation of another set of circumstances. Thus, the existence of sport and religion are not directly related to the *practice* (which is so often believed to be true) of life as much as the character of the conceptualization.

Simply, it is the *essence* of both sport and religion that is comprised of events and program. *Existence* is a function of conceptualization.

From this discussion the astute reader might well argue that neither religion nor sport does exist (the concern with "God is Dead" is not all popularization). That is to say, sport appears to lack absolute meaning or at very best is paradoxical relative to means and ends. Thus, sport, as *described*, could *not* exist. While apparently an acceptable argument, it is not a convincing one. One cannot dismiss the existence of sport, or for that matter God, on the basis of "lack of meaning"; for it is the *description* of sport that lacks validity and certainly not the *existence* of sport. To continue in the process is, in a sense, to *maintain* the religious.

Sport: Morality and Ethics

Philosophy has always been interested in exploration of the "good life." Given the absolute thinking of the idealists, man's behavior has been often measured against a scale of perfection. This system of thought has undergone some marked discussion and alteration among scholars from many disciplines. It is not surprising that today we hear such men as Bishop Pike and others advocating a new form of "situational" ethics.

Sport has been duly involved with this very same argument. At times one would think that "philosophy of sport" and sportsmanship are one and the same. From the time a child is old enough to play with other children, he soon learns about *sportsmanship*. Yet a review of the literature indicates that perhaps theory and practice are greatly removed from each other.

No doubt part of the problem rests in the "realistic" expectations of the participant. It has been fairly well demonstrated that individuals might well *know* the "correct" pattern of behavior; but indeed they act another way. However, a second and greater problem exists—namely, is there such a thing as *the* correct or right way? If there is, one must conclude that an independent system, divorced from the environmental forces that man is subjected to, is in operation. Unless we assume this form of "super-structure," or inner voice, we must give up the ideal of an absolute morality. If it does not come from this basic source, the chances are good that it does not exist at all.

When considering the *existence* of ethics, it is most direct to perceive them from a sociological viewpoint. To develop ethics from the basis of a deity is neither convincing *nor* desirable. It simply becomes a merry-go-round of perfection. To assume the role of the freedom of man, within his environment, might well be the place to start. The importance of freedom in sport can hardly be overemphasized. To consider a morality divorced from freedom is simply not just. Since the very meaning of the term *absolute* indicates the existence of an ultimate *beyond* the validity of man, it appears fruitless to pursue the end of absolute ethics. This is not to indicate we should not be concerned with "right" and "wrong." But the search for value structures is not one of looking for the perfect, which is not really attainable. Certainly our world of sport asks for an evaluation, based upon a standard, which greatly goes beyond the powers of man to fulfill. No one person should assume a perfection, or be troubled that he has not reached it.*

One often hears the uncertain and vague person, desiring structure for the security of his world, indicating absolutes, "I want 100 per cent of the best; I am 100 per cent Italian." As Sidney Hook pointed out in the *Hero of History*, "There is no such thing as absolute health, absolute wisdom, absolute democracy, an absolutely honest man—or an absolutely fat one" (Hook, 1943, p. 23).

Of course this does not indicate that we do not work for the best. But it is more important to recognize that the ideals of life must be adjusted to the capacities of the performer within the structure of his world. It is indeed dangerous and rather foolish to urge the absolute heights of perfection in a survival world of action. This, again, does not mean we neglect value theory or a high sense of ethics as much as we develop them realistically.

In a sense, values become a map. The ones we hold did not suddenly develop; rather, they were developed out of many years of experience. To think about them and develop relative structures is all one can ask of man. And certainly of the participant in the world of sport can be expected no more or less than this.

* For a most interesting "lay" discussion on contemporary values see, "On Having a Sense of Values," The Royal Bank of Canada, Monthly Letter. December, 1962.

When looking at sport, one is generally tempted to focus at "situations" and deduce ethical structures from these happenings. The problem with this method is that it produces only general guidelines for the individual but does not resolve the problems in the "gray" areas of life. How does man resolve the choice between two "goods"? Frequently, the answer is resolved in terms of the "greater" good. Yet this complete discussion comes close to employing an externalized structure. In the sport situation the ethical question is usually resolved during the "action." These are usually emotional times. Traditional ethics would ask the man of sport to beware. Yet I think it is here that the decision tends to be *easiest.* Simply, man needs to listen to the inner forces that direct one. Let no one be deceived. These "inner forces" are not an ultimate power. They simply represent man's feelings. Again, we face a constantly recurring theme; namely, that man is not all rational. Thus, why be afraid to let our "guts" speak for us? If man is to be *really* free in his choice, it is important to recognize that the "rational" part of man might well be greatly influenced by his previous experiences. Therefore, he might not be, indeed, as "rational" as he thinks he is.

The world of sport is often a lonely existence. Perhaps this is the way it best be if man is really to develop a theoretical value structure with some degree of "honesty." It would seem that when man is alone, his actions reflect a normative basis that is as "free" as one could hope it to be. Man, as he exists, demonstrates his value structure. If he argues with the official, holds an opponent illegally or covertly manipulates a situation in his favor, he determines the realm of ethical basis. Some might see this as some form of anarchy; however, it is quite the contrary. In truth, since man develops the criteria for morality, he is thereby *responsible* for these standards of action. It is again important to stress that man comes to sport with a prior value structure. In an emotionally charged setting, which sport frequently is, man makes decisions based upon the dynamics of the situation. It is little wonder that the sport situation acts as a type of "projective" instrument, telling a man and all the world about his basic morality. It is entirely proper that values accruing in action should be judged as authentic, for often it is not until man acts that we really know personal fact from fiction.

From the prior discussion it can be seen that morality is not a listing of rules for each and every situation that may possibly confront man. Rather, morality is to be viewed as a type of "promise in process" that one makes to himself. The parameters are certainly broad; and transfer is assumed. Thus, a difference is viewed between moral "law" and the application. It is in the world of sport that man is constantly reminded not only of the variance in application but in the law itself. Football coaches, for years, have developed the ethic that one does not "run the score up" on an opponent. The idea is simply when you "have enough," you do everything within your power not to let the other squad look too bad on the scoreboard. This might well look like a principle of "sportsmanship," but in truth it is founded on the "Golden Rule"—namely, the next time the "tables may be turned"; don't do anything that is going to hurt you tomorrow. If one looks at the pure facts of the situation, man is being highly immoral. He is thus curtailing, voluntarily, his own performance. To do this because of a "point spread" is illegal. To do the same act because of survival is morality. Relativity? Situational ethics? I am afraid so.

Of course one might say, "This is all well and fine but because this is the way things *are* does not mean this is the way things *should* be." But indeed it *can* be no other way. Man's experience is all we know. This does not imply objective cognition as much as it demands honest subjectivity. Again the term *honest* implicates man's responsibility for choice.

The hunter, as he stalks his prey, must make his decision. Is this a kill? Or is it truly sport? Do I engage in this activity through an ethical dimension personified by the sporting life? Or is my activity highly immoral? Obviously, the choice is *his*. He can either pull the trigger or not. But to be responsible, as a sportsman, implies that man will weigh the question of morality. Not only is he responsible for the choice he makes, but he is responsible for all the choices potentially to be made. This is a far cry from immorality. It might well be the deepest morality known to modern man. The responsibility is man's.

It is obvious that the man of sport, as all men, cannot honestly consider all the available alternatives. Thus, no matter how conscientious man really is, the practicality of each situation must lead him to extreme anxiety. The paradox faces him at each turn. The more one employs concern, the greater the awareness of each and every choice. However, morality implies action and yet man cannot possibly act really morally because of the enormous choices that are available to the free man. "Taking responsibility for the choice I have made while yet recognizing the imperfection of my awareness signifies the fact that my choice gave this alternative actuality and not some other" (Bugental, 1965, p. 45). Thus, the man of *existence* falls prey to anxiety and *despair*.

Sport is integrally concerned with the business of achieving. And in so doing, the act must be one of volition in order to be truly moral. It appears this is the only way that man can really maintain the freedom that is rightfully his. In truth, the ability for man to escape his immediate world and therefore *to free* himself *for and into* freedom is one of the enticing elements of sport. It is perhaps *the* true morality of sport. Certainly it appears that sport, itself, does not possess a moral structure. To confuse the element of "sportsmanship," for example, as *belonging* to sport appears to be a stretch of the imagination. When one's actions are "sporting," he is not necessarily reflecting the essence of sport. In reality he is acting as one would expect any civilized individual to behave. Perhaps our acute awareness of this cultivated action in sport is but an indication that we really *don't* expect man *to be human* in the sport situation. For certainly I expect the same form of behavior from my opponent in tennis as I do from my business competitor. If there were not a certain degree of honesty and respect for the general rules of civilization, sport, as well as all mankind, would become quickly anarchistic (Umminger, 1963). Perhaps this is what is meant by "gamesmanship and one-upsmanship."

To speak of ethical choices in sport it becomes necessary to understand the experiences within which these decisions must be made. Value decisions are partially dependent upon the analysis of the existing time. To talk of absolutes is to admit to a static world when the evidence that constantly confronts us indicates profound change. It seems only justified that the conduct of man in sport be evaluated in keeping with the "changing times." The very essence of sport, as a collection of dynamic events involving the participation of man as both object and subject, speaks to the commitment to the transitional nature of man; and therefore available to the subjective. Absolute values, in sport, are simply an attempt to hold onto a "neat" world, one in which we are all allowed "to keep our cool." The determination of any value decision is to utilize *both* reason and emotion.

To even hint that the "Christian ethic" is to be maintained in modern sport is to contradict the very existence of sport as we know it. At the risk of sounding greatly "used," I must indicate that in sport, traditional *Christian ethics are dead.* One simply cannot expect two tennis players to place their shots in such a position, provided they did possess the necessary skill, as to assist in the increased development of the opponent. This is simply not the *reason* for sport as we know it today. The name of the game *is* win. Any effort to read in the noble aims of the naive is to be unjust with what is. Grantland Rice was noble, but wrong, when he indicated they remember you for "how you played the game." They remember you for sixty-one home runs, 9.1 seconds in the 100-yard dash, 18-foot vaults, four-minute miles and over one-hundred stolen bases. Achievement, conquest, victory, and performance—these *are* the heroes and the gods of sport. Mr. Durocher, in saying that "nice guys finish last" might not have been right, but that is only because he confused values with placement.

The real world is revealed to real people and sport offers dividends to the realist. The man of sport makes both rational and irrational decisions. Reality is treated cognitively only if it is *practical.* Values indicate man's *feelings* and his prejudices. Because his decisions are founded on internal aspirations, makes them no more meaningless than those developed scientifically—*provided* they bring about expected achievement.

In an analysis of the sport situation, man typically makes the emotional decision. When the choice is made *in action,* it tends to be an inner reaction. Therefore, the obvious conclusion one must reach is that the man of sport is both more and less moral than his fellow man. He is "more" moral because he trusts his impulses and tends to minimize rational conditioning. However, he is less moral in that he tends to make an *unexamined* choice.

It has always been my *personal* feeling that sport is *not* the place to teach moral virtue. Choice in sport tends to be pragmatically oriented. To consider that man will weigh "druthers" on the basis of responsibility of the authentic life is a bit naive. Again, morality and immorality are not based on an absolute scale, but are *situationally relative*. Their validity is grounded in concern and responsibility in an *authentic* existence.

The man of sport is compelled to act with little or no knowledge of the future of his actions. To a great degree they depend upon chance and the interactions of others. "That is the way the ball bounces," has become an American cliché, in part reflecting upon the accidental-realistic causation of the *will* and *things*. In few areas of life is chance and the immediate conflict of man and nature so directed and, at the same time, so circumstantial. Thus, choice is a quality of potentiality, while morality is a dimension of realization.

In this sense to be immoral is to not realize the self. For the athlete to say he plays to *win* when in truth he attempts to conquer, is to admit immorality. It matters little how close man is to altruism. But it does matter how close he is to real self. One cannot consider the action of the gymnast "good" or "bad" prior to the commencement of the movement experience. To "judge" after the event is acceptable provided one is not evaluating the "absoluteness" of the movement. To decide upon the morality of the performance demands a sensitivity to the communication of self. Once aware of the "inner man" we can attempt to locate the existing degree of closeness between *the mover and the moved*. If the movement *is* man, then it is moral. If the movement disguises man or misrepresents his self, it is immoral.

For the average man sport provides an opportunity to escape the risk of freedom. He enters into sport perceiving a system of rules, regulations and order. To play the game is to regulate oneself to the rules. Participation in football obviates man from moral decision. Or so he thinks. If this position is *really* representative of the self, then he is already immoral. It matters not if he plays according to the rules or not. He is immoral as soon as he fails to see the self as it really is. To say one would act another way if conditions were different is to say man does not have responsibility for his environment. Although he might not be able to alter the situation of sport, he still maintains the *dread* of *his* world. For he is in part responsible for what it is. Moral man, as a being, recognizes the reciprocal interaction of the self and the world. The relationship of individual to environment cannot be naively conceived as one of mallet to stone, to be shaped by continuous blows and stimulation, but rather like two meshing gears. The movement of *each* determines the movement of the other and the self. It is typical, through false humility, for the coach to blame the players. It is not infrequent, generally on losing teams, for players to indicate that "perhaps" their team was "out-coached." Small gymnasiums, tail winds, excessive heat, hostile spectators and poor weather conditions are but a few of the elements used as "reasons" for defeat. Soon man comes to lie to himself so often that he loses real being. It is at this point that freedom has been immorally used.

There is still another aspect of sport that is morally frightening. I see it most often when man plays the role of a *performer* rather than being a person of sport. Sartre refers to this quality as the "spirit of seriousness." Although difficult to put into words, I have seen this quality in operation when performers *play at* the activity, or when coaches play God to *their* (possessive pronoun *most* intentional) athletes or constituents. Somehow there is a thesis of "hard work" that is conveyed. This is not to say that sport does not demand hard work indeed; but individuals falling into this class appear to be obsessed with making certain everyone *knows* how serious sport really is. I am almost convinced this might be one of the reasons why man trains so hard for a particular swimming meet or soccer match. Obviously, this does not deny the necessity of training relative to performance. But it is to warn of what might be interpreted as man's desire to be *more* than what he is. All that becomes necessary is a mixture of motivation and masochism. When the man of sport becomes *so* involved, *so* engrossed and *so* absorbed, one wonders if he is not assuming a *role* of a performer. Most often this is easier than *being* one. This absorption of self into self is an affliction; it is a "neat" way for man to avoid the more penetrating questions of sport and existence. Why do I really play? Not why I tell myself I play. What do I really want to do when I participate? Not what do I do. How do I find out who I really am? Questions more easily avoided than answered. To walk away from the necessity of answering these questions, man finds it easier not to be disturbed while concentrating on a shot. Certainly it is easier and *more* comfortable to be pounded by a two-hundred and fifty pound linebacker, or take a series of left jabs in the nose, than to "fill time" with queries that threaten man's basic existence. It is far simpler to immerse oneself into "seriousness" of the activity than to relate the problems of a real life. Sport affords most of the answers. So why worry? If you need to develop social relationships, engage in sport. If you need a feeling of security, attempt a self-testing endeavor. Whatever your ills, come to the panacea. *Humbug*. It is about time man realizes that to be moral is to *use* freedom. To hide from choice is to deny any opportunity of actualization. To be anything less than you are is to deny existence! To rob oneself of existence is to deny life. If life is refused, then certainly the unexamined and unauthentic life constitues hell.

It can be seen that morality is *more* than religious affiliation. It is more than the worshipping of abstract absolutes. It is certainly more than pre- and post-judged suppositions, by whoever the judge is. For man it becomes what Buber would call "our ultimate interdependence of each other." Sport demands and challenges man to "harness the total." Each man knows he pays the price whatever the choice might be. Facing loneliness, as does the long-distance runner, man must decide by himself what the *value* really is. To say this is good for all of mankind is to be quite presumptuous. Yet to deny its possibility would be to refute one's own stomach for the possibility of accepting one's own mind. Indeed, this *would* be immoral.

A Symbol of a Materialistic Morality. The field of human meaning is inherently interwoven in the web of personal morality. As we have seen, the absence of a despotic system of imperative demands places man in a most *responsible* position for action. This point of view demands the renunciation of the arbitrary and emphasizes the re-creation of life founded on an ethic that is relative to the situation.

Sport, as an ever-present part of everyday existence, is greatly influenced by the *total* situation or environment. To be sure,

American culture is characterized by its materialistic and concomitant economic desires. Therefore, it is not surprising that sport takes on the veneer of an economic materialistic culture. When this desire for the "concrete" gets translated in terms of "how to achieve it," we fall right into the American industrial value of *work*. Although talking of *play*, as interchangeable with sport, Kwant makes some interesting observations pertaining to the "work credo."

> Not only work but play also takes place in an orderly field of worldly meaning. Playing requires a playing area, and within this field the objects are given a very special sense. In play also the possibilities of the human body must be channeled. The man who plays with the world plays also with his own body. Such play, moreover, usually requires certain implements, such as a football, tennis racket, or playing cards. Hence, play also takes place in an orderly field of worldly meaning. The same applies to all typically human activities that take place in the world. It is impossible to conceive a purposive, meaningful and circumscribed human activity without a world adapted to it; the orderly character of our actions is indissolubly connected with the organization of the world. By becoming acquainted with the way in which people have organized their world, one knows also how they are accustomed to work. (Kwant, 1965, p. 223)

It makes one wonder if man is still not Puritanical. That is, desiring to play on one hand and feeling guilty on the other, he organizes his play in a work-like manner and therefore can live with his choice.

To say sport is work oriented is only the beginning. For work, in our culture, looks toward commercialism for its fulfillment. The American has recognized and fostered this direction. From "wholesome" Little Leagues to our professional organizations the work cult has taken over sport. Can one pass a Little League, Pony League or Babe Ruth League without being plagued by commercial billboards? Everywhere, nine- and ten-year-olds can be seen sliding into second base with a reminder, on their backs, that the local barber shop, bank, dairy or dry cleaner is making this all possible. Babies learn to be boys and boys learn to be men. But how many of them learn to be human? When "backed" (pun intended) by industry, it follows that man will be industrious. I have seen all too many well-organized and highly mechanized forms of sport participation. I have no doubt that the child receives superior coaching and learns to play the sport in a more *professional* manner. Furthermore, I am reasonably assured that his physical health receives greater safeguards than would ever be possible on the sandlots. About this there can be little to complain. However, one wonders if "playing professionally" is so important for the child's development. One wonders if he is *really* not being *used*, as a means toward an end. The ethic of sport, again, is not the ethic of a total society, but rather of a specific situation. I express a doubt that children need be "readied" for the "hard cruel world." Perhaps by so conditioning them we maintain the kind of world that many espouse we should not foster; yet who is man to say what kind of world we *should* have. He *only* lives in this world.

It is no wonder that on almost every level man associates with a world of materialism and technology. At the highest level of proficiency man has been super organized into professional leagues with subdivisions. It is of interest that frequently these "feeder" systems are referred to in technological language, *farm* systems or *taxi* squads. Although the sociologist has had a "field day" in the analysis of team names—animals (Lions, Tigers, Rams), battle symbols (Bullets, Chargers, Blades), local patriotic symbols (Knickerbockers, Seventy-Sixers, Forty-Niners) and others—little has been said about the development of rather artificial representation and loyalties. About this we will say more later; however, it is of interest to note that a city might give little realistic local support to a team. It matters not. Before the people themselves know it, a new industry (the word "franchise" seems to be popular) is now *representing* the city and the citizens are supposed to demonstrate their "loyalty," a loyalty they did not perhaps desire or encourage.

Materialism, as such, is not necessarily united to commercialism. "The materialists want to achieve the greatest happiness for the greatest numbers . . . (They) want everything to be of advantage . . . but what is to our advantage?" (Roubiczek, 1964, p. 89). Should man be a rogue and hide or should he pretend to be deeply concerned in human welfare? Afraid to reply to this type of question man generally talks about being "happy." But certainly happiness is not an end but rather a process. Man *lives* happily. In sport the question of "most good" gets reduced to the *tangible*. Thus, it is not surprising that the story of sport is told in statistics, "phony" national rankings, and artificial attempts to evaluate beauty and grace. An example is the judging of gymnastics, diving and ice skating. No one would dream of assigning points to a piano concerto or a ballet. Yet the man of sport must be subjected to a materialistic form of evaluating his efforts. John Underwood almost recognizes this "boring" aspect of sport when he wrote about the National AAU Women's Cross-country Championship, ". . . sitting around the motel coffee shop bragging times and discussing times, that singular, most wearisome aspect of the track athlete's makeup. If it were not for minutes and seconds track athletes would be pretty good conversationalists" (Underwood, 1966, p. 30). Sport is indeed an intricate part of our culture and reflects the layman's stress on material possessions. To win a letter, cup, trophy, plaque, cup, or bowl is important. To achieve this end the athlete fortifies himself with the material and objective "proof" he knows best, "the stats."

To achieve the increased performance that is measurable, statistically, man has to give up much of his authentic nature. Training one muscle, like a machine, so that one can jump higher; developing powers of concentration so that he can reduce his association with the crowd; and developing strong daily regimens in order to condition the machine; all are examples of the loss of humanity. Man moves forward technically—his product becomes better and more efficient—but in so doing he destroys his dignity. It is a question of moral values. Man must make his choice. Either man lives humanistically or mechanistically. The *extent* of one's participation in sport is not simply a preference; it is a moral decision.

Although the "way" in which man participates in sport is a moral decision, *good* participation requires *more* than morality. Sacrifice, drive, dedication and appreciation are not necessarily moral traits but they are qualities that are associated with the good performance.

The dilemma of materialism as a moral dimension of sport brings us to a consideration of man's *will*. If morality tells us what we *ought* to do, then *will* speaks to our ability to achieve. In sport the *will* appears to be quite strong. The popular image of the "sportsman" characterizes a man of independence and strength, a man of will. Yet, the social commitment of *mutuality*, implied in most if not all sport situations, demands that man, *realistically*, is not afforded the *last* choice—death. When one plays tennis, he enters into a social contract that he will participate along *expected* avenues. His original choice structures the future. If man *is* free in sport, he *is* to a limited context. What matters are man's actions. But this is not the end of the argument because, as we have seen, morality is personal and yet beyond the self. If this is valid, we must address ourselves to these mysterious influences that occupy the man of sport.

If nothing else, we can see that the body adapts itself to special function. The experiences of life form the conditioning by which man adapts. If one is to be a long distance runner, he will be prepared differently than if he participates in golf. A mystery? No. This is expected. But what is mysterious is the original choice. How did man know he must be a runner, or a golfer? Was it simple preference? Or did other factors operate? Is it possible that man could be exhibiting something beyond a value decision? It does not seem possible or plausible that man would restrict himself to the rigidity and sacrifice demanded by sport if an element of *transcendence* were not present. Yet materialism alone has proved to be an extremely strong motivational force in our culture. The real heart of the moral dilemma rests in the fact that morality is a personal experience, a type of private calling. There is nothing as confining to the man of sport as when he is asked to follow rules that do not have personal meaning to him. Tell the hunter *why* and you will get his cooperation. But *meaning* is more than a list of reasons or objectives. Meaning somehow unites what *is* and *why* it should *be*.

> The last temptation is the greatest treason:
> To do the right deed for the wrong reason
>
> (Eliot, 1935, p. 44)

To ask *why* man participates in sport is almost wasting inquiry. The typical answers are the development of leadership, spirit, comradeship, and recreational benefits. Yet one *really* has to wonder if there is not something more. If there is not something that man recognizes—perhaps in his solitude—that he wishes not to reveal to himself and certainly not others. Might it not be related to something called "inner fulfillment"? Somehow we *fake* our life, because we attempt to live in keeping with an abstract absolute, rather than admitting to ourselves what and who we really are. If sport is in our behalf, admit it! If man coaches for selfish reasons, say so. Why play a game that one can't win? This is a value no culture, not even a material one, would maintain. We need to cry out for sport to be what it is, whatever it is.

Morality needs to consider the *totality* of man's existence. The moral decision must be man's. But to be moral it must bring to man *Existenz* (*true* existence) and not *Dasein* (*mere* existence). To be in sport is to have reached *Dasein*, for there can be little doubt that life is present. *Existenz* indicates that in sport participation man must *stand out*. He must be aware and open to the potential of the situation. As Jaspers indicates in his writings, it is this quality that allows man the possibility of his potential. It allows the realization of *being*. Without this quality sport could not be human. With the incorporation of this quality sport could not help but be human.

Many of our decisions in sport are made through the obvious. When we experience an encounter that is not "black or white," we meet the serious realities of the world. All we can do is decide in keeping with our personal nature, which our discussion has indicated to be part social. We know that avoiding the issue is in itself a choice. Since it is one that works to negate *Existenz* and avoid authenticity, it is an immoral decision. I think each man who has *experienced* sport feels a hint of recognition when facing the potential of morality in attaining *real* being.

On Ethics. Modern life is new and dynamic. The advent of modern science and technology, coupled with shifting populations and rapidly altered social codes, has renovated the citizen of the latter half of the twentieth century. To assume that man will act as he did yesterday is to demonstrate an unrealistic outlook germane to today's culture. From a simplified and relatively quiet past man has passed to a quickly changing society of dynamic dimensions. Modern decisions are overwhelmingly complex and as such reflect a compromise between the polarities of practice and theory. Thus, man finds little security in looking to the past. The "ideal" decisions of yesterday are no longer applicable. Not only is there an existing difficulty of *making* a decision. The modern choice is complicated by man not being "sure" what the decision *is* that needs to be made.

In the sport situation a slightly different picture is presented to the participant. There is extensive "security" offered to the man of sport because the sport scene is one of *order*, even if it is not idealized. Man learns *what* the rules of the game are. During the contest the rules remain fixed and decisions become a matter of "living-up" to the known. Man comes to sport from a fickle society of changing mores and fluid traditions. Now, present in sport, he faces a cosmos of regulation. The security he lost in "real life" is quickly regained in a stable world of sport. Not only does he *know* for "sure" what is expected of him, but now he has a group of officials, umpires, commissioners, and the like to make certain he remains within the rules. Deviation is permitted but one soon learns *just* how far one can stretch the rules.

Unlike the "real world," where conscience has been transformed from a mediator between id and ego to law itself, and where action is evaluated on the utilitarian functional scale, sport attempts to make man adhere to predetermined ethical constructs (needless to say this is not always carried out). During the sport event the performer is asked to evaluate or at least be cognizant of each happening, in keeping with rules, as an occurrence which has its roots in prior happenings. Thus, not only is their security in the known, but there is security in the comparison. Unlike the decisions he is asked to make a social setting, which calls for him to evaluate events as unique phenomena, thereby each standing on its own, the man of sport can look toward objective and rational order. He can determine the "norms" and make his own decision within the context of an "absolute" system. In social settings, decisions may agree with morality. But if they do, it is purely tangential to the act of immediacy. In sport the immediate must comply with the rules. This type of forced security makes an "artificial" world of *sureness*, if not comfort. It is "nice" to have an established order; at least it is consoling to know where one stands.

In place of fuzzy standards determined by a cross between ideals and norms, sport affords *deduction* in a *realistic* sense. It admits the abstract of the common good (sport even demands officials to "interpret" same), thereby necessitating man to be aware of the "higher and inner voice," while it asks him to act on an individual value bringing about a "good" for personal existence rather than an abstract omitting evaluative feedback. In this way previously established false images of good and bad are avoided. Sport thereby combines the paradox of the polar extremes of absolutism and relativism. It is interesting to note that professional wrestling, once a sport, now an "exhibition," always provides this dimension of polarity. There is always the "good guy" against the "bad guy." It is of interest that "good" normally gets defined in keeping with "clean" or ethical, while "bad" is synonymous with "dirty" and therefore unethical. Perhaps professional wrestling needed "to be arranged" so that the naivete of life could be demonstrated in "sport." Is it not the "Batman" of sport? Namely, the sublime highlights the foolish reality!

It must be pointed out that rules in sport are more than guides for decision. They actually direct the *way* of doing things, if not the choice of doing. The participant is usually suppressed by a God-like official, who rather than provide an image of the "loving father" becomes a dogmatic legislator (the umpire is *always* right). In a manner of speaking, every personal decision must be interpreted in keeping with that which will be made by the official. Likewise the man of sport really does not need to develop his own ethical existence. The rulers of sport do this for him. This is much different from everyday life where man must "go by" the rules of the social order much like the rules of the game. The difference rests in the immediate response. In life man is *eventually* "ruled on," but he does not live with a *constant* whistle to remind him of what he *should be* doing. Pragmatic rationale, and not morality, undergirds the real ethical choice in sport.

In reality, sport does not really concern itself with absolute, for if it did it would relegate itself to an abstract audience. It must consider *hic homo* (concrete man) rather than *homo ut sic* (abstract man) (Poppi, 1957, pp. 3–63). The *practical* way is neatly woven together with *traditional* regulations to form a basis for *ethics*. Thus, in a way, the sportsman is truly representative of Nietzsche's *Superman*. Static morality is present, yet personal existence is that which ultimately gives causation to decision. Each decision is based on *the* happening along with the *emotional* determinants of the individual. Through development of the spirit and emotion an ethic of absolutism is tempered from "formalism" to relativism. As an area greatly involved with *system* and conversely dependent upon individual existence, sport calls upon regulated freedom and relative choice to develop an ethic that above all is *workable*.

It must be emphasized that the *basis* of morality is in the *authenticity* of man. Once the participant *examines* his life, he commits himself to a constant search, not for truth, but to the *meaning* of truth. Since sport is a dynamic and changing situation, and there is no established order of values, it follows that moral decisions are founded on a system of *relatives*.

Do these normative structures have an objective? Is there a target man can shoot at? The answer is both yes and no. If one perceives a goal as a stationary archery target, the answer is an unequivocal no. Again, the very nature of a changing environment and a developing man necessitates a modulating structure. Thus, if morality is viewed as a system of "audibles" in football, man might well make appropriate decisions. The quarterback will call a play in the huddle. This decision is based on numerous factors including the expected defensive alignment of the opposition. When standing at the line of scrimmage, prior to the snap of the ball, the quarterback may well see a different situation from the one he thought would exist. To run the same play as called in the huddle is sure defeat. To perceive the different environment, to be flexible enough to alter and decide on a new "play" are the marks of a *winner*. Man must learn to react to the situation. For the quarterback the goal is victory; for man it is a meaningful life. Morality must not only be true to the situation, it must also allow for purpose to man's life.

In this light it can be seen that a relative ethic is not, if authentically derived, a symptom of ambivalence or moral seasickness. Situational morality is not an attempt to avoid problems; rather, it is an effort to have man face the realities of life. If anything, sport "teaches" man it is life that must be faced as it *really* is in existence. One cannot run away or deceive oneself in sport or in life. Self-deception might work for a while, but only a short while. Meaning is diffused and life becomes a *nothingness*. Our safeguard is human concern for being. To say it will *work* is to fuse the pragmatic and the idealistic into the unreal. We have to evidence, in any sense of the word, that this "new" system will contribute to a higher level of life. Yet to *settle* for what we have is to admit our destiny. I, for one, am willing to place my faith (concern) in man rather than believe (statement of probability) in the supposed "goodness" of man. We must ask the man in sport to risk *defeat* (after all it is only a *game*). He must be willing to say *no* to his conscious, as a rational power, and beat down the false self. Once rid of the demigods of societal influence, namely "MEPSKY" (M is for money, E for energy, P for power, S for Sex, K for knowledge and Y for youth), man can use this newfound *freedom* truly to actualize the self. No doubt this requires extensive self-regulation.

It should be pointed out that this form of "discipline" is inherent to the sport scene. The athlete learns to "do without." However, the sacrificial aspect of this form of morality might not be as inherently valuable as the realization of what the Freudians might call the sadistic/masochistic desires of the individual. Certainly this aspect of sport cannot be denied. Thus, it is easy to recognize the simple transformation that is necessary for the performer to achieve this desired morality. The track performer, as well as the fisherman, learns to "pay his price." This "new morality" is *really* not new to him. Perhaps it has never been verbalized, but he knows it well. Perhaps only too well.

I have not attempted to show the possible causation of human morality. Morals, like life, might be a product of qualities. But so what? What is important is their existence. They are present. To admit their existence is not to confirm their absoluteness. But rather to implicate the evolutionary dimension which is demanded by the nature of the modern world. In truth, it appears that man's insistence upon absolute structures is an attempt to mirror symbolically man's uncertainty, his insecurity, and his incessant attempt to achieve peace the "easy way." But to settle for the unreal is not to bring peace but to bring a sword.

To look at the "lessons" of sport in this way is to question the basic meaning of human existence. It places great importance as to the *basis* of value decisions. Is sport simply a *battleground for human conquest?* Or is it possible, through the use of freedom, to make choices leading to authentic *being?* To be tied to "a power beyond" might well cause man to rationalize and sublimate *what he is doing.* To live a false life, when real self is "good," is unexcusable. I see great potential for achieving this end in most situations in sport. Simply, it lends itself to this form of ethic. But it will not come until the performer becomes aware of the relationship of his action to the authentic self. In so doing he must renounce prior conditioning and search for meaning in each activity of life. To not search in this manner is to play the game (of life or sport) without any *extensive* purpose. If man acts without being "bugged" by the attempt for constant meaning, then life and sport might well be, as Sartre indicates, *absurd.* But it is not life or sport that *is* absurd. They are *nothing.* They don't exist without man. It is in man's hands to make each act meaningful. He is morally *free* to do so. If he does not, then he must shoulder the responsibility for *making* it absurd. Man, therefore, *creates* sport. Through a relative value structure he *re-creates* the life process. He makes sport, again and again, what it potentially is. To say any more is not necessary.

Morality as an Intimate of Sport

Working within the structure of *personal concern* the morality decisions that face man in sport are most personal. They provide the *intimate* fiber of communication between man and the activity. In order to actualize the ethic man must ask where he *is* within the totality of the sport experience. For all of life begins and ends with what he experiences in existence. If one espouses the thesis that you "treat your opponent as you would desire to be treated," then the *meaning of the truth* of that statement is a dependent variable. Its validity is determined by the *intimateness* of man to the experience.

The word "intimate" is being used to connote that which is beyond human thought. The value is not achieved, *really*, if man just *thinks* that is the way to act. Or even if he says that is the way I would like to be treated. This quality of the "intimate" goes into the depths of existence and certainly extends itself beyond modern Christian Ethic. The implication is that man *cares*, not merely intellectually, but with an involvement that extends to the very root of his personhood. If man is not treated in this manner, one is not *just* disappointed, he becomes *nauseated*. He *suffers* because his involvement was more than what was stated—it was *all* of life. Sport is, generally, an act of initial volition. Man participates with *all* of his complexities. This completeness leads to a seriousness of involvement. Only too often the "intermediate" goal of victory blinds man from seeing the eventuation of his participation. To become intimate is to initiate morality. Real morality cannot be achieved until man is willing to *risk* his self in the sport experience.

In achieving this morality man cannot treat man according to usual role expectancy. One does not treat one as an umpire, bowler, boxer, jockey, skier, or basketball player. One is treated *intimately*, as an *individual*. Too often, in our complicated and mass culture of mechanization, we forget that man is not a collective noun. He is a person with a unique identity. Sport must be wary that, in its zest for *ends* and results that are indicated on the scoreboard, man is not relegated to a *mean*. Again, I trust this thought is in keeping with Buber's moral imperative:

> One cannot treat either an individual or a social organism as a means to an end absolutely, without robbing it of its life substance. . . . One cannot in the nature of things expect a little tree that has been turned into a club to put forth leaves. (Buber, 1953, p. 17)

The *intimate* relationships of sport provide the raw material for the most "humane" of all ethical structures. However, one must wonder if the potential is being realized or prostituted. The question is not one of the normal means/ends dichotomy. No matter how good or bad is either the means or ends, man is *immoral* if he attempts to structure any form of dualism which segments, and thereby injures, the authentic existence of man.

Our experiences and our goals need be one. Our dreams and our realities need be fused. To say they *are* not is to admit *reality*. To say they *cannot* is to admit *defeat*. We might make choices that are less than what we would hope them to be. But we must not close our eyes and our hearts to those that are *not* chosen. An ethic of *existence* is personal; it is intimate. In sport man can free himself *in* the closeness of another: in his relations with man, in his empathy for skill development, in his appreciation of dedication. All these qualities *bring* him closer to the door of being. Whether he *enters* into life or stays behind a closed partition is a matter of *choice*. A choice of none less than life or death, for man and sport.

In making the choice we cannot run away from the obvious question. Is the authentic life both "good" and "right"? When man is trying to find *real* self in the world of sport, does the *sport* itself encourage man in a world of good and right? In talking about modern sports, The Rev. Edward Hildner, who at ninety-three years of age is the sole survivor of the first basketball game, said, "There are too many whistles, too many interruptions because some silly little rule is broken. The same is true about baseball—all that baloney that makes the game too long" (Scorecard, 1966, p. 22). Well the game may now be "right." But is it "good"? Is this what James would call a difference that makes no difference and therefore it makes no difference? I think not. Man does not find any sure and clear roads to follow in journeying toward the *real* life. The subtle differentiation between "right" and "good" affords insights into the sport situation as an arena for the development of *being*. Choices are difficult to make when the scope of the question is clear. But in the complexity of the sport world we are talking of another issue. It is easy to see how man could "settle" for a world of absolutes. When life becomes intimate, man needs to deal with the "gray areas." Black and white will not do. The importance of *relatives* becomes both obvious and terrifying. But now the decisions cannot be avoided. They are close. They are intimate. How do you regulate between the good of the team and the rightness of man? It might be right for man to hunt (the deer will be injured due to overpopulation is the usual reason that is given); but few would say it is good to kill a defenseless animal. Hopefully the reader is not expecting any type of ethical panacea. The only answer I know is that man must do what *he* feels is good. Values and ethics, as moral derivatives, need be unclouded so that man can act with a decisiveness that indicates position and reflection. But this is only the start. For the more immediate and intimate man becomes to sport, the greater will be the effort to reach the zenith.

Physical Fitness as a Moral Quality. To talk of *physical* fitness as an aspect of sport is to be obviously and almost hopelessly out of date. Obviously man needs some form of physical tonus to engage in all activities of life. But in sport it is all the more imperative. Yet to talk of *physical* fitness is to relate to an "old" concept. Now the vogue is *total* fitness. But really one can't help but hear the intonations of a guilty dualistic culture giving mouth service to those elements that *also* compose man.

Fitness is basically a survival technique. It is necessary for day-to-day living and receives special attention during a period of increased stress. War and sport have been special modes of human life that have stressed the demands of fitness. To talk of the importance of fitness to any individual concerned with survival is much like "bringing coals to Newcastle." But to see fitness receive extensive stress is to recognize the moral structure of survival.

Since fitness is necessary for survival, we can understand that fitness is a desired *means* for the achievement of a specific end. Accordingly, it becomes a *relative* dimension of morality. How fit should one be for football? How fit should one be for squash? Is the same type of fitness required for sailing as mountain climbing? Obviously, the answer to the dimensions of fitness are dependent upon the *ends*. What is your aim? Obviously the end is not mere participation. Nor is it victory. Somewhere, someplace we come to recognize there is *more* to life than the obvious. We have not forgotten fulfillment, righteousness and self-realization. All this indicates that when we conceive of fitness for the purposes of a sport we are saying it is a *means for a means.* The question that needs to be asked deals with the end to which fitness is an appropriate mean. Is fitness a moral quality, serving as a handmaiden, of sport?

Darwinism has established the principle of survival of the fittest. But the "fit" in sport are not those with qualities of concern, love, empathy, care, passion and respect for personhood. To survive in the world of sport man better *not* have these qualities. To be hard, to be tough, to be strong and to be rough—these are the qualities that pay dividends. Again, the accent is in different kinds of strength or relative values. The truth of the matter is that the Bible would not have a chance against the likes of Darwin in a war or in sport.

Now the preceding conversation begins to haunt us. It might be "right" to develop a level of fitness that enables man to conquer; but is it good? Is it good for *mankind*?

Much is often said of the *social values* of sport. Certainly such moral structures facilitate our social life. About this there can be no complaint. Love, warmth and kindness assist man in his attempt to be human. Yet the qualities of fitness lead man to anything but a social life. They serve as a means, not to the ends of actualization, but rather toward achieving a conquering soul. I think few would deny the apparent necessity for fitness in sport. In so demanding we must readily see that the original choice commits us to further choice. We select sport. We must choose fitness. When we select fitness, we commit ourselves to a "warlike" environment. From this choice little in the way of "tender loving care" can emerge. Morality assists us toward social awareness and compatibility. Fitness facilitates our preparation for war. Since social harmony and war are opposites, it follows that morality and fitness are also at polar extremes. I cannot go quite as far as some who insist fitness is *immoral* (since it is nonsocial). But, from the immediate discussion, it is obvious that I can *almost* go that far.

The morality of man is a consequence of the *existing* social order. Alter the order and you possibly alter the morality. This does not necessitate that the morality be recognized by the social order at the time it existed. To be there is to demonstrate its existence. If it is "right" and "good," it will activate the society toward the appropriate end. But it never will be right for all.

The preceding has demonstrated the social dimension of morality; however, basically, morality is a personal and individual matter. In this regard sport gives man the choice of participating in "individual" activities such as golf, riding, swimming, bowling and skiing. If man desires the social setting, he turns his attention to team sports such as baseball, basketball, football, volleyball, hockey and soccer. It is interesting to note that no matter whether man participates in individual or team activities the social code continues to dictate. Officials, umpires, referees are employed to make certain the "just" receive their due. They are a symbol of the rules. In essence they represent what is *right*. Although they have little direct concern with the *good*, at times they temper their decisions *with what ought to be*. It is quite frequent for an official to "miss" a foul (not right) when it does not affect the direct play of the game (the good). When this action becomes repeated, it soon becomes an expected tradition or custom of the game. Thus, as the social order changes, sport, and the concept of right and good, makes similar modifications. While morality is not completely a servant to changing times, one could hardly deny the rightful effect of the environment upon the morality of any given time.

Allowing for the Existing Morality

Morality is directly related to its environment. However, this does not mean the social matrix always affords assent to the expressed value. Since the realm of sport is atypical from many other endeavors of life—one would expect a varied ethic. That is to say, it is hard to believe that one would even dream that the sport participant would exhibit the same value structure on the gridiron as he does when visiting friends. Each situation calls for its own judgments. This is not to say that this system of relatives is right or wrong. But it does say that it is internally consistent with prior analysis. We might not like ourselves for making certain value decisions. Nevertheless, man makes the choice. Yet, it has been my impression that educators, laymen, sports writers, and sometimes even coaches act surprised and even shocked when a value is demonstrated that is contrary to the Judea-Christian Ethic. All of this in spite of the accepted thesis of situational ethics.

This expressed horror is not naiveté. In fact, it is more probably a reflection of associated guilt which is manifested in another. Any individual who has been around football for any period of time knows that "elbows fly" on the first play from scrimmage. This is when each man tells his opponent "who is boss." Yet let a player get "caught" for punching and everyone exhibits great shock. "How could such a nice boy do a thing like that? Why he goes to church every Sunday." Yes. But this is Saturday. And on Saturday the name of the game is *kill*. Do we really expect him to practice the Ten Commandments in front of 60,000 people? I think not. We might *like* him to. But we don't *expect* him to. Yet overtly we give the impression that the morality of sport is identical to the morality of the choir. It seems it is high time we either change the nature of sport (which is highly unlikely), or stop the hyprocrisy and *admit* to ourselves the existing ethic. To condone, covertly, and punish, overtly, is not my idea of authenticity.

Our expressed purpose and preference in sport is clear. It is not comradeship, self-discovery or aesthetics. I don't care what the "level" of participation is—be it six-year-olds or sixty-year-olds—man plays to succeed. And success is measured by pushing the other guy down, just a little, so that you, as you harness the forces of nature, climb a little higher. Each time we climb a little higher. Each child learns that some day if he works hard and is lucky (but he also learns he has to *make* his own "breaks"), he might grow up to be the champion.

The athlete *knows* the acceptable moral code; however, within this frame he might make many varied value decisions. While he might select to play professional baseball as opposed to seeking a college education, it is not an unethical decision. It is simply an expressed preference. This is what he *likes*. Values are *not* moral imperatives. Since man is *not*, in any sense, forced into action, it would seem wise that we make room for the values we locate in sport. Again, no one is saying this is what we *want*. All that is being said is this is what *is*. Let us not make the mistake of so many who preceded us. Let us recognize *situations* in sport as they exist; and let us stop in the game of self-deception. No life could be more immoral than where one refuses to be aware of his own existence.

The Element of Silence

In searching for the "sounds" of sport one quickly hears the roar of the crowd, the crack of the bat and the thundering of racing feet. But if one listens a little harder and a little longer, one comes to hear silence. There is silence within the performer, in the tenseness of the crowd, in the fear of the hunter and in the beauty of the ski slopes. Perhaps silence is communicated because it is an expression of a multitude of personal feelings; but whatever the reason, it appears to be a meaningful splendor.

Man soon learns that silence is an integral part of life and that certainly it is prominent in sport. Silence is not simply the absence of sounds. Rather it is presence. It is the presence of the dimension of time. A realization of the instant and the situation. Furthermore, it is an expression of the completeness of the situation. In a very real way, silence is heard as an integral part of existence and, as such, provides for many combinations of feelings in the man of sport. The hushed quiet at a crucial moment in a sport contest is only too apparent. It does all but tell the exact status of the situation. Rather than perceive it as the absence of sound, silence can be viewed as a highly intensified element of participation. "Silence is not just 'unspoken' . . . Silence comes from attention, concentration, recollection, meditation, and prayer" (Sciacca, 1957, p. 287). Any serious sport participant knows only too well the difference between a "quiet" performance and one that is *silent*. The former is marked with omission, while the latter is most inclusive.

When aware of his existence, the participant becomes aware of his being and starts to experience all about him. He again starts to ponder the questions of his existence. If one authentically searches in these directions, he might well reach the level of authentic anxiety. As one feels this sensation he comes to the realization of his commitment to being as fundamental. Suddenly we press for answers. Our existence comes to encompass our being. But this is still a long way from the realization of meaning. Silence, not quiet, allows the performer the opportunity to reflect upon reason as he faces being. Sport no longer is *just* the place where man feels he can escape the humdrum world that has become his existence. Now he must face the "why" of life. He musters his powers of thought and fortitude and regroups his experiences into another relentless round of activity. Hoping in some way he can escape the *loneliness of silence* that speaks to him so earnestly. For most performers there is a *chance* for reflection which in turn could abate the ultimate anguish; but for most the "easy" answer is pursued. Compete with strength, speed and cunning—nature is defeated by man—and one does not have to listen to the silence of his existence.

Again, we can see the matador, symbolic of grace and elegance, facing the deep and dark beast within himself, portrayed by the bull. It is as almost as if man must maintain dignity in the form of silence or allow himself to be defeated by the "enemy within." The actualization of athletic skill and prowess requires essence, but to a greater degree it calls for the depths of human emotion. Within the action of unification, mind and body phenomena develop which are not rational and not always deducible from experience. Nor are they always logical. Man's silence brings him closer to his needed existence.

In the perfomer's confrontation of sport he extends *outward*, from self to others, as his existence takes on a newly created and intensified form. This in no way robs the person of his individuality but rather adds a dimension to his existence. To kill the bull does little for the matador. But to do so "in the way of sport" is to add to all of life. Basically the man of sport stands before himself, ready to meet every unknown obstacle and challenge which the situation is to place in his path, and his personhood is reduced by little, including rule. No longer bowing to God, or to the pressures of society, or even to the pagan symbols that control his "usual" daily routine, man recognizes that complete independence of forces is only academic. He becomes the complete man that he is. When one skis, his complete being takes on the composite of nature and self. To speak of this as body development or spiritual development is to forget the unification of man. Yet to recognize man one does need to be silent. Man is *the* one who makes the decision; he is *the* one who acts *on* the structure of the sport and thus he is the conceiver of the *relative* "good." Again, decisions of this magnitude, if they are to be *really* made, require something more than the loudness usually associated with sport; indeed, they require the silence of reflection.

Interacting with the other, man turns *within* his self. All one needs, to be convinced of this quality, is to listen to the inner silence of football players prior to a "big" game. Some in prayer, some entranced in solitude and still others in private communion, all listening to their selves. Their thoughts focused on reason, complete with scientifically determined strategy, they are fully aware that their concentration is not on the rational but on "something else." Man will know if he is "right" in sixty minutes, but really he *knows* already. He needs only to find the way to release what is already within. Sport provides this mechanism of release. It is a place for trial. Here man will learn if indeed he needs to reject his own freedom. It is in sport he can become what he is.

When seen in this light the man of sport is a lonely figure. But his loneliness is not a function of exclusion but one of inclusion. Man's ability to relate to others can be emotionalized and intellectualized in the loneliness of his existence. The locker room, the huddle, the top of the slope, the rough canvas are all lonely places, no matter how many others are near. As is true with the "distance runner," most men need loneliness. Isolation from the surroundings is not so much superimposed by the "nature" of sport as much as it is an inherent quality sought and cherished by the men of sport. The athlete enjoys this wonderful dichotomy.

He is alone with himself but simultaneously shares with fellowman and environment the peace and turmoil that makes sport sport. It is in loneliness that he can think and, to a great degree, it is in loneliness that man attains the ideal. Yet he always has the "other" at his call—a necessary ingredient if man is to achieve the actualization of self.

For the participant loneliness is not *to be* lonely. Rather it affords the individual self an opportunity to reject the stable parts of human existence without feeling unnecessarily guilty or shamed. In so doing he comes, or might come, to a greater comprehension of others. The performer, especially in team sports, stands together with the other. Man goes within his self and comes out with causation for relation, appreciation of his "mate" and perhaps a greater sense of meaning. Sport can be individualistic, nationalistic or what-have-you, but for man, preparing for the event and during the action, the world of silence and loneliness transcends actual existence. Confronted by the situation and self man must face his own existence. In a sense the whole of the human effort is fused before the performer. He either rejects his authenticity or he commits himself to the freedom of his inner self. To achieve in sport man must achieve his own awareness of personal horizons. Anything requiring this depth assumes a communication with the self, requiring the utmost of silence in order to be really heard, to be heard by powers that, somehow, are more than human.

SPORT: EXISTENCE AND DECISION

THE traditional philosophical differentiation between that *which is*, existence, and that *what is*, essence, is clearly demonstrable in the world of sport. Specifically, when one talks of existence he refers to the quality of individuality. On the other hand, essence refers to the composition of humanity. Typically, the men of sport have been aligned to the world of the rational (and at times the not too rational) animal. In this way, man *naturally* runs through the woods to hunt other animals; he jumps in the air in an attempt to contest the forces of gravity; and he meets fellow man to test his worth. Thus, he is conceived as existing. However, only a heightened degree of sophistication separates him from other living forms. Some say the quality that does divorce him from other animals is his essence. It is this quality, his "character," that marks him as one of humanity.

There is an essence of sport and certainly, there is an essence of the man who participates in sport activity. Man's efforts are generally indicated in seconds, minutes, miles per hour, weight and even something perhaps as *artificial* as the Power Efficiency Rating recently used in baseball. Man becomes a mixture of essences to be evaluated and recorded. In this way, hypothetically, man can *measure* himself against all men, past and present. The fact that the essence of the performer's tools are not alike does not seem to bother man. One admits, but not for long, that diet has changed in the last thirty years; condition of running and jumping surfaces has been greatly altered; and that there might well be a difference between arrows, paddles, rackets and bats. It would appear that sport could best serve man and man best serve sport (if this is not too "inhuman" a thought), if individuals recognized the relationship between essence and existence. They are frequently confused, on the one hand, and improperly related on the other.

Perhaps nowhere is man's fate sadder, but clearest to demonstrate by example, than in the world of track. In a sport potentially saturated with experiences for self-discovery and human fulfillment the expressed direction of the activity has been toward the location of *what* is occurring. Take a look at the average printed track program. It is almost certain to list, for each event, individual records, meet records, school records, conference records, national records and world records. The four-minute mile, once a psychological milestone for man's fulfillment, if not a physical apex, is now almost an expected outcome. If man does not achieve this "mark," all are disappointed. I have often heard many spectators and performers remark, "It wasn't a good race." What they really meant was the objective evaluation of the performance indicated *less* than what they had hoped would occur. Spectators, sports writers, and, most sadly, the performers themselves are no longer concerned with *the* event as much as they are focused on the barrier. What was the "split"? This becomes the password for almost any track buff. If the race is under "four minutes," it was a "good" race. Any other effort leaves a little to be desired. Exemplifying this attitude is the great track performer, Jim Ryun.

> If you set up a goal of something like 3:50, say for the mile run, it gives you a target to aim at. You think what a 3:50 mile really is—four 57.5 quarters—and you realize how much work you have to do to be able to run a mile at that pace. It's important, of course, not to get too discouraged if you don't make it. (Brown, 1966a, pp. 42–43)

The amazing dimension of this remark is not the instrumental approach to sport; for this we have recognized as symptomatic of our culture, but rather Ryun's warning of despair. In reality he is saying don't feel *too* bad if you can't *measure* beyond human *expectancy*. If anything is true in sport, it is that man is not recognized as "good" if there is a lack of *action* to validate the assertion. But one wonders if there is not a responsibility that each performer maintains; namely, that action is secondary to the totality of the world. As the man *of* acts, is he not responsible for the self? If the world of the performer is a rather naive concept of "perfection of being," one must wonder how sport yields to true bonding of essence and existence. It would appear this effort is attainable through an effort beyond awareness. Even if the latter were true, it would need be founded on "relatives." Perhaps it is time that man runs a mile for reasons of *relation* and not one of competition. But then this would *not be sport.*

Perhaps the height of prostitution of humanity is symbolized in the rather strange phenomenon of track's "human rabbit." It is not accidental that the grammatical construction of the prior sentence indicates a passive quality in the sport, for truly it is sport that "owns" man. As anyone who has ever heard of Jess Owens or Rodger Bannister can tell you, a "rabbit," in track, is a *man* placed into a race for the sole purpose of setting a fast pace so that other more talented performers will be able to run a fast race. Not only does man no longer run with man, nor even against man, now he runs against an artificial standard *using* man to assist his efforts. Is this not the height of human decay? Man *uses* another. And perhaps what is worse, man allows and offers himself to be used. Perhaps one might argue that man is not being used. But rather the "rabbit" is cooperating with fellow man. To argue this way is to admit human sacrifice as a form of desired human action; and to deny the basic motivation for the race. It is not enough for man to run for the sake of running or even for victory. Man now becomes the *tool* and even the slave instrument of measurement. Man is not important. Records are important.

Perhaps this can be expressed in another way. It is the attempt at *becoming*, rather than *being* that says the same thing. Nowhere is this more vividly highlighted than in organized sport for youngsters. Without getting involved in the relative virtues of Little Leagues, Pop Warner Leagues and the like, let us inquire into the *nature* of this form of activity. The usual arguments, pro and con, focus on levels of competition, maturation of the children, spectator involvement, organization and structure. But these aspects are not ones that have personally troubled me; yet I do find myself "shrinking" from this form of participation without really knowing why. Upon closer inspection I find my distaste is centered in the *pretending* element of the participants. Somehow I receive the idea they are acting or even faking. In terms already used they are *becoming*—without being. Most of these youngsters focus *outside* of themselves. This takes the form of *mimic*, but it is truly more than copying a "big-leaguer." They play as if they are fulfilling some sort of *obligation* to someone or something established as a demigod of what they "ought to" be doing. Play for these children *appears* not to be spontaneous or even voluntary but rather a necessity, a compulsion to act out what their culture tells them *should* be. In most cases these children are not aware of *being* and the sport activity becomes an artificial device to increase the obscurity of self.

The other day I had an opportunity to view a Pop Warner League football game. These children were approximately ninety to one hundred pounds and probably in the sixth grade of their schooling. My attention was first drawn to the linebackers, they were *kind of* "jitterbugging." I say *kind of* because, unlike their college or professional counterparts, there seemed to be no reason besides *imitation* for their action. It was almost like watching a bad theatrical production. One could watch a child's play and not expect high level performance. In fact, because of the "childish nature" of most of these productions they become "cute." But one does not think an "imitation" is cute. It is simply ridiculous. Imitation, prefabrication and an attempt to *become* like "others" were the marked features of this "bad" bit of play-acting. Unlike most theatrical performers, these youngsters did not know they were acting. They fool themselves into believing they are *something* they are not. *Something* rather than *someone*, because in this act they *use* them*selves* as instruments and lose their *personhood*. They destroy their own humanity by substituting *becoming* for *being*.

Why can't these *children play*, and not *perform*, football in a style depicting their age and maturation rather than that of a fancy night club entertainer? One might well argue that professional athletes need to entertain (an argument I admit having little credence in); but certainly children do not. In one game, within *one* series of downs, I saw no less than a single wing formation, a shift into a straight *T* formation, a shift into an *I* formation and three variations of a "winged," "slot" and "double-wing" formation. During this same contest I witnessed inside and outside reverses, halfback options, gap and slant blocking, looping on defense, safety "blitzes" and numerous "cross-bucks," "slants" and the old stand-by, the "statue of liberty" play. I saw more *things* than any professional team would dream of including in one game. Was the play of the children "bad"? Was this why I was bothered? No, it was "good." It was *too* good. It was so good that I had the feeling I was watching a *machine* at work. (In talking with the coach after the game I was interested in the fact that he indeed did refer to his team as a "well-oiled machine.") These were not boys playing, as they are; they were robots moving as they were told they *should* react. These were youngsters attempting to grow *out* of their selves. It was impressed upon them how important it was to be more than themselves. They were motivated to *become* something they were not. If this type of human development is present at this age, where does it start? And, what is more important, does it ever stop?

The grade school child imitates the prep school performer who in turn copies from the collegiate stars who, of course, look towards the professionals. At each and every step they can never be satisfied with who they are; for they never do know who they are. They are always living in the future world of *becoming*.

At each level man falsifies the values of the sport and of his existence. Man goes *through* the stages of life, often not taking the chance and/or time to reflect upon his own *being*, each person trying to look and feel like something he is not. Perhaps this is the one advantage of "sand-lot" sports. Each child plays as a child. It is *more* voluntary, in its true sense, than the highly organized activity. The child is truly given an unhampered opportunity to be aware of his *being*. The pressures, both self and externally imposed, are not so great. In a word he is more *free*. He is free to exist.

Perfection in Sport

It is a strange anomaly that for all those almost infinite numbers of individuals who have participated in some form of sport, at one point in their life or another, most have attempted to reach the "perfect" performance, regardless of how it was determined, without really conceiving of the ideal as real. This is the lesson certain academicians have been preaching for years; namely, that no matter how earnestly man pursues "the ultimate," the completeness of existence will always elude him. In sport, as in all aspects of life, man attempts the attainment of the not yet achieved. Man becomes condemned to an inescapable fate. Thus, it is the very freedom that we desire, to pursue and attain, which ends up by condemning us.

This might well explain the popularity of surfing among "young" people. The challenge of surfing is the challenge of extreme forces. The necessary sensitivity to nature not only demands aesthetic elements of form but requires precise balance. On the other hand, the ruthlessness of the wave demands strength, power and a degree of endurance. The surfer is endlessly free. He is distant from himself by the apparent barriers of nature; yet, what he really is involved with is *nothingness*. Whether he is "just riding one," or "hanging ten," he is forsaken by the past. The experience is new, the conditions are fresh, yet he must put forth his self. The tradition of history cannot assist him. Each and every encounter is new and fresh. Man stands on his own as he faces the unstructured and unique forces of nature. Man's freedom is his own when he takes the wave. The experience is released from the demands of precedent. And in all of this freshness man is called to put forth a *viewpoint*. In constant excitement and in recurring sets of fear man is constantly challenged. One loss of consciousness and the end is immediately presented. Yet the surfer is not really in consciousness but rather has transcended the conscious. His mood and feeling are beyond the board and even the wave. He is estranged from the material and senses a type of spiritual excitement. He knows *of* the real. He must relax but not *really*. He is alone; he is by himself and free *from* the world. He determines his own destiny. If *he* has the ability, *now* he can demonstrate it. If he makes an error, he is "wiped-out." The responsibility for his self is his. The action is a constant reminder of his own truth This is a frightening responsibility. Failure cannot be blamed on a sudden gust of wind or a strong current. This is part of the sport. In fact, this *is* the sport. These forces make up the *whole* and comprise the *nature of the act*. This is what man asked for and this is what he is free to determine. The anxiety of his freedom actually assists him in the situation. His *concern* causes him to remain attentive to the situation. While he *needs* to "ride it in," he would like nothing better than to relieve himself of his situation. However, in surfing, no act of God, no environmental force, no "other" human action is an allowable scapegoat. It is an experience of wonder. It is an experience of man meeting nature in its most intimate setting. The surfer *is* what he makes himself *to be*. He alone is counted responsible. And this is the way it should be; for it is man who has the freedom, and thus the responsibility for his actions.

Regardless of the recent trend in surfing, to objectively score performance, it is most unlikely man will ever attain perfection in this *real* sport. In many ways surfing speaks to the "loner." Thus, it does seek cooperative excellence as much as personal development. In surfing, man's existence offers an opportunity to attain true *being*. Being, as is, might well be called the personification of perfection. Not only is the object perfected but all conditions of nature are perfected *toward* the meaning of the good world. The existent cherishes his existence because of its inherent value in comprehension of the world as a *unity*. There is a kind of *necessity* in surfing that pulls man toward an awareness of his existence.

In this way, *to be* becomes a factor of *existence*. Together they mediate in the development of the *good*. "Conceptions can only be seen as good as having existence in the mind but this is not strictly their being as they exist" (Salmon, 1953, p. 37). The surfer knows well that an *idea*, to attain truth, must be placed into existence through the immediate realm of action. The importance of the *immediate* decision and reaction to the new is a characteristic of surfing; nature and the individual are stressed as necessary ingredients for the *good* existence. To sense surfing deeply as an area of human concern is to consider nature and man, as a reciprocating subject/object relationship, constantly reacting to the good of truth.

When one sees the unification of *truth and good* in surfing, there is little necessity to explain the immediate and necessary transcendence from the material to the spiritual. Unification of man becomes a focal point for most actions. The experience of man on the surf board extends into the development of *being as being.* From here it is a short step to understand the *significant meanings* which are the *perfections* of sport. In surfing man can become aware of all that is. All of nature is before him in his freedom. It is for the surfer an imperative to make sense out of the whole. In this approach the surfer reaffirms his action. He cannot consider the act unless he sees it in the unifying form, and this is the only form that is possible. Perfection, thus, is an act of existence. It is *not* an idealized movement. Being is captured by the surfer, not only as an act of *his* own but as a force of the *wholeness* of existence. It *is* perfect not because it mimics another motion, or approaches the theoretical perfect, or, for that matter, is rational or workable; rather its perfection is a factor of its "goodness." That is to say, not because it is perfect, but because it is perfect*ing* what it is. Sport does *just* this. It allows for the *process* of betterment.

It therefore is understood that *being* must relate to *existence* if man is to achieve the unity of life he desires in sport. The importance of *skill* levels is herewith inherently indicated. Specifically, the surfer comes closer to unity of self and nature when he increases his ability and knowledge. He is not perfecting sport as much as the self, but the latter is not achievable without the former. The attainment of high skill proficiency in no way guarantees even the slightest awareness of perfection of the whole. Existence, of the surfer, must be captured so that being can be significantly determined.

The surfer, in some way, must be convinced of the value of being. Being and sport need to be perceived as important *in its own right.* Otherwise sport will become destroyed as an *instrument* for man to *use* in the attainment of other qualities. This simply is not what is called for in the perfection of existence. There is *good* in the sport, as it is, and meaning of one's personal existence is achievable through authentic concern with the activity. In this case, surfing is; it is truly a vehicle for transcendence. But the *summum bonum* is not the perfection of surfing, it is the perfect*ing* of surfing. There is a truth of man's being which is essential and not the value of surfing. This perfection is an expression of being. This in turn gives significant meaning to the performer's existence.

A Production of Work and Play

Sport, as is, exists! At first, this statement might appear to be superfluous. One might ask, why even state this rather self-evident truth, much less exclaim it? The answer lies in the fact that sport has so commonly been viewed as a medium, a tool, a way of life and a cultural expression that it is often forgotten that sport itself exists *as itself*. It maintains a being as that what it is. To recognize it as intimately related to the existence of man is not to refute this premise as much as to recognize the total nature of sport. Secondly, this is not to infer that the existence of sport cannot clarify other aspects of life and as such be "employed" as a universal element. Certainly, in specific instances this might well be most appropriate. But this is a long way from indicating that sport is some magical algebraic symbol which has implications for all human experiences. In this way sport can be viewed as providing man with an opportunity to locate his own being. And in so doing takes on its own existence, a form that combines the familiar elements of play and production. In a sense it is voluntary and yet not really so. Great performances in sport are never made through externally compulsive techniques. To achieve desired goals in sport, demands are placed on man that require voluntary commitment to a world of strenuous discipline and movement. In this way, man, by taking part in a free act, comes to remember his freedom, a freedom his societal form of living has since caused him to negate.

In his "play" element, man involves himself in *un*productive ends, seeking no specific and direct result, except development of self. Turning a deaf ear, for the moment, to Freudian psychology, we can see that play is undertaken for reasons of pleasure. In a real sense the concept of sport, applicable to both amateur and professional, is one implicating man to "play for the fun of it." Again, this is not to deny the obvious, that many forms of remuneration are extended. Yet it is hard to believe that one can be "successful" in sport if he does not "enjoy" his involvement. Any "product" to be associated with play is, at best, tangential to the motive.

On the other hand, if one looks at sport as "work" (as we know it in our culture), it becomes production centered. The individual who works at sport is interested in creating some form of reality, whether it be material, abstract, and/or appealing to the senses. In both work and play *creative* production can be facilitated when man achieves independence from the immediate. The trick is to learn what one can *realistically* achieve and in so doing each participant in sport becomes an *answer* to life rather than looking to sport to provide the answer to man.

Sport combines the elements of work and play. It is at once production and non-production oriented. Like play it is oriented to the activity itself; however, similar to work, its *meaning* extends beyond the activity. The game that is played may well be *completed* but it is not *finished*.

Within the framework of sport is a call for *order*. This is one of the aspects that allows all sportsmen—be they beginner or Olympian—the ability to achieve. The athletic *drive* is one of desire to improve one's own performance through the magnificence and *pleasure* of movement. And in so doing man pushes beyond the present barriers. Activity, as such, proceeds according to rule, without which there could be no sport. "The explanation . . . lies in the instinctive response of the mass of people to the rule of fair play without which games would degenerate into tribal warfare" (Umminger, 1963, p. 259). Man might well decide to play without a given rationale. He might attempt to avoid arbitrary rules and not direct himself toward a *productive* end. But this is most improbable. For sport incorporates elements of play and as such becomes a *total activity.** The play activity, as it is developed in sport, takes on an element of necessity and order. Sport is serious. From the hunter to the tobogganer, from the hockey player to the figure skater, and from the skeet shooter to the golfer, the participant "engages" play toward a directed product. The commitment enriches the performer's participation, for again it is a voluntary activity. But as such it demands great devotion, as if it were indeed a compulsory act. It should be of little surprise in a

* For further discussion on games and play the reader is directed to: Jan Huizinga's *Homo Ludens* and Roger Caillois' *Man, Play and Games.*

material, mechanized and technological culture that sport takes on an appearance of our production-oriented society.* It is a reflection of a "having" and "becoming" populous. A premium is offered to the man of aggression, of force and of stay-to-it powers. Sport is not a world for the loving and tender.

In this relationship, it is interesting to note that the "inner" man reacts differently to play than he does to sport. Sport, perhaps because of the product-end phenomena, tends to "harden" man. He becomes divorced from his own humanity. Victory, glory, personal achievement, and sometimes money, become desired values. Almost always focused on "turning it out" and achieving, the man of sport has little time and/or emotional desire to stop and reflect on the innate values of sport. His time *is* spent in execution and production. Secondly, the product of sport tends to be less than authentic. It is shaped by external forces to man and in the final analysis *concerns* itself only superficially to man as a man. Its obligatory demands and freedom-negating regulations cause man to seek glory rather than internal consistency. Although John Steinbeck does not differentiate between sport and play, he no doubt senses this dimension of existence.

> I am particularly drawn to the game of rounders, which we call baseball. I would be wrong to call it a sport. I don't think the players have a sporting attitude toward it. Mostly they want to win because if they win they get more money. (Steinbeck, 1965, p. 100)

Baseball as it is played in America, from sandlots to the majors, as Steinbeck intimates, is truly not sport. But yet by common usage it is a sport. Perhaps the distinction is the lack of "spontaneity" of baseball, a quality that almost indicates there is little *play* in sport. It becomes an example of the unification necessary in a production-centered culture. (It appears that even congressional legislatures, involved with anti-monopoly legislation, cannot differentiate between a sport and a business.)

* See Renny C. Kwant's, *Phenomenology of Social Existence* for discussion of work and play as body orientation and as all encompassing social characteristics of man.

Sport yields self-esteem. It welds man to himself and to others. Its true mark rests in the ability for man to engage in the activity for *its own sake*. The opportunity for intrinsic value is present but the degree that the existence of man is opened to the self is highly suspect.

> Certainly no climber attacks a cliff like that in order to measure himself against it . . . to call this an experiment in self-trial is an arrogant denigration of what is in fact a healthy and honorable sentiment, and bears no relation to the silent inward appraisal to which a climber subjects himself and his actions. It is utterly false to suppose that self-trail is the motivation of climbers. Incorrigible complex-mongers invented the idea because they could think of nothing better for explaining away the unexplainable. (Harrer, 1960, p. 73)

The worth of sport is specific to the individual. But the opportunity is presented for man to explore what is. And this is sport. The opposition is there. Mountains are there. The bull is there. It is for this reason, their *existence*, that man confronts them and the existence of sport is presented to all.

Certainly any attempt to establish categorical differentiations between sport and play would be, at the very least, guilty of oversimplification. Man is never purely *homo faber*, *homo ludens* or *homo sapiens* (Jolivet, 1961, pp. 114–120). Sport, stimulated by play motivation, can be a funnel for joy. Like most forms of production, sport provides man with a pleasure principle—one that makes it all worth it. "It is hardly conceivable that any of those who made their way to the top . . . did so for the thrill of it" (Umminger, 1963, p. 295). The involvement required in sport does not allow the superficial to remain for long. It is not enough to participate for the "thrill of it." Most sports ask for a more authentic *motive* if not an act of participation. Through the involvement in sport man indeed does locate being of self as well as others. "The ordeal (mountain climbing) is of such a nature that a man is truly searched to the very kernel of his being" (Umminger, 1963, p. 296). The climber who is in *existenz* is able to "take in" the surroundings. He assembles his potentials and brings this all to actualization in the form of a magnificent set of movements in his assault on the summit. To a degree he plays, but the internalized sensations tell him that his *production*, like that of the gymnast, skier, figure skater, or most other performers, is one of the *sportsman*. He produces an idea of the external that at once reflects and is him. This form requires both play and work and is to a great extent the composite of sport.

On the other hand, the circus performer who like the man of sport attempts to perfect his skill, might well see his nightly *routine* as just work, compulsory and almost "unsporting." In his non-play realm, pleasure is a side factor. His satisfactions are not evaluated internally. They are measured by applause, glory and the size of his "billing." Indeed one has to wonder if baseball is a sport. Is the golf circuit a sport or a circus? Is the "big time" collegiate athlete a sportsman or a workman? A sport *is* what *man* makes it: yet *men* are frequently made *by* sport. Too many of our modern forms of sport might be lacking what play possesses—namely, a free and joyful existence. The *spirit* of sport has been replaced by the *product*. In the final analysis it is not that the spirit of amateurism in sport is a naive ideal but that the spirit, or lack of same, of sport is missing not only in the amateur but in all men of sport. Perhaps what is needed is the development of a *spirit of play* and not a *spirit of sport*. Indeed this was the symbolic nature of Babe Ruth. He was not only an outstanding athlete but one who enjoyed playing. In modern baseball Willie Mays is about the only athlete who symbolizes this quality of existence. "Play . . . involves contemplation . . . its grace, its harmony and its specific beauty" (Jolivet, 1961, p. 913). At the heart of the existence of sport is the warmth and joy of voluntary participation, in its real sense.

Freedom as a Function

The world has long witnessed man, in the name of freedom, commit massive injustices. Is not war between nations engaged in the name of freedom? Are not principles of destruction rationalized in the name of freedom? Under the guise of freedom massive breaches of rule and social contract have occurred.

On the surface, it appears that "freedom" in sport bears the same relationship as does freedom in cosmic concerns. However, because of the individual's voluntary involvement in the sport process, freedom assumes a rather unique perspective.

Freedom is a pivotal force by which man can comprehend the perspectives of sport. Initially, one might well argue that the rules and regulations of sport negate any serious discussion of freedom; however, freedom must be seen as a *function* of man's involvement and not as an *end* in itself. Freedom is *used* in sport; it is not protected. "For I . . . am a man, and, every man must find out his own way" (Sartre, 1956a, p. 85).

To be definitive, freedom can range from the negative "absence of constraint" (one does what he wishes), to the positive construction of "fulfillment of the nature of man by reason and morality" (relative to a hierarchy of powers) to, finally, the existential development of "free choice" (one acts without causation but with responsibility). Typically sport has been involved in one of the first two modes. Indeed it is unusual that man, in sport, should not be viewed as *what he makes himself to be.* The freedom to choose, so basic to the existential position, implicates man toward ultimate truth and despair; in that being free to choose, man needs to consider *what is to be chosen.* Obviously, this implies an infinite involvement in the "right" decision, an alternative that finite man could not consider. Thus, he makes choices without being completely free and without considering all the alternatives. An authentic man could do little but suffer with this type of responsibility. But the man of sport can absolve himself in the helter-skelter of sport.

Free choice, ontologically inspired, could conceivably result in no "sport." The participant's actions are so developed as *his* without regard to the structure of sport that it is easy to predict nihilistic normative structures, reducible to chaos. Man's individualism quickly turns to anarchy and sport becomes truly an arena of the absurd. This is not because rule is not adhered to, but rather because man has acted without authentic involvement in the perimeters of available choice. And yet practicality allows little else.

If the "nature" of sport so establishes choice of alternatives, man must submit, revolt or adjust to the system. However, no choice is so developed to protect or abdicate one's freedom; rather, it is a choice which *extends* man's use of freedom. The choice of man is one of *operational* significance and *theoretical* breadth.

Sport, to be sport, must afford man free will and in so doing not only allows, but encourages, freedom of choice. This freedom, to be conceived as absolute, does not infer anarchy; for freedom of choice is one of *conception* and not *execution* (Sartre, 1956a, p. 87). Freedom in sport is a necessity, not because of the ability to achieve desired *ends*, in terms of victory and defeat, but because of the *for-itself* autonomy. Man, and his sport, cannot be what he is unless man is free to choose the alternatives. In this choice, man's freedom, through self-revelation, opens and does not negate the freedom of others. It is interesting to note that sport generally does not free man by itself. Rather, man is *left alone*. The guide lines are present, the rules are established, but he is there in the vacuum of his existence to inquire and discover his own truth.

This implication of personal truth commits one to an aspect of reality. Within this complex world the performer is *limited* by real conditions. The responsibility of freedom is not really constricting, for without it things would not have form. Thus, even those who are most Zen-minded among us would admit to the use of a goal in basketball, with all its impending limitations on freedom. We might not *use* the goal in the same way, but without it *the* sport takes on a different appearance. The man of sport cannot theoretically speculate, he must act. His existence is tightly bound by the matrix of forces that bombard him. External factors greatly refute his "free act." But at the same time it is imperative to recognize that man *thinks*. He is not simply a resultant "wave" in the environmental ocean. His thought does not guarantee him independence of the forces of the ocean.

It is obvious that freedom in sport requires man to produce his own act. It is here we see a great potential for the contribution of sport. In its medium for "self-mastery" it *provides* and encourages exploration. This is more than superficial *spontaneity* (sometimes taken as synonymous with freedom); it implies more than "nature" as emphasis is placed on responsibility in the form of discipline. For sport, if it stresses one thing, stresses control of one's total self. Add to this element of *mastery* the quality of *determination* and one can see a profile of the man of sport. To choose is important. But to *be* the choice is a most impelling credo. My strong suspicions of organized athletic leagues for grade school children are partially based on this premise. Organized sport asks the child to master himself at an age when he might well be involved in a process of exploration requiring little determination but a great deal of *creation*. Taking the youngster and causing him to *become* a form of stimuli-reacting organism, of robotized will, is not my idea of sport for the youth of America.

The sports performer must be free to become *more of what he is* (not what he sees others to be). In a word, man is "not all he is." He is enough, yet not enough. He is never enough and thus he can never really be free.

Deny freedom and sport is denied any meaningful place in the realm of existence. "The meaning of life lies in the values which we can find in it, and values are the products of choice" (Kaplan, 1962, p. 105). Man is bound by nothing, save regulations, which really do not as much negate as they guide. Man attaches his own values to sport and in so doing achieves a personal identification in what might well be one of the most impersonal modes of life. The value is formed from a situational ethic that further implicates the personal realm. For example, professional football players soon learn that they don't take "cheap shots." Even the men of the "violent word" make a most reasonable choice; it may be legal but if it is not "right," don't hit. Man is free and is thus given the awesome responsibility of maintenance of the personal and self-discovered truths. Man is not even protected by the rules. His freedom has allowed him to reach a new height of existence, one based on awareness of the *realness* of the situation. Man involves himself in self-discovery, and takes a big step toward a meaningful actualization of the person.

As the sport event unfolds, each situation presents itself with a number of potential choices. The "successful" performer has the awareness necessary to place himself in a position where his skills could be best used. Choice is a function of awareness, performance *only* a concomitant of skill. The dynamics of sport are such that it is near impossible to refrain from choice. One might say it is within the "rules of the game." Limited to the prowess of the performer, man's potential is a condition of his choice. The "tighter" the rules, the more narrow is man's development. The greater the scope of freedom, the greater the opportunity for development, creativity and actualization. Thus, it appears that the performer is faced with Kierkegaard's *Either/or;* but not really, because his original choice of sport commits him to certain further choices. But in a sense it is not possible for him to be "choiceless." In assessment of the varying conditions man must study the alternative choices. Freedom is not infinite (although choice might well be). It is a product and a limit of the action situation. We can now view freedom as basic to the being of the performer. He develops through it and, in the process, sport develops because of it.

As we have seen, human behavior is not a permanent state. Freedom, itself, is a human reality; therefore, it is not so much a condition of existence as existence itself. In order for one to be a good performer one needs to be free. The participant must *really* feel free. If man allows another to take his freedom from him, then his performance will reveal man to be less than what he is. Since existence does precede essence, it follows that life is only what it is made of by the individual. Since man exists first, the performance is created by man as he "makes" *for-himself* what he makes himself to be! There is no universal essence to duplicate or "live up-to." All actions and values are found alone within *being*. "Man is condemned to be free and . . . to create . . . his course of action in accordance with the situation" (Mihalich, 1960, p. 40).

To be free to create one's style, movement or form does not afford one license. Freedom brings with it the immense concomitant realm of responsibility we have already discussed. Since the performer creates his world in keeping with other realities, the finished product is an indication of his awareness. The individual is always operating in the reality of the environment. In his choice and actions he must be cognizant of all of mankind. Just as there is no "correct" picture, there is no correct dive or shot. The performer is free but he cannot be arbitrary.

It is easy to see that the free man almost needs to suffer. In a society where man must perform to righted standards, the *initial* anxiety is reduced by the known, thus allowing for a pragmatic life if not one of meaning. Likewise the free performer also suffers from what might be called the *anguish of the enslaved.* In a way, his actions are the same as all others. But there is something else he *feels.* To express this feeling is not easy, for words tend to reduce the meaning to trite oratory. Yet he knows the feeling of restriction is in part committing his self to *non-being.* But how does he communicate this emotion? At least the dancer can move "it out." The athlete must play within the circumference of acceptable rules and form. The *anguish* becomes rooted in the awareness of each choice; but what is more tension producing is that each *action* involves a further reduction of self. Sport incorporates this action. When the performer ceases to act, he ceases to *be.* Yet when he acts, he becomes less of his *being*—a dilemma that is not easily resolved. How does he draw from his existence in the process of transcending the situation and the self? "... The motive, the act, and the end are all constituted in single upsurge ... and its upsurge the pure temporalizing nihilation of the in-itself which is one with freedom. It is the act which decides its ends and its motives, and the act is the expression of freedom" (Frankl, 1963, p. 87). Perhaps this is the best answer we can give. We can't have what we want but we can "settle" for honest action. To expect more than this from sport is to ignore reality. It is only too frequent that we are "acted upon." Thus "to act" is rewarding in itself.

As man participates he soon finds his level of involvement is one that mitigates against indifference, for this quality is quickly transformed to indecision. And if anything is a cornerstone of sport, it is the emphasis upon decision-making or choice.

To be free is the form of the existent. *Being-free-for* leads to essence. The sport situation not only allows man to be freed, but condemns him to freedom. The choice itself is not the basis of freedom of sport. Freedom is the "symbolic trophy" that represents fulfillment. *Being-free-for* affords true *existenz.* As the sportsman is open he is available to explore and discover, in an attempt to make gains for utilitarian ends.

Since theory is only true as measured by experience, reality transcends the situation and presents itself to man. And man remains ready and open to accept that which he is free to accept. On the other hand, the more the individual is "closed" to the potentials of the specific situation, the less the opportunity for reality. In this way we can see that sport goes beyond the individual and touches existence itself. "But to go beyond something is to have that something as your basis" (Frutos, 1957, p. 104). This is simply fundamental to sport. It goes beyond man, but it is man, in his singleness, who is the basis of sport. Perhaps the highest degree of freedom is that afforded man in sport when he is freed from himself. The skier coming down the mountain goes *beyond* his equipment, his ability and even the mountain itself. The needles of the wind and the cold-aliveness of the snow are all quickly before man. He must yield to the sport and transverse (no pun intended) to another world. It is a world of motion, delight and magnificence. As man is free he absorbs his being and goes beyond himself, as he enters the self! Sport provides man with a freedom *not instinctually* natural, but "his is a freedom in the midst of a nature which binds him to an obscure tendency which permeates his being" (Fink, 1960, p. 99).

A Realm of Anxiety

Modern man is quickly approaching the era when he will be capable of controlling the external world of physical and biological forces. He already has attained a higher standard of living than any of his ancestors. His application of science to modern systems of mechanization and technology have, to a great degree, been responsible for the comforts he enjoys and no doubt will continue to enjoy; however, somehow the *real* desires of man have escaped him. Deceived, as *a person*, man realizes he needs to turn into himself and gather the fibers that will allow him to endure. Today the hope that science will be the all powerful panacea has lost its appeal for many. The supposed stable order that was to be achieved by science is not so stable.

In our rapidly changing world with its shifts in population bringing about new moral codes as well as new methods for accomplishment, man is reaching out for a *personal* answer to some of his very personal questions. He no longer can listen to physical explanations on the one hand and mental explanations on the other. What is needed is a theory of human nature which would comprise the somatic as well as the mental aspects of man. No matter how theoretically valid is the fact that man is composed of such and such a chemical, the crucial question is always that the individual exists at the given moment in time and space, and the problem is how he is to become aware of that fact.

The plight of the man in sport has paralleled mankind in general. The use of science has made his activity reach heights toward perfection that were previously thought to be impossible. In face of this increased level of performance, because of modern scientific applications, his activity has become safer. Again, it appears we are on our way to solving all the dilemmas relative to human performance, except one, man himself.

Sport, through its very preoccupation with competition and combat, encourages man to *live with anxieties* as opposed to the psychiatric school advocating the "cure" of anxieties. It must be recognized that nothing exists as a priority to man. Man is nothing but virgin wax before he creates his history. But the wax *does* exist! To define man by his desires or needs might well be "useful," but it does assume the abstract when only the concrete is revealed. Man must be viewed as the *whole* that he is. Any attempt to reconstruct man on the basis of his "inclinations" has the ultimate effect of proliferating man. His most insignificant and superficial behavior must be considered as an integral part of his total expression. *All* of his actions are revealing. Sport reveals the anxious "shaping" of the wax.

As it is in most aspects of life, anxiety is present in sport. Rather than a negative force, anxiety can be seen to bring about basic satisfactions inherent in sport. Each time man "takes the field" he lives his life in performance. Each and every time, he faces the reality of *extinction*. He is constantly in a process of survival. Always protecting and defending that which he believes to be his "territory," the performer not only lives with anxiety, he embraces it. It allows him and, in fact, motivates him toward greater realization of his skill in the contest.

Anxiety should not be mistaken as a "defensive reaction" of the performer. It has been my observation that the athletes I have known use anxiety as a type of warning signal. It is almost as if man needed to cross the tracks but was not sure if the train was approaching. Seeing the "green" he plunges across. Once man starts to cross the tracks he is fine. But, oh, those prior moments of decision . . . "Butterflies" are there before the game, but rarely during. Sport involvement actually dissipates anxiety. Once the contest has started man escapes the immediate and anxiety is decreased. In a way, anxiety reveals to man his inner thoughts, as if man almost would divorce himself from his *being* provided he were so allowed. It seems that anxiety reappears whenever man is faced with living up to his potential (an almost constant factor in sport). It is not surprising that man comes to *recognize* anxiety most when he takes the "time-outs" of life. It is at this point that the inner relatedness is brought to the conscious. The athlete recognizes anxiety as highly *personal*. It will not leave man *alone* until he reveals his connection to the *future time* in a way that is ultimately authentic. In reality, the athlete's expression and reply is as much a reduction of anxiety as a lack of realization of all the compelling factors. "The threat of non-being cannot be eliminated. It belongs to existence itself" (Tillich, 1952, p. 39). Therefore, it follows that no healing can cure it.

Time, in the language of sport, is a paradox of the most specific and highly abstract. The expression of achievement in hours, minutes or seconds is indeed concrete; but on the other hand, it is almost imaginary in that time is best thought of as an opportunity to achieve ends. The future, with its endless freedom, is potentially menacing or ecstatic, depending on the design of *ends*. It is rather ironical to note that "times" in swimming and track events, to mention just two examples, are expressed not only in seconds but in tenths of seconds and there is presently consideration of hundredths of a second. One might assume when a man runs the mile in four minutes and one-tenth of a second, he has taken a little more than four minutes to run this distance. But the time measurement hides a dimension of the meaning of time to the performer. In reality the athlete, *during* the running of the race, needed one-tenth of a second more than four minutes to reach his goal. Time is now a *conceived future* with opportunity as opposed to a measured standard of the past. In a sense this is inconsistent with the *becoming* nature of sport. It would seem that man should not run a set distance in an attempt to better his time. Rather he should see how much ground he might "acquire" in four minutes. It would seem that this would be more in keeping with the realm of sport as we know it today. This would keep time static and space fluid. And thus man could further delude himself in thinking of his presence as *being-now*.

Anxiety, as a fundamental human emotion, facilitates the athlete's desire in his search for *being*. Its specific role, however, is related to an awareness of *non-being*. As an inner conflict between the performer's attempt to locate and separate *being from non-being* anxiety makes *available* to man his own true potential for life. In a real sense the threat of defeat, which man faces in each sport encounter (in the broad sense of singular non-success), produces a great deal of the anxiety. Since man comes to measure his potential by victory or defeat, it is not surprising that anxiety develops out of a symbolic representation of the awareness of a compelling potential for weakness. Since this form of anticipatory behavior is, by definition, of the future tense, we have an intensification of the situation. Man in sport lives not knowing the self; realizing the decision will *soon* afford concrete evidence, he *becomes tomorrow* oriented. When tomorrow finally reveals the decision, it is almost anticlimactic, for man is already focused on new tomorrows. It is during the "lulls" that the performer *realizes* his anxiety and perhaps even expresses it as being present. The participant, conscious of the eventual threat of defeat which he identifies with non-being, proceeds to an elevation of anxiety levels. In a way he is always conscious of his impending death (Beck, 1958, pp. 451–470).

The athlete's anxiety is, typically, all encompassing. Anxiety says to the performer, "Succeed or nothing is left to you but hopelessness." One can play the game over and over again—in his head, after the contest is completed—but to no avail. The time to play is during the game. Of course, this brings to mind that the anxiety found as an integral part of sport is most often *apparent* as opposed to *actual*. It is not a pathologic condition as much as a recognition of the *lack* of meaning in *this* aspect of my existence. This form of "existential anxiety" can be viewed not only in the performer, but in all participants in sport. It has always been my contention that it is this element of anxiety that is falsely manufactured by coaches to give them a *reason* to win. In a sense, it affords meaning to what may well be a meaningless activity. I can hear the roar now. "Reason to win! I don't need a reason. Lose and I am out of a job." Of course, this in itself is an unusual explanation: man wins to keep a job that demands of him to do something he *hints* is not the reason he is there! A rather confusing circle, to say the least. To be certain, there are many coaches on all levels who need to win to maintain their posts. A professional baseball manager or football coach would not be in the post too long if he cannot demonstrate he has the winning way. With these individuals, personal threat is most real and therefore anxiety is real. However, this group is in the distinct minority. Even at the collegiate levels, *most* coaches do not need to win to keep their positions. Again, depending on the institution, the specifics are quite varied. But there are not too many fencing coaches or wrestling mentors that *must* win to keep their jobs, their own pride, yes, but not their jobs. Most of these individuals initiate their own pressure. They even tell themselves "the pressure is on" so often that they develop some until it *really* is there. Certainly "people" would like victory; however, in truth, the alumni, the president, the faculty, and the student-body couldn't care less. Who cares if the collegiate golf teams win or not. The coaches *do* care. They want to be part of the big time. They start recruiting when no one demands it. They adopt tactics and organizational features that indicate their importance. They seek schedules that will place them under the big tent. Most often these pressures are *self-imposed.* Man is not satisfied with his "lot" and so he seeks to be more than he is. What better place for immediate results than the world of sport. Anxiety develops from a need for ego-fulfillment and self-realization. It does not come from the situation *as it is.* What is apparently pathological anxiety, brought about by the circumstances of life, is more often an expression of self-imposed neurotic behaviors. A behavior drummed-up out of feelings of inadequacies centered in non-being (defeat in *life*), but internally and in reality a feeling of the fear of *being*, a fear to be what one is. This is indeed the stem of existential anxiety. It continues to revolve around the delicate balance of being and non-being. Both neurotic and existential anxiety are related but the differences are worlds apart. It is the same difference which exists between authenticity and unauthenticity. The coach, operating under what is *now* neurotic anxiety levels, places himself under bitter harassment from within the self. He is now *condemned* to this life and feels the *closeness* of constriction. In a way he stands before himself, as both judge and defendant. The anxiety, brought about through non-realistic happenings, now takes over. Man cannot get away from himself. Thus, we have the classic form of depression brought about through estrangement of the self. Now man has not only lost meaning, he has lost self. Anxiety takes over as non-being is rampant and seizes man's existence. Man can now feel the marked displeasure of his own self. The feeling is vague and appears to have no form, but it *is* there. It is rather ironic that man should reach this most *personal* stage of life, in which anxiety is most definite, because at a previous time he was not capable of locating *his authentic person.*

Anxiety is most reflective of *real* personhood. It is an integral part of each and every *being*. In Kierkegaard's words it comes *through* the self as well as *about* the self, a distinction that is most significant.

Anxiety and the Ego. So much of sport is focused on the self-affirmation that it is no wonder that coaching is not as much ego fulfillment as it is egocentric. The *will* is nearly destroyed and so is basic humanity. All individuals involved in the sports world must somehow recognize the integrating function of the media. To deny man's ego beyond the body is to assume nihilism. We all need to adjust the ego boundaries so that *man* is the center. "Ego feeling first creates the ego by encompassing all experience and experience traces" (Federn, 1952, p. 291). Upon reflection and a continuation of purposeful thought a normative system might well develop that is uniquely comprehensive of anxiety. The armor, worn to protect the man of sport, must be constructed so that its permeability affords meaningful achievement.

This form of "openness" will bring about a common identity of desires. The pronouncement will be localized in the violence of each performer's existence. The creative will transplant the rigid, thus affording a unification of purpose and means. Both the coach and the player can be true to "demands" as well as to the self. Thus, not only is there personal satisfaction in participation, regardless of the level, but there is also the realistic opportunity for the achievement of human existence. Anxiety is now replaced by a kind of "joyful tension." When man comes to this point of awareness, it is perhaps the best evidence that he has attained a realistic expression of his *being*. Man has attained a realistic expression of his *being*. Man is accountable for everything. No wonder sport provides for "anxious times." Everything is in the process of being affirmed. There is no way to escape it. It happens in front of all in a most concrete manner. Self and time are merged in the reality of the sport event.

The development and expansion of the ego must overcome "security." In this way existence escapes *meaninglessness*. If man loses existence, he loses ego. Anxiety is now seen as deeper than the form associated with *non-being*. We are faced with the unending tunnelization of Sartre's *Nausea* (1949). The soma functions of sport are continued but now man has no normative criteria and an associated absence of meaning. Perhaps this is what is meant by utter "annihilation" (Fenichel, 1945).

The solution to this situation appears almost too simple. First, man needs to recognize the virtue of authenticity. Without this awareness of *the mover to his movements*, there can be no hope of attaining meaning. Secondly, there must be an appreciation of the place of sport in the development of humanity. The result of this development would be, I trust, a realization of the meaninglessness of the "scoreboard." The end would be a consideration to escape annihilation by employing *virtue*, a virtue of process and not end. In this way self-affirmation will be truly achievable. This will be accomplished not by an accumulation of points necessary to fortify a neurotic ego, but by achieving the summit of values with each individualized ego. This approach recognizes anxiety as an unavoidable aspect of human existence. But as long as man is free to choose, anxiety and resulting guilt is a necessity of man's life. But this is part of what it means to be human.

Critics of this approach might well counter by indicating how easy it is to "aim for the best." But how is this possible when the subjectivity of man's mind limits his perception of all that is real? The solution rests in a comprehension of man's *power*, namely his mind.

We all need to be sensitized to the far-reaching experiences of man. It is the human self that apprehends itself as it becomes aware of the environment. The "percepts" are realized and hopefully actualized. If the "charges" (a most unfortunate name for man, as he is controlled by another) are *to live* meaningfully, *as defined and confined*, it appears that a value structure is a necessity. In this way, the "essences" of *being* will complement one's inner existence. "So we have the identification of actual essence, power of being and self-affirmation" (Tillich, 1952, p. 38). The experiences of all sportsmen must encompass the expansion of *thought* that incorporates the depth of life. The greater the quality of the ego and the more it is expanded, the greater does one live.

Nietzsche's *Will to Power* is a statement of the indication of self-realization. Anxiety is not necessarily a concomitant of aggression; it is the individual affirming his existence potentialities. "Man's task is simple: He should cease letting *his existence* be a thoughtless accident" (Kaufmann, 1963, pp. 372–373). The sport performer knows only too well that he must turn anxiety into his *being*. While the ego is a reflection of the outside world, *being* is rooted in one's experience. A performer's sense of *being* is not his capacity to assess reality and to perform—it is rather his capacity to perceive himself as an individual in the world, so he knows himself as the being capable of specific movements. Finally we come to understand *nothingness*. We see "the other side of the coin." Without awareness of what man *is doing* in sport, defeat becomes unreal. But when defeat is brought to the conscious, existence takes on immediacy and the individual has a broader view for consideration of personal significance.

For the performer fear is certain and concrete, while suffering, like dread, is an abstract emotion derived from the feeling of nothingness. Most performers experience a genuine sense of fear within the sport encounter which is *definite*. The common understanding of fear is that it is an expression of "lacking." In a way, fear is a defeat already suffered for something that in actuality has not been experienced. Thus, what is really feared is not the actual, which is linked to future time, but the performer's *being*.

The athlete uncovers his immediate world by his affiliations with the objects and others involved in the sport situation. Meaning is attained *after* he *considers* the reality of the form, whether it be a dive, a figure on the ice or a kick-turn. It is up to the performer to find a *reason* for action, thereby relieving dread and increasing meaning.

Sport, initially viewed as pleasure-ridden, can be seen as a haven for anguish. For each man who is victorious, another loses. Frequently, the losses are more vital than the score might indicate.

Suffering is not easily described. Perhaps this is because it is not voluntarily achieved and/or reflected upon by man. It is normal that man reflects upon the *cause* of suffering but rarely the *process*. For the man of sport it is taken as part of the game. Something to be endured. It is almost in the classification of an "occupational hazard." The pain that is produced from suffering affords man a separation (Buytendijk, 1956b, pp. 282–297). It allows man to have an *achieved meaning* beyond himself. Yet knowing that fear, pain, anguish and suffering are part of sport, man voluntarily participates. Its all part of the game. And it can be justified by the achievement of the ends of sport, whatever they may be for the individual.

Prior to, during and after the actual event man is made to live with the intolerable. Once committed, by choice, he does not quit. All that can save him are the limits of the event. The round will end. The inning will soon be over. Time will run out. The tragedy of personal suffering is recognized as a part of life. Then why not sport? The inequity of the rules, the imminence of defeat and the collapse of expected conditions all will result in anguish. Yet, each has its place in the tragedy of existence. What is more tragic than the fate of a bull? Suffering is inflicted upon both nature and man, yet each with a reason affording meaning. Tragedy is true and in its truthfulness it rings of authenticity.

Of course the suffering that is integral to sport can be both relative and absolute. When meaning is achieved, suffering can be seen in a relative dimension. Unfortunately for too many individuals, the *why* of their participation is not brought to awareness and absolute suffering is the result, an end of meaninglessness.

As anguish develops, frustration is often conceived as an integral part of the "naturally" aggressive demands of sport. More often than not, this is not a result of the failure to achieve *pragmatic ends* of sport, but a dimension achieved through the frustration of a lack of *meaning* for the specific pursuit. Thus, when man misses the "head pin," he misses *everything*. His goal is restricted to the finite, and he has nothing beyond the "pin" with which he can associate "success." Yet with meaning established in a less pragmatic direction man can pursue an authentic life with actions that are implied to do *more* than knock down pins.

Of course, in a discussion of suffering, one cannot belittle the place of physical pain. If one were to accept modern psychological thought, physical pain could be conceived as a "cathartic price." This is the performer's ticket of admission to the arena of sublimation, masochism, sadism and other forms of "adjustments." To be sure, physical aches and pains are very much a part of sport. But the Freudian explanation is refuted because most of the experiences of sport do little more than depict the existence of man as an *open* entity. Physical pain unites the participant with himself. Through pain he learns to attach to the world. Pain obliterates the ego and man becomes, at once, more and less sensitive to the self. He can now reach out to the world as he never has before. It is almost as if he shares a secret with the pulse of mankind. He comes to know himself as never before. The outward projections are realistically turned inward, and man becomes aware of the inner self. And yet it is difficult fully to comprehend the whole. "Substantial unity becomes so difficult to understand that you can only call it a mystery" (Borne, 1957, p. 99).

Although not fully understanding all, man indeed does understand. Pain does not lead to absurdity but to meaning.

It is truly a catharsis; but more than a cleansing of emotion and spirit it leads toward meaning and reason for sport. The responsibility is typical of existence. The performer must authentically appropriate the self so that suffering can make man clean and available for meaning.

The performer, like others, is consistently faced with the dichotomous place of his existence. As he struggles with the conceptual complexities of the world, he is invaded by sport's most interesting demand that he be the meaning of his existence and at the same time be the object of same. Consciousness-unconsciousness, substance-abstraction and mind-body are but a few ways of presenting the problem. To find meaning in existence becomes the challenge and the reason for life.

The shot-putter engages in seeming endless sessions of "lifting" in typically claustrophobic pits called "weight rooms"; he sacrifices many pursuits of human pleasures from the dinner table to personal relations; and his constant spartan-like obedience to training rules prepare him for the desperate hour upon hour of actual practice. "Put," walk, retrieve, carry, sweat, grunt, lift, bend, force and put again. All of this, not for what, but for why? Why the investment in time, effort and direction? And secondly, how is he able to continue? No doubt part of the answer is centered in the meaning man achieves from events.

If "tossing the shot" is a meaningful structure, which it must be, then it cannot stem from non-meaningful events. It seems the athletic drive toward *this* meaning can be described in naturalistic terms.

> This assumption of a drive toward meaning corresponds to the assumption in psychoanalytic theory of the primary autonomy of ego functions, especially of the synthesizing ego functions. For "ego" is the name for this unifying drive toward meaning and the specific forms and outcomes of that drive. The ego's unity, ego-integration as such, is a unity of meaning. Its primary energies are its being. (Fingarette, 1963, pp. 26–27)

We can assume the shot-putter propelling sixteen pounds of steel is not expressing a concealed unconscious drive, devoid of meaning, but rather is attempting to restructure unorganized "patterns of meaning." The usual frame of the subterranean realm is hereby rejected. This act *is* its totality. It is its conscious. It is this *organization* of effort that is indicative of the performer's attempt to locate meaning. In his vigorous action he finds comfort in the extreme individualization of his effort. The structure, routines and organizations are his conscious pathways for determining a concept of self that has relevance and insight into *meaning*.

Frequently the "ego" of the performer is perceived as a stabilizing force between the id and superego. In a kind of human compromise it attempts to bring unity to the individual's seemingly unrelated drives. It appears the existence of the ego, in itself, means that balance has *previously* been achieved. Since we recognize no priorities to man, the ego of the shot-putter is indicative of his meaningful unification of the essence or substances with existence. In itself, the performer's actions are "ego-integrated" and therefore form a basis for unification of meaning. As exemplified by the shot-putter, the ego is a unification mechanism and synthesizer of all the "inner drives" of the individual and therefore allows external reality to be objectively determined, in this case, by feet and inches. This measurement however is not the *end* as much as the symbol of the efficient "summation" of potential and organization. The participant may now have reasonable integrity since he is the *agent* of the symbol and can thereby derive meaning.

It should be made clear that the tension and anxiety, previously discussed, and generally thought to be an "integral" part of the activity, may be conceived as fear of disunity. When the shot-putter suddenly becomes aware that there is a blade of grass near the "toe board," or that his trunks are not quite "right" or that he just can't get "loose," he might well be losing the *integrated* pattern that is so important to his *wholeness* of effort. It is this threat of disorganization, commonly released in tension symbols, that promises to draw man away from himself and his efforts. He becomes a barrier to his own freedom and thereby reduces the potential for meaning as well as production. "Ego and anxiety are the opposite faces of the same coin" (Fingarette, 1963, p. 79). To maintain open horizons the *intentional* structure must be abandoned and *total* reality must be comprehended.

When we can see that the performer's anxiety is more than a result of psychological pressures resulting from "future-time" orientation, we come closer to understanding the intentional experiences given as both object and subject. To coin a term we might call this occurrence a "metapsychological" phenomena. In this way anxiety is not something that requires what mental health experts would call *adjustments*, but a product of awareness necessary for the *flow* of performance. If man is unable to extinguish or maintain anxiety, as is needed, then the performance is threatened by disorganization of effort, resulting in a meaningless experience. This *appears* in the form of poor rhythm, timing, and balance. Translated into a state of existence, it is indicative of results that are not in keeping with *desired* meaning. Thus, anxiety becomes a direct sign for the presentation-to-the-world of the striving for meaning. To say that man *derives* meaning from the specific substance of the event is not valid. But at the same time actualization of the ego—and thus reduction of anxiety—can be suspected. To be is to act and to become is to be acted upon. It is rare when the man of sport desires to be acted upon.

Sport and Death

Typically, man views death as an external phenomenon. He sees it as something away from the self. It is the one thing that man cannot and has not *experienced*. He can experience pain; or he might be near death; and he even knows of some person who has died. But for him, *as a person*, death is one phenomenon he does not experience during his existence. It is not surprising therefore that death is normally viewed as not *immediately* imperative. It is real. We know it is present. But it is removed from man's realm for he only sees it as a spectator.

> When death appears in its true form as the lean and joyless reaper, one does not behold it without terror; but when, to mock men who imagine they can mock it, it comes upon the scene disguised, when only the spectator sees that this is death, this unknown figure which captivates all by his courtesy and causes all to exult in the wild abandonment of pleasure—then a profound horror seizes him. (Kierkegaard, 1944, p. 83)

Indeed, the presence of death keeps most men as viewers of the future. Knowing we will all die, *at some time*, man enters into life almost laughing at death, for it is not to be regarded as *specific*. Yet all his laughter and talk about death, plus his obvious avoidance, implies the importance of death.

In a way, sport flirts with death. We have already seen that sport encourages the *intensification* of actual experience in a real-unreal world. The drama of competition encompasses the extremes of joy and suffering, and rightfully "toys" with death much like a little girl would tease her big brother.

Most often sport provides man the opportunity for false bravado in the name of death. For all the ruggedness and fierceness of football, soccer and rugby, *real* death is much an accident and not really a transformation of the actual probabilities. The athlete may well think he is a noble warrior facing the perils of death, while in reality he is greatly protected from the ultimate. Thus, actual death is indeed accidental to sport. Certainly it is a realistic possibility for the baseball player to be mortally injured when "beaned." The basketball player can take a final vicious fall. And the skier may well meet his end on the slopes. Yet the thought of death is not a *reality* for most sport participants.

Notice what occurs immediately following a serious injury on the football field. After an initial, almost "I-hope-nobody-sees-me," look at a teammate or opponent the performers will turn away from the injured athlete. Their action almost indicates a kind of refusal to admit the obvious. Namely, that injury and death are *real*. Man faces death almost as a *nonentity*. He tries not to acknowledge the unpleasant, much less death. Man must face death as an individual. There is no one or thing that can share this with him. He is *finally* alone.

In the so-called death-centered sports, performers overtly talk about death only in the rarest of situations. They tend to act as if it does not exist. One should not mistake this for a lack of concern, for they are *all* aware of the *coming*. But death is treated as something that is there but not *recognized* as tangibly affecting their lives (overtly). It simply hounds them. It is in this area that one can see how much man refuses to face the truth of his own existence. Authentically to encompass death is beyond the grasp of personal reality. "Death is the impossibility of possibility" (Heidegger, 1929a, p. 19).

Prior to his tragic death, Donald Campbell, England's great speedboat racer, told reporters, "You boys will see me carried away in a box one of these days. That's what you're all really here for" (Scorecard, 1967, p. 7). Perhaps when the sportsman relates daily and directly to death he comes to recognize, with a little greater clarity, the almost inhuman desires of his fellow man. In a way, Campbell seemed aware of the certain desire for man to almost *wish and know* that nature cannot be continually thwarted. But when man is really *compelled* by the spirit of sport, life becomes a risk we all must take, for without the risk there is no *real living*. There is only *mere* existence. "There are things in life you must do . . . It's darned difficult to get inside yourself and find out why. All you know is that there is a fire burning inside" (Scorecard, 1967, p. 7). After reaching speeds of almost 320 mph, *Bluebird*, his boat, started tramping. Suddenly the end was there. Campbell lost to nature.

Indeed, Donald Campbell probably did not know why he remained in this sport. Many of us do not. Perhaps it *is* the uniqueness of the being of each sport. But one must wonder if like life, death brings a meaning to our existence, that is, in part, responsible for this uniqueness. And in so doing, man lives as if he is almost awaiting death. "All life is colored by the expectation of impending death" (Kaufmann, 1956, p. 87). It is really difficult to know. Is it not? Our intense efforts are to ignore this final departure; yet, we can't really escape from its prevailing presence in the world of sport. It becomes an *inclusive* segment of the total experience; and as such must be assimilated within the realm of realistic choices that are to be made. Its presence is both real and personal. Its significance lies in the "availability" to man, an availability that renders our efforts meaningless (Storer, 1966, p. 2).

Sport is to be lived, by the living and for the living. Death is the end of life and thus irreconcilable with sport. The athletic is his life; and he becomes little beyond his performance. In truth, the athlete lives constantly with the *thought* of death. However, like most men he knows not the *fact* of death; nor will he admit the *concept* of awareness. In such sports as boxing, auto racing, bobsledding, and speed-boating, man is constantly performing in the shadow of death. Performers in these areas are constantly arranging a rendezvous with the ultimate. More often than not, the desire to participate in "high-risk" sports gives man the attitude of "complete" living. The feeling of excitement is generated by what might be called an attempt to escape *death*, and not life as is more commonly thought. Man hides his anxiety about death through a process of actually testing the *object* of death. Death, in this way, is not a reality; rather, *fear* of death becomes the reality. By facing fear the performer is more often than not stimulated to new heights. In defeating fear he assumes he has defeated death. In truth, he has done little more than suppress and conceal the actual. His performance is enhanced and man sees himself as more than what he is. As Kaufmann indicates the expectation of impending death actually does enrich life.

Sport, unlike many other areas of human involvement, provides for increased satisfactions and wonder as the participation is repeated. In too many of man's habitual day-to-day activities life is little more than a "daily routine." Life almost appears to be commonplace if not a bore. It almost appears that the more years man lives (is endure a better word?), the closer he comes to merging the extremes of novelty and repetition.

When man faces death, he really faces life. Sport provides for a voluntary and regulated expression of this confrontation. Man tends to be most authentic when close to death. At this point there is no need to fake. The hunter must stop "playing at being a hunter," when he awaits the charge of a wild boar. Now the superficial and superfluous are not necessary. There is no one to impress. Now he faces the ultimate reality. Is man capable of passing the test? It is *real* ability that counts. It is rather paradoxical that man needs to escape the "real" world (which might not be so *real* after all) and enter into the artificial realm of sport in order to determine the authentic self. He now must admit real existence to the self, something he can usually manage to avoid. To this degree, the man of sport is closer to truth. He learns his potentiality. He realizes what, perhaps, he has already and always known—namely, who he is. He no longer needs or can fool himself. He faces the finality of life and in so doing sees the *Gestalt* of his existence. To the degree that he can be "objective," in what was and presently is a most subjective existence, man is forced to realize his own worth.

The sportsman faces life with one last moment. How does he use his freedom to mediate between the *worthy* life and mere living? Death is not faced as a "just" sentence to the evils of man's ways. Rather it is the result of one of many choices man has made. Apparent finality is little more than one truth in the life of men. Perhaps it is with value that sport presents this opportunity to achieve meaningful inner discussion—a process that might well yield a significant impact to personalized existence.

Facing death makes the man of sport available to an awareness of authentic existence. Performance, faced with such extreme stakes, will tend to represent authentic being. Putting it another way, man is rarely as moral as when he is facing death. Death tells man to "face up" to life. Meaning comes to the performer when he becomes aware of the end. The totality is taken into account.

No one is "short-changed." Sport now becomes real for man. "Authentic action is not a chaos, but an ordered pattern based upon the structure of human nature" (Wild, 1955, p. 240). The man of sport is not as acutely faced with this problem. In fact, he often enters sport to find escape from boredom. Each event, each day, is *new*. Tomorrow *is* another day. The event of today is never quite like the one of yesterday. And tomorrow's encounter will be still different. Each *meeting* on the field reveals the elements of nature and man as an experience that refuses to allow man the opportunity to become blasé. Death therefore is paradoxically present and not present. It *is* there but not of the conscious. In this light sport provides a realm to escape the boredom of years and the necessity of common tasks. Sport acts as a solvent, dissolving the constant experience, which can be truly repetitious and thus lead to boredom, by providing *cycles* of activities (Lamont, 1965, pp. 29–36). These full patterns, such as innings, seasons, rounds and periods provide both completeness and variety. Thus, looking at sport as an exciting venture, man can face each activity with a type of heroic encounter. Lose—well at least I played. Win—and I am the one who did the unexpected. I am the hero! With courage and fortitude man can face battle and still maintain the relative security guaranteed by the "controls" of the situation. If one can be frequently successful, then truth begins to leave the subjective. Man's efforts become regular and thereby expected. If success is extremely constant then, in a sense, man's efforts live on.

The Hero and Immortality. Death is always a reality. But sport provides man with "everlasting" life. It offers the common man *immortality.* The great performance is remembered and man's name becomes a part of all the stages of time. The performance on the high school football team keeps man alive. It places him in *retrospect* to the unfolding history of time. In a sense he attains immorality because of his identification as a "football player." But in another way his *performance* is what lives, not the performer. In some small, but significant way, each participant is related to the unfolding history of sport and life.

For example, in talking of one of golf's greatest upsets, Jack Fleck defeating Ben Hogan in the United States Open Championship of 1955, Jim Murray the perceptive sports columnist of the *Los Angeles Times* more than hinted at the "unforgiveables" in life.

> The public doesn't forgive guys who beat Jack Dempsey, break Ruth's record, replace Stan Musial in right field. People who thwart romance dispel myths, flout legend, get to go stand on a corner the rest of their lives. To paraphrase a British earl, not losing to Ben Hogan is a kind of agnosticism that has no place in a decent society. (Murray, 1966, III, p. 1)

Indeed, man does not enjoy facing death. To maintain immortality in the sporting hero is one way for each of use to keep our association with the far-reaching past. In this way, we each stay alive a little longer and our life is also that much richer.

Perceiving the sport performer in this manner brings to attention the image of the daring and the brave. To this degree all performers possess a quality of heroism. Certainly this is most obvious in sport folklore. Gipp, Grange, Thorpe, DiMaggio, Mikan, Cousy, Richard, Owens, Bannister, Palmer and Dempsey are only a few of the numerous examples of performers personifying heroic stature. The legend of sport is the legend of heroes. But let this not be misleading. That is to say, it is not that sport is founded in the image of the "Saturday Hero," as much as man looks to sport for heroic realization. It is the rare youngster who, in his fantasy, did not hit the 3-2 pitch "out of the park" to win the world series.

No matter if the hero be romantic or realistic, the performer in sport is forever mindful of the *individual.* Through *one* stroke of the bat, one last-minute shot from half-court, or one desperate lunge for the over-thrown pass, each man *can* be a hero. The fact that this is rarely achieved only increases the perception of glory.

The reader could well be skeptical. Certainly man doesn't really expect to be the "one in a million." Does man play golf on weekends so he can be the hero? Do youngsters play on the sandlots because of heroic desires? The immediate answer must be a resounding no. But I say, yes! I don't pretend to know the motivation of man. But I do *feel* that the chance for the "hole-in-one" keeps many a man returning to the golf course. And it is not the rare youngster who constantly daydreams, while playing the outfield, of his opportunity to make the leaping catch against the outfield wall. *To a degree,* man seeks the spectacular. Sport provides for the rational possibility.

The quality of existence is not foreign to analysis of the sport hero. The performer of heroic magnitude is theoretically self-directed. Yet the obvious paradox is present. Namely, man enters sport via externalized stimuli and proceeds to internally discipline himself toward heroic ends.

Because of the "tomorrow is another game" doctrine, sport gives man an opportunity to be a hero each and every time he participates. It is important to note that this explanation admits no qualities to man. He *is* neither a hero nor a coward. He is what he is. Each and every sporting phenomenon gives him the opportunity *to be* a hero.

> Man is free. This means he cannot be a coward in the same way, for instance, that a table is a table. He may be a coward on some particular occasion, but every new occasion that presents itself offers him a completely clean sheet, to be a coward again, or to be a hero. Observe . . . the phrase "be a coward *again*" rather than "continue to be a coward." He may have acted like a coward on *every* occasion, yet it is still not true to say he *is* a coward. He is free . . . for in his essence he has no qualities. . . . he just is. (Wilson, 1959, p. 110)

Thus, man's involvement *characteristic* is a function of choice. Each and every decision points to his existence and not his essence.

The *immortals* in sport are legends known to most men. Joe McCarthy, Amos Stagg, Nat Holman, Dean Cromwell, Knute Rockne, Babe Ruth, Ty Cobb, Lou Gehrig and Florence Chadwick are only a few of the many who will always be linked to the past. In each case they are *symbolic* of a sport feat which in some significant way their performance stretched beyond the bounds of the ego. These are individuals who have actualized, fulfilled, affirmed and lived up to the maximum potential. Their bodies have passed on or will pass on, but their self (*being*) will continue to live. The ego immortalizes the *concept* of man, if not man. The Owens, Cousys, Gibsons, Hudsons and Rudolphs will continue *to be*.

Since man knows of death, it is with great courage that he accomplishes more than mere survival. Not many baseball fans will forget the final speech of Lou Gehrig, a man knowledgeable of his immediately impending end. In his last dark moments he maintained the courage that was indicative of the quality the immortalized all that he represented. The "Iron Man" is gone but his being is ever with us. He affirmed the pinnacle of selfhood, much beyond skill as an athlete. He remains, as he was, a deathless spirit.

Death is non-relative. But its potential, as a reminder of *life*, is all the more significant. To say life can again be duplicated by the same mortal is beyond the scope of this analysis. But to recognize for each of us that there is the *hope*, in sport, no matter how average our ability that perhaps, just perhaps, someday we might make *that* leaping catch, or bowl that 300 game. In some little way we might have an association with both the past and the future. In a way, this softens our responsibility toward that end which we know will come to us, as it does to all.

Death terminates existence. But somehow it is part of the game. Tragic? Yes. But only for the moment. It is an element of integration. Certainly the tragedy is registered on the individual, close relations and friends. Even those who are not known personally are shocked. The *deaths of immortals* (a rather unusual phrase) such as Thorpe, Gehrig, and Ruth grieve us all. But this is what it means, in part, to attain a meaningful existence. The despair of the actual end for each of these individuals gets transformed into the lives of the living. Even when death is not caused *in* sport, and is a "relief" from painful illness, the *end* is tragic. All that is left is solitude. If it does occur *in* sport the feeling is perhaps even more distasteful. In a sense we ask, "Was it really necessary? Did he really have to take this chance?" Of course this attitude is one that recognizes the "make-believe" quality of sport and the real quality of life, as if man can separate his necessity from his need.

The element of death stands in man's path as a barrier for actualization. Not only is the performer cognizant of advancing age, which in itself is related to the approach of death as a deterrent of his *being*, but he must face the possibility of each performance being his final *appearance*. What sport does for man is bring this awareness closer. The "death sentence" makes man aware of his wholeness in that as long as the awareness of death is present, man is *not* whole. It is a rather unusual turn that projects the performer into his own recognition of what he does not possess. It is only when man takes time, a feature not often afforded to the man of sport, that he can *really* consider his total existence. When man finally encompasses death, he is then said to have *ceased life*. Once man is aware of his death he can understand the self in a way that sport typically does not encourage. It is almost sublime that man thinks of sport participation as the cultural avenue where he faces death and stares it in the face, when in truth it is sport that negates his view of death in any meaningful way. To bring death to an awareness is to pursue the authentic life.

Death is uniquely personal. Perhaps this is another reason why it honestly is not faced in sport. Namely, sport does not lend itself to sensitivity of *the personal*. The emphasis is placed on the impersonal, the collective, and man's ability to demonstrate his skills on and to the mass. Always seeking fulfillment and perfection man realizes that the very concept of death is a direct contradiction to the process man must undergo to really be *of sport*.

The indefiniteness of the *time* of death leads the sportsman into the pain of this inevitable conflict. The dynamics of sport allow man to "lose" himself and to forget his personhood; but at the same time he loses the sensitivity that is essential to the development of the impending crisis—the crisis of non-awareness. In this light, we see that the recognition of death becomes a personal responsibility. Man must appraise his personal world and decide if sport is going to be *used* to hide the inevitable or if it will be a mecca for the attainment of actualization. To run away is not to escape but to delay.

> If, therefore, the ordinary man reacts to the thought of death with numbing fright, it is not because the consciousness of death is intrinsically paralyzing, but because the ordinary man resists the consciousness of death, flees from it, in order to protect the mundane values which he has not the courage to abandon even though the consciousness of death has revealed their pettiness to him. The courageous man, on the contrary, will embrace the consciousness of death as an agent of liberation. He will not flee from it nor from the anguish which accompanies it because he knows that it is absurd for a finite being to expect fulfillment and well-being as traditionally conceived and because he is aware of the values which the consciousness of death carries with it. (Olson, 1962, p. 72)

Death is a human experience. To avoid its realization, by participating with vigor in sport, is to avoid the former and misuse the latter.

Death provides man with a viewpoint for sport. It asks man to accept death as a *real happening*, and to develop the necessary abilities to thwart death. But typically this just does not happen. Man naturally wishes to escape death and thereby develops his skills with extreme precision. But in the forestalling of death, through competency, the process of means and ends are reversed. In man's refusal to approach death, and take it into his existence, his high degree of skill reflects not his ability as much as his refusal to encounter the primary concern. Running in a frenzied effort for greater development in sport, he hopes he can shut out the reality of finitude. But he cannot. The anxiety increases and, as with any doubt, leaves little room for authentic living. All the trophies, medals and recognitions provide increased layers of "glare," not allowing man to focus or, for that matter, see the reality of life.

It is easy to see that man usually participates in sport in an unauthentic manner, hiding from his person the thoughts that are most related to him. Therefore, it is not surprising, if man lives and plays unauthentically, that he should die unauthentically. Always running from reality, attempting to avoid the final confrontation, man never allows for affirmation of his own existence. "To die authentically is to live in such a way that death is constantly anticipated in one's projects" (Heidegger, 1949, p. 188). The sport performer must see beyond the immediate. To think the game *is* life speaks most sadly for life. Man will not be afforded the opportunity to have a substitute take his place in the final game. He must be there at the end *himself.*

Then why play each game from the bench? Why, in the avoidance of death, do we allow ourselves to "get" less from sport than we easily could achieve? What is needed is man's honest insistence upon the responsibility for his own life. By becoming aware of death, he unites himself to his parts and to the elements of time (history as well as tempo); he comes closer to making both sport and life personal.

Since we cannot avoid death, it seems reasonable that it be brought into the consciousness. In sport man *can* (it is within his potential of *being*) become aware of the authentic life. I don't think it takes a restructuring of sport as much as it requires a new orientation to conflict. To say it takes concern, courage and awareness is to state the minimal. To speak of its importance in the development of humanity is to state the obvious.

To recognize death as a part of sport is to admit it is part of life. This is hardly enlightening. But what is crucial is man's appreciation of death and his perception of the *awareness* of death as a sign that one is capable of freeing the self for meaningful pursuits. Each defeat that is suffered in sport, and what is more important, the recognition of the potential for defeat, gives man the opportunity to achieve *meaning* for all of life. As he embraces defeat, as he must death, he learns, indeed, the structure of life. It is a shame that many "play" at sport for many a year and never come to this anticipation. But then there are many more that "play" at life and, too, never recognize their own self until the game is all but over. To say that sport is a reflection of life is, perhaps, not admitting the whole story. But then maybe the whole story is not known, that is until man knows the end. It is odd, but maybe not *that* odd, that the *recognition* of death itself provides the man of sport with *life.*

POSTSCRIPT

THROUGHOUT this book I maintained my belief in the dignity of man. It was my contention that both the individual and sport existed. Both could be experienced. Sport began and ended with man. *Being* was not at the center of sport but rather it was deduced from sport by man. Through this process sport and man could be viewed within a relational context.

Sport was intimate, profound and even spiritual. It reached the root of human existence and, as such, provided an arena for the discovery of personal truths. Neither man alone, nor sport alone provided the completeness of existence. Sport and man revealed to each other the opportunity of determining meaning. In this way, once again, man located a realm of value formation. It was *a* source of worth and meaning.

I have little doubt that far too many participants in sport did not question the meaning of their involvement within the sport experience. One came to accept his environment in the best of the stoic tradition. However, my personal experience, with extremely well-skilled athletes, specifically in football and track, indicated a perpetuality of concerns that were most relevant to their existence. In fact, it had been my impression, in athletics, that strongly self-imposed forms of dogma were often used to contain the encroachment of existential doubts. Why did I run? What was the meaning of my participation in sport? These questions, and others like them, have plagued many a performer. Sport was real. Abstractions have little place in the world of action. It was not infrequent that the former was superimposed on the latter. In this way thought was repressed and man came to learn of the pragmatic advances of his efforts. He replaced *meaning* with achievement. If one tried "hard enough," he could even come to the point of unification of thought and action.

Historically, sport has appealed to man. Meaning, however, was another matter, as it was not an automatic element given to us by the Gods or clever little men of science. It was a part of our existence but, without concern and awareness, the potential could return to us in as much dross as gold. "The world appears to man so that it may acquire a voice to speak of the meaning of the existent" (Van Peurson, 1959, p. 35). For modern man sport *can* assume many roles—some perhaps analogous to religion, art and music. Namely, it can be an arena for the location of a *meaningful existence* rather than a hell of conquest and survival.

Traditionally, philosophy has been concerned with the problem of essence and existence. The relationship of sport to this dilemma has been presented if not emphasized. Sport was, in existence, both subject and object. Man was not inanimate. Nor was he a statistic within an impersonal world of control and experimental groups. He was a dynamically affirming being. He was in the process of reaching out in order to direct his own destiny. Each and every experience in sport provided man with an encounter causing him to make a choice. But the magnificence of sport was in the process—for man never did *attain* as much as he was *within* the act. He was *homo viator*—never at the goal, but always on his way toward "becoming what he is." His decisions, within the process, link man's essence to his authentic existence. Not only did man possess his existence, but he was acutely aware that he existed. Within very broad limitations he was free to determine the direction of his existence. The mastery of force, space, time and matter compose the *essence* of his reality but meaningful being was achieved through endeavors to discover personal existence.

The importance of dualism, in its multiple aspects, formed another thread in this book. The emphasis of the body in sport was quite evident. But certainly man cannot deny his mind and spirit. But neither can man escape the "other" as part of his totality. Whether the "other" was a thing or object, to be used for instrumental purposes, or was to be accorded status of *personhood* as an integral aspect of sport, was a dilemma of human existence.

Man no longer found his world as one of an unchanging intermediary environment. Frequently he accommodated himself to the situations of life as he located them. Sport afforded opportunity for alteration of position in the *immediate* world. Here man can harbor emotions within a relatively short-lived experience. The attitude of "it is only a game" was indicative of the "passing" dimension of sport. The *real* world was somehow separated from the realm of sport. Yet, in spite of this attitude, true existence transcended all realms of life and sport was a very real thing.

Involve oneself in sport and one was involved in a critical reflection of life. Sport confronted man with challenge and, at times, threat. These simultaneously provided for self-realization and achievement. Whether the act involved a fisherman's apparently endless fight with his catch or the baserunner's daring in stealing a base, *being* was the *risk*. To what degree did sport assist or detract in this process? Was irresponsibility encouraged? And was man to achieve the discovery of his own worth? These were but a few of the questions that were basic to the *concept* of sport. Sport accented the individual's attention on basically self-engineered concerns. Sport *was* and *mirrored* the venture, as both a sublime and realistic form of human ambivalence, revealed within a *very* human predicament.

"It's not a matter of life or death. It's a little more important than that" (Hall, 1966, III, p. 3). Red Sanders, the late and great football mentor, was not referring to war, peace or even love. What could be so important? Naturally, a sport contest. The USC–UCLA football game, that is what. To some a football game could be slightly more than life or death. Yes! It is both sublime and real.

While most people certainly would not entertain this form of literal extremism, most have to admit the cultural import of sport on the American scene is socially, economically, politically and culturally significant. The objective evidence is present. Tremendous sums of money are spent each year for sport equipment, admissions, and instruction. Special sections are set aside for sport coverage in most newspapers. A ticket to the Rose Bowl, Super Bowl, Army-Navy Game, or the World Series is a sign of social status. Increasing numbers are both participating and spectating at varied sport events.

Yet, with all of this expressed interest sport remains a mystery. A frequent subject for popular writing, sport has undergone relatively limited serious literary inquiry. The need for this form of analysis is all but obvious. It is hoped this attempt, in some small way, will encourage others in this area, eventually leading to a comprehensible theory of modern sport.

Sport cannot be completely understood from a rational foundation. Sport is violent. It is full of emotion, excitement and irrationality. If anything it is highly non-logical (which is not to say it is illogical). To attempt to comprehend the world of sport through a nice pat system of psychological variables based on basic drives and needs is to suggest a prior commitment that might not be valid. Nor can one assume a moral or educational basis for sport. To attach any absolute structure to the world of sport is to deny limitations to its known reality. This is especially true, then, if a system of scientific truths is used to demonstrate the presence of sport in our culture.

This is not to deny our present knowledge of instincts, impulses, and the complete realm of modern psychology. What is needed is to explain in some way the highly *personalized* experience of sport, a "way" that is, perhaps, *beyond* the impersonalized forms of known psychological theory. After all it is the scientist who insists upon neutrality. Yet, in sport man simply cannot be neutral.

The scholar of sport needs to be vitally concerned with the same areas of human existence which concern all mankind. Namely, how does freedom of the will really affect the sport participant? Are elements such as faith, doubt, relationship, choice and love an integral part of the decision-making process in the realm of sport? What does it mean to be *re*sponsive, and to be *re*spectful of the man of sport? Is there such a question as morality of sport (even the casual reader is aware of the almost neurotic lip-service that is given to sportsmanship)? Does sport place a premium on the rights and wrongs of human action? Certainly we all, *rationally* and *objectively*, know that one does not cheat in sport. We all *know* "it is not whether you win or lose, but how you play the game" that counts. Or do we?

We live in a world where reason has been traditionally thought to be supreme. The world of sport does not place its "bouquet of flowers" in the lap of *Athena*. Combine the emphasis of the subjective with that of the physical, in a world that pays homage to the mind, and one can well understand the lack of sincere scholarship related to sport.

If anything, sport is *not* ethical in the traditional manner of thinking. At best ethics are *situational* and private. Man plays the game according to a code of "common acceptance" and only the naive and/or ideal would even consider the transfer of Christian Ethic. Like theology, sport interprets commonly accepted "knowns" of the social order. Sport needs to develop a system that is not haphazard. A system of life, if one will, that places man and his responsibility in the foreground. This requires acceptable postulations and theory based upon *what is* and not what *should* or *ought* to be. As soon as the *absolute* is introduced, sport loses its very importance; namely, the relativity of structure.

In this way sport becomes truly *ethical*. The man of sport can now be perceived as one who operates within a world of free choice. *He* is truly responsible for his actions. "Holding" in football, a "near touch" of second base on a double play, the moving of the ball from the rough to the fairway, all are not actions to be prevented, they are simply *happenings*. Thus, a value structure cannot be founded on reason. Rather we must use intuition and feeling, the subjective vehicles of morality. Perhaps this was the motivation that prompted Kierkegaard when he demanded a "leap into the unknown." The man of sport is in an excellent position to attain this level of morality. He is in an avenue of life which accepts the emotional. He must stop relying on the heaven of reason and seek a reality that is based on "inner feelings." To objectify these thoughts, or demand "proof" of same, is to miss the point. Man cannot objectify his life. To accept this form of activity is to require scientific evidence for a non-scientific entity.

The system of analysis that was employed in this book attempted to reject complete reliance on absolute empiricism. In its place I tried to determine how man, in his existence, could locate an authentic being in sport. Sport was perceived in its present form. The perspective is modern, not in the attempt to negate the rightful place of history, but rather to focus on the world of sport as it now exists. The ultimate conclusion, hopefully, will result in a *way of life* that *is* lived.

Sport provides for extensive forms of *experiential* living. Situations are volatile and dynamic. Action is exciting and complete with the necessity for instant decision. At times the consequence of a "wrong" decision can be rather tragic. But then so is *life* filled with the potential for tragedy. Sport must be considered from the realm of man. It is in man that sport is actually perceived and experienced. To start with thoughts that are only speculations is to take time and effort from the real and immediate problems of man. Thus, the constant necessity to relate to *experiences* of the man of sport formed the background of this work. For the man of sport, like so many of us, that which is personally perceived is that which is real. Therefore, the concern was with the *reality* of sport. The book is useless if *just* read; it needs to be taken within the self and *experienced*. To stand away from the presented thoughts is simply not *sport;* nor is it a quality of *existence* for the real *man*!

In the consideration of sport, one could hardly begin the analysis without a clear understanding of the differentiation between essence and existence. Traditionally, sport, as most areas of human inquiry, has centered on the ideology of the nature of things. But, perhaps, to a greater degree than commonly understood, sport has revolved around the personal and the concrete. To comprehend the "inner world" of the performer and to understand the reason why each man, as an individual, chooses to partake in sport activity, is to pursue inquiry into personalized forms of *meaningful and significant existence*. In truth, I couldn't accept the typical fragmentation of essence and existence that one finds as a basic tenet in most existential writings. In a way, this smacks of the very *dualistic* overtures this position works so hard to refute. However, I do believe the emphasis on *personalized authenticity* is so central to the analysis of sport that one could do little but recognize basic humanity and proceed with admitting the presented *emphasis* (not sole inclusion) on existence.

Most men recognize that this world is not all *reasonable*, that methods using completely rational thought have not worked in education, nor in solving the daily problems of living. Men of sport often recognize that there is *something* beyond "having the horses." And only the foolish would assume the *something* is restricted to coaching. Man is not all rational. He plays and lives with emotion. It becomes important to recognize this intriguing element.

It is here that sport could provide a lesson for all of us. Perhaps we all need to get "up" for certain games. Perhaps we could all remember the world is not all deterministic. Is there not room for the depth of human feeling in each and every one of us?

As man controls his universe he should be "better" able to live *his* life. But Orwell, Reisman and Whyte are but a few who have pointed to the relative fallacy of this type of thinking. Is man to be truly an instrument for others? Does sport demand that man hide himself from the rest of humanity? Do we need to be the "cold men" in order to score points on *all* the fields of life? Can sport in some way assist man in learning more about himself? Or does this become an "improper" function of sport? These are not questions that will, or should, be answered by science. They will be answered by man. They *must* be answered by man. Solutions to these problems are not achieved in the laboratory; but rather they are a function of human discovery, a product of the search for the inner, and perhaps authentic, man.

Does sport provide a *living* and vivid atmosphere for man to reach himself and his fellow man? If one would read the Sunday supplements, we might come to believe that anything is possible before "the last out." But the truth of sport might well be far from the romantic idealization. Certainly, we know we experience a spectrum of emotions. But to say sport facilitates the attainment of authenticity is, to me, not demonstrable in the literature of sport or life.

I hope the reader was not misled. I did not intend to indicate any form of *causality*. If I did, I was guilty of establishing a tentative assumption that I am not prepared to support. The only place I can honestly start my inquiry is in the realm of *experience*. What is sport? How does it present itself to man? What are man's reactions to sport? In a word, how is the *real* game played? Certainly, this inquiry *relates* to cause and effect; however, never could the present form of induction/deduction achieve such farsighted ends.

To consider experience is all we could do. Is sport something that is really a correlative of other forms of human experience? By necessity, I had to draw upon theoretical conceptualizations in other related fields. This is not as much to demonstrate possible relationships as it is an admission that the life of man is truly *whole*. If the reader was often puzzled by the lack of *unique* or *novel* outcomes, perhaps I again must re-emphasize that this should be hardly surprising. Sport is but one phase of human existence. Its importance rests not in its *difference* but in its *agreement* with other realms of life.

The sport world is stimulated by many influences. However, I illustrated, hopefully, that this was not to be used as an "excuse" for habitual responses as much as an underscoring plea for the development of *personal responsibility*. To assume this quality is to know sport. To integrate this quality into self is to know man.

The remaining questions are enormous. Perhaps they are of as equal importance as their solutions. What values are communicated to man through his sport participation? Do we really believe in the "theory of *relativity*" when we discuss man's normative structure? Does sport contribute, positively, to the attainment of basic truth? Perhaps a prior concern is germane to the existence of basic truths.

One wonders if this is not all a bit *beyond* sport. And perhaps this is the lesson, if there is one, of the book. Namely, that morality, truth, existence, being, self-realization, despair, relationship, and creativity are as much a *by-product* of social and historical phenomena as they are "deliberates." Perhaps the battle on the sport field indicates that man is little more than a defenseless urchin caught in the tide of life. Indeed, this might be it. Man, in sport as in life, is a "piece" available only to "controlling forces." It may well be that man, in his own right, is little but a bottle floating on the ocean. There is no more "rightness" to assign the values and outcomes to sport as to any other determinable force. In the words of Camus, "If we believe in nothing, if nothing has meaning and if we can affirm no values whatsoever, then everything is possible and nothing has any importance. The murderer is neither right nor wrong. Evil and virtue are mere chance or caprice" (Camus, 1954, p. 5).

To say that sport presents values to man does not establish the reality of right or wrong. Certainly, the values of sport could be established upon a non-valid group of assumptions. The only hope for sport, as is true for art, drama and music, is that man lives a life that could be considered by the self as personal. A world apart from this would dehumanize sport as well as man.

In using a systematic approach, I did not use *a* system. To remain in the confines of any *one* realm of philosophic thought is to hint again of *dualism* and, what is worse, to deny the validity of other approaches. Hopefully, now that I have concluded, the reader will have advanced some insights relative to *Man, Sport and Existence* that will give some basis for *personal action.* There was no attempt to achieve a unified point of view or even a position without paradox. To have done this would refute the complexity of established human thought. Instead, analysis was achieved by, to use a cliche, "calling them as I saw them." But we cannot afford for long to be on the sidelines, umpiring. We must all enter the game—even if a little "dust and heat" is caused To say the game has only started is to admit the truth and to express hope in tomorrow.

REFERENCES

Arnheim, R.: *Art and Visual Perception.* Berkeley, University of California Press, 1954.

Bannister, R.: *First Four Minutes.* New York, Dodd Mead, 1955.

Beck, S. J.: Implications for Ego in Tillich's Ontology of Anxiety. J. Philo. Phenomenol. Res., *18*, 451–478, 1958.

Becker, E.: *The Birth and Death of Meaning.* New York, The Free Press of Glencoe, 1962.

Berdiaev, N.: *Slavery and Freedom.* New York, Charles Scribners & Sons, 1944.

Bertocci, P.: Existential Phenomenology and Psychoanalysis. Rev. of Metaphys., *28*, 690–710, 1965.

Borne, E.: The Meaning and Meaningless of Suffering. Philo. Today, *1*, 98–101, 1957.

Boss, M.: *The Analysis of Dreams.* New York, Philosophical Library, 1958.

Boyle, R.: *Sport: Mirror of American Life.* Boston, Little, Brown & Company, 1963.

Brenton, S.: From Phenomenology to Ontology. Philo. Today, *5*, 65–69, 1961.

Brown, G. S.: A Special Brand of Fame. Sports Illus., *25*, 42–43, 1966. (a)

———: America's Gritty Guinea Pig. Sports, Illus., *25*, 42, 1966. (b)

Brugger, W.: Togetherness: A New Dimension for Traditional Thought. Philo. Today, *1*, 22–26, 1957.

Buber, M.: *Between Man and Man.* (R. G. Smith, Trans.), London, Collins, 1961.

———: Distance and Relation. Psychiatry, *20*, 102, 1957.

———: *I and Thou.* (R. G. Smith, Trans.), Edinburgh, T. & T. Clark, 1953.

Bugbee, H., Jr.: The Inward Morning. Philo. Today, *4*, 265, 1960.

Bugental, J. F. T.: Humanistic Psychology: A New Break-through. Amer. Psychologist, *18*, 563–568, 1963.

———: *The Search for Authenticity.* New York, Holt, Rinehart & Winston, Inc., 1965.

Buytendijk, F.: *Allgemeine Theorie der Menschlichen Haltung und Benegung.* Heidelberg, Springer, 1956. (a)

———: *General Theory of Human Carriage and Movement.* Utrecht, Spectrum, 1948.

———: Le Sens de la Douleur. Revue D'Histoire et de Philosophie Religieuses, *4*, 282–297, 1956. (b)

Caillois, R.: *Man, Play, and Games.* London, Thames and Hudson, 1962.

Camus, A.: *The Myth of Sisyphus.* New York, Knopf, 1955.

———: *The Rebel.* (A. Bower, Trans.), New York, Knopf, 1954.

Christain, P.: *Das Personverstandnis im Modernen Medizinischen Denken.* Tubingen, J. C. B. Mohr, 1952.

Coe, G. A.: *The Psychology of Religion.* Chicago, University of Chicago Press, 1916.

D'Arcy, M. C.: *The Mind and Heart of Love.* London, Faber and Faber, Ltd., 1945.

De Ruggiero, G.: *Existentialism.* (E. M. Coeks, Trans.), London, Secker and Warburg, 1946.

De Waelhens, A.: The Ontological Encounter of Human Science and Philosophy. Philo. Today, *3*, 52–64, 1959.

———: Phenomenological Concept of Intentionality. Philo. Today, *6*, 3–24, 1962.

Doherty, J.: *Modern Track and Field.* New York, Prentice-Hall, Inc., 1953.

Eliot, T. S.: *Murder in the Cathedral.* New York, Harcourt Brace, 1935.

Farber, M.: The Phenomenological View of Values. J. Philo. Phenomenol. Res., *24*, 552–558, 1964.

Federn, P.: *Ego Psychology and the Psychoses.* New York, Basic Books, 1952.

Fenichel, O.: *The Psychoanalytic Theory of Neurosis.* New York, Norton, 1945.

Fingarette, H.: *The Self in Transformation: Psychoanalysis, Philosophy, and the Life of the Spirit.* New York, Basic Books, 1963.

Fink, E.: The Ontology of Play. Philo. Today, *4*, 95–110, 1960.

Frankl, V.: *Man's Search for Meaning.* New York, Washington Square Press, 1963.

Freud, S.: On Narcissism: An Introduction. *Collected Papers, IV*, London, Hogarth Press, 30–59, 1950.

Frutos, E.: La Liberdad como Destino de la Persona Humana. Augustinus, *2*, 99–107, 1957.

Geiger, L. B.: On Freedom. Philo. Today, *4*, 126–136.

Gendlin, E. T.: *Experiencing and the Creation of Meaning*. New York, The Free Press of Glencoe, 1962.

Glasser, W.: *Reality Therapy*. New York, Harper & Row, 1965.

Grene, M.: *Introduction to Existentialism*. Chicago, University of Chicago Press, 1948.

Guardini, R.: The Phenomenology of Religious Experience. Philo. Today, *6*, 90, 1962.

Guitton, J.: The Psychology of Religious Experience. Philo. Today, *6*, 93, 1962.

Hall, J.: Not Life or Death. Los Angeles Times, LXXXV. Part III, 3, November 19, 1966.

Harrer, H.: *The White Spider*. (H. Merrick, Trans.), New York, Dutton, 1960.

Harper, R.: *Existentialism: A Theory of Man*. Cambridge, Harvard University Press, 1958.

Heidegger, M.: *Being and Time*. (J. Macquairre and E. Robinson, Trans.), New York, Harper & Brothers, 1962.

————: *Existence and Being*. Chicago, Regnery Co., 1949.

————: *Holzwege*. Frankfurt am Main, V. Klostermanny, 1950.

————: *Wom Wesen des Grundes*. Halle, Max Niemeyer, 1929. (a)

————: *Was Ist Metaphysik?* Bonn, F. Cohen, 1929. (b)

Herrigel, E.: *Zen in the Art of Archery*. New York, Pantheon Books, 1953.

Hesburgh, T. M.: The True Meaning of Sport. Sports Illus., *25*, 56–57, 1966.

Heschel, A.: *Man Is Not Alone*. New York, Farrar, Strauss & Young, Inc., 1951.

————: *Who Is Man?* Stanford, Stanford University Press, 1965.

Hoffman, K.: Existential Philosophy: A Study of Its Past and Present Forms. Unpub. Doct. Diss., Harvard University, 1949.

Hofstadter, A.: Truth of Being. J. Philo., *62*, 167–183, 1965.

Hook, S.: *Hero of History*. New York, John Day, 1943.

Hora, T.: Existential Psychiatry and Group Psychotherapy. Amer. J. Psychoanal., *21*, 58–70, 1961.

Huizinga, J.: *Homo Ludens, A Study of the Play—Element in Culture*. (R. F. C. Hull, Trans.), London, Routledge & K. Paul, 1949.

Husserl, E.: *Ideas: General Introduction to Pure Phenomenology.* (W. R. B. Gibson, Trans.), London, G. Allen & Urwin, 1952.

Jaspers, K.: *General Psychopathology.* (J. Hoenig and M. Hamilton, Trans.), 7th ed., Chicago, Chicago University Press, 1963.

————: *Man in the Modern Age.* New York, Anchor Books, Doubleday, 1957.

————: *Philosophie.* Heidelberg, Springer-Verlag, 1948.

————: *Vernunft und Existenz.* Groningen, Batavia, Wolters, 1935.

Javet, P.: Sartre from Being and Nothingness to a Critique of Dialectical Reason. Revue de Theologie et de Philosophie, *1*, 51–60, 1961.

Jolivet, R.: Work, Play and Contemplation. Philo. Today, *5*, 114–120, 1961.

Kaelin, E.: *An Existentialistic Aesthetic: The Theories of Sartre and Merleau Ponty.* Madison, University of Wisconsin Press, 1962.

Kant, E.: *Critique of Practical Reason and Other Works on the Theory of Ethics.* (T. K. Abbott, Trans.), 4th ed., London, Longmans, Green & Co., Ltd., 1889.

Kaplan, A.: *The New World of Philosophy.* New York, Random House, 1962.

Kaufmann, W.: *Existentialism from Doestoevsky to Sartre.* Cleveland, World Publishing Co., 1956.

————: *The Faith of the Heretic.* New York, Anchor Books, Doubleday, 1963.

————: *Nietzsche: Philosopher, Psychologist, Anti-Christ.* Princeton, Princeton University Press, 1950.

Kierkegaard, S.: *The Concept of Dread.* (W. Lowrie, Trans.), Princeton, Princeton University Press, 1944.

————: *Concluding Unscientific Postscript.* (David Swenson, Trans.), Princeton, Princeton University Press, 1941.

————: *Either/Or: A Fragment of Life.* (David and Lillian Swenson, Trans.), 2 vols. Princeton, Princeton University Press, 1949.

————: *Fear and Trembling: A Dialectical Lyric.* (Robert Payne, Trans.), New York, Oxford University Press, 1939.

————: *Journals.* No. 614 (Alexander Dru, Trans.), New York, Oxford University Press, 1938.

————: *Repetition: An Essay in Experimental Psychology.* (Walter Lowrie, Trans.), New York, Oxford University Press, 1939.

Kleinman, S.: The Significance of Human Movement: A Phenomenological Approach. NAPECW REPORT. Washington, D.C., National Association for Physical Education of College Women, 123–128, 1964.

Koufax, S.: The Customers Come to Watch Us Live a Part of Our Lives. Look, *30*, 90–92, 1966.

———: Koufax on Koufax. Sports Illus., *23*, 36, 1965.

Kwant, R. C.: *Phenomenology of Social Existence.* Pittsburgh, Duquesne University Press, 1965.

Lamont, C.: Mistaken Attitudes toward Death. J. Philo., *52*, 29–36, 1965.

Langer, S.: *Philosophy in a New Key.* New York, New American Library, 1948.

Lavelle, L.: Introduction to Ontology. Philo. Today, *9*, 182–189, 1965.

Lemos, R.: Immediacy, Privacy, and Ineffability. J. Philo. Phenomenol. Res., *25*, 500–515, 1965.

———: Sensation, Perception, and the Given. Ratio, *6*, 74–80, 1964.

Lerner, M.: *America as a Civilization.* New York, Simon & Schuster, 1958.

Luce, R. D. and Raiffa, H.: *Games and Decisions.* New York, John Wiley & Sons, Inc., 1957.

Lukas, J.: Poker, An American Character. Horizon, *5*, 56–62, 1963.

Marcel, G.: *Le Coeur des Autres.* Paris, Grasset, 1920.

———: *Man Against Mass Society.* Chicago, Henry Regnery Co., 1952. (a)

———: *Metaphysical Journal.* (Bernard Wall, Trans.), Chicago, Henry Regnery Co., 1952. (b)

———: *The Mystery of Being.* Chicago, Henry Regnery Co., 1960.

Maritain, J.: *Neuf Lecons sur les Notions Premieres de la Philosophie Morale.* Paris, Tequi, 1949.

Maslow, A.: *Motivation and Personality.* New York, Harper & Brothers, 1954.

Maule, T.: A Cool Masterpiece. Sports Illus., *24*, 14, 1966.

May, R., Angel, E. and Ellenberger, H. (Eds.).: *Existence: A New Dimension in Psychiatry and Psychology.* New York, Basic Books, 1948.

Merleau—Ponty, M.: *Phenomenologie de la Perception.* 4th ed., Paris, Gallimard, 1945.

Metheny, E.: *Connotations of Movement in Sport and Dance.* Dubuque, William C. Brown Co., 1965.

Mihalich, J.: *Existentialism and Thomism.* New York, Philosophical Library, 1960.

Mitchell, C.: The Fad and Fascination of Surfing. Holiday, *35*, 122–130, 1964.

Murray, J.: Fleck's Infamy. Los Angeles Times, LXXXV, Part III, 1, June 17, 1966.

Olson, R. G.: *An Introduction to Existentialism.* New York, Dover Publications, Inc., 1962.

On Having a Sense of Values. The Royal Bank of Canada Monthly Letter, *23*, 2, 1962.

O'Neill, W. F.: Jean—Paul Sartre's Concept of Freedom and Its Implications for American Education. Unpub. Doct. Diss., University of Southern California, 1958.

Parain-Vail, J.: Notes sur L'Ontologie de Gabriel Marcel. Critique, *158*, 636–652, 1960.

Parks, B.: Skiing. Unpub. paper, University of Southern California, 1966.

Pascal, B.: *Pensees.* (M. Turnell, Trans.), London, Harvell Press, 1962.

People. Sports Illus., *25*, 64, 1966.

Poppi, A.: Le Morale de Situatione. Miscellanea Francescana, *57*, 3–63, 1957.

Proust, M.: *A la Recherche du Temps Perdu, A L'Hombre des Jeunes Filles en Fleurs.* Paris, Gillimard, 1943.

Quinn, C. H.: The Readers Take Over. Sports Illus., *23*, 18, 82, 1965.

Rank, O.: *Will Therapy; and Truth and Reality.* New York, Knopf, 1950.

Reisman, D.: *The Lonely Crowd.* New Haven, Yale University Press, 1950.

Reulet, A.: Being, Value, and Existence. J. Philo. Phenomenol. Res., *9*, 448–457, 1949.

Rilke, R. M.: *Selected Works.* (J. B. Leishman, Trans.), Norfolk, Conn., New Directions Books, 1960.

Roberts, D. E.: *Existentialism and Religious Belief.* New York, Oxford University Press, 1957.

Rogin, G.: An Odd Sport . . . and an Unusual Champion. Sports Illus., *23*, 104–106, 1965.

Roldan, A.: The Absurd, the Paradoxical and Human Understanding. Philo. Today, *1*, 29–32, 1957.

Rotenstreich, N.: Some Problems in Buber's Dialogical Philosophy. Philo. Today, *3*, 155, 1959.

Roubiczek, P.: *Existentialism.* Cambridge, England, University Press, 1964.

Rousselot, P.: *L'Intellectualisme de S. Thomas.* 3rd ed., Paris, Babriel Beauchesne, 1936.

Salmon, E.: *The Good in Existential Metaphysics.* Milwaukee, Marquette University Press, 1953.

Salvan, J.: *To Be and Not To Be.* Detroit, Wayne State University Press, 1962.

Sarte, J. P.: *Being and Nothingness: An Essay on Phenomenological Ontology.* (H. E. Barnes, Trans.), New York, Philosophical Library, 1956. (a)

———: *The Emotions: Outline of a Theory.* (B. Frechtman, Trans.), New York, Philosophical Library, 1948.

———: *The Flies.* New York, Vintage Books, 1956. (b)

———: L'Homme et les Choses, *Situations I.* Paris, Gallimard, 1947.

———: Materialism and Revolution. *Literary and Philosophical Essays*, London, Rider and Co., 1955.

———: *Nausea.* Norfolk, Conn., New Directions, 1949.

Schmidt, R.: Husserl's Transcendental Phenomenological Reductions. J. Philo. Phenomenol. Res., *21*, 238–245, 1960.

Schrag, C. O.: The Lived Body as a Phenomenological Datum. The Modern Schoolman, *39*, 203–218, 1962.

Sciacca, M. F.: Il Silenzio Significativo. Giornale Di Metafisica, *7*, 285–291, 1957.

Scorecard. Sports Illus., *25*, 22, 1966.

Scorecard. Sports Illus., *26*, 7, 1967.

Sheets, M.: *The Phenomenology of Dance.* Madison, University of Wisconsin Press, 1966.

Slusher, H. S.: *Toward a Meaningful Existence.* Dubuque, Iowa, William C. Brown Co., 1964.

Smith, H.: *Condemned to Meaning.* New York, Harper & Row, 1965.

Smith, J.: Los Angeles Times, LXXXIV, Part II, 76, February 28, 1965.

Steinbeck, J.: Then My Arm Glassed Up. Sports Illus., *23*, 99–102, 1965.

Stierlin, H.: Existentialism Melts Psychotherapy. J. Philo. Phenomenol. Res., *24*, 215–237, 1963.

Storer, D.: Significance of Death in Sport. Unpub. paper, University of Southern California, 1966.

Sykes, G.: *The Hidden Remnant.* New York, Harper & Brothers, 1962.

Szasz, T.: *The Myth of Mental Illness.* New York, Hoeber-Harper, 1961.

Tillich, P.: *The Courage to Be.* New Haven, Yale University Press, 1952.

———: Existential Philosophy. J. History Ideas, *5*, 44–70, 1944.

Tyner, G.: Surf's Up. Unpub. paper, University of Southern California, 1966.

Umminger, W.: *Superman, Heroes and Gods.* (J. Clark, Trans.), London, Thames & Hudson, 1963.

Underwood, J.: Chasing Girls through a Park. Sports Illus., *25*, 30, 1966.

Van Den Berg, J. H.: The Human Body and the Significance of Human Movement. J. Philo. Phenomenol. Res., *13*, 159–183, 1952.

———: *The Phenomenological Approach to Psychiatry.* Springfield, Thomas, 1955.

Van Peurson, C. A.: Phenomenology and Ontology. Philo. Today, *3*, 35–42, 1959.

Von Weizsacker, V.: *Der Gestaltkreis.* Stuttgart, Theime, 1947.

Wahl, J.: *A Short History of Existentialism.* New York, Philosophical Library, 1949.

Watts, A. W.: *The Way of Zen.* New York, Pantheon Books, Inc., 1959.

Webb, L.: *On the Edge of the Absurd.* New York, Abingdon Press, 1965.

Wild, J.: Being, Meaning and the World. The Rev. Metaphysics, *18*, 411–429, 1965.

———: *The Challenge of Existentialism.* Bloomington, Indiana University Press, 1955.

Wilson, C.: *The Age of Defeat.* London, Victor Gollancz Ltd., 1959.

———: *The Outsider.* Boston, Houghton-Mifflin Co., 1956.

Wolf, R.: The Absurdity of Sport. Unpub. paper, University of Southern California, 1966.

Wolff, W.: Selbstbewiteilung und Fremdbeurteilung. Psychologische Forschung, 7, 251–328, 1932.

Wolstein, B.: *Irrational Despair.* New York, Free Press of Glencoe, 1962.

Yevtushenko, Y.: A Poet Against the Destroyers. Sports Illus., *25*, 126–128, 1966.

Ziff, S.: Bruins Confident. Los Angeles Times, LXXXV, Part III, 3, November 18, 1966.

Zuidema, S. H.: Gabriel Marcel. Philosophia Reforma, *22*, 78–94, 1957.

Zutt, J.: Vom Gelebten Welthaften Leibe. Congress Report, 2nd International Congress for Psychiatry, IV, Zurich, 444–445, 1957.

INDEX

L

M

N